Richard Walker

Biography of an Angling Legend

BARRIE RICKARDS

With a personal perspective by Patricia Marston Walker

ELLESMERE
THE MEDLAR PRESS
2007

Published by The Medlar Press Limited,
The Grange, Ellesmere, Shropshire.
www.medlarpress.com

ISBN 978-1- 899600-58-8

First published 2007
Reprinted 2007, 2008

Produced in England by The Medlar Press Limited, Ellesmere.
Designed and typeset in 11 on 12^1/$_2$pt Garamond by
Jonathan Ward-Allen.

DEDICATION

I do not share the pessimistic viewpoint that there will never be another Richard Walker.

Some day, somewhere, there will be another revolution led by one angler.

I dedicate this book to that person.

Acknowledgements

My warmest thanks go to the Walker family for their unstinting support, especially to Pat Walker who has had to put up with me a great deal, yet has remained unfailingly hospitable; Tim Walker and his wife Lynn too, as well as Simon, Robert and Richard. Pat and Simon have written pieces for the book, as you will see, and Tim has also contributed. One or two others have done a great deal to assist me and I must single them out for my gratitude, in particular Kevin Clifford (who also contributed the Foreword), Chris Ball, Alan Brown and his wife Jeanette, Richard Brown, Fred and Margaret Buller, and Craig Pickles who ferreted out manuscripts for me. My thanks also to all the following for their anecdotes, letters, tapes and photographs: *Angling Times*; Keith Barker; Gemma Bentley; Geoff Bucknall; Roger Buss; Bob Buteux; Nicky Butt; Sharon Capon; Jim Carfrae; Chub Study Group; Bob Church; Brian Clarke; Ron Clay; James Cox; Dave Cursons; Jon Dwyer; Terry Ellmore; Jim Gibbinson; Roy Goddard; Gonville & Caius College, Cambridge; Frank Guttfield; Jim Hardy; John Harding; Andrew Holmes; Dave Ivey; Pete Jackson; Susan Jackson; Gordon Johnson; John Langridge; Alun Lewis; Derek Lewis; Peter Liam; Sarah Lincoln Smith; Denis Loveday; Keith Makin; Graham Marsden; David Melland; Chris Mitchell; Pete Newman; Wally Prior; John Reynolds; Hugh Ross; Paul Salmon; Trevor Sawyer; John Searle; Anthony Shepherdson; Andy Stafford; Dave Steuart; David Stocker; Paul Sykes; Phil Wakeford; Andy Warers; Donald Williamson; Mark Wintle; Fred Wilton; Justin Wood; Dave Woods.

I should also like to thank the many people who have helped with the photographs of this book. Most of those used are Pat Walker's or come from Dick's own files, and are used with Pat's permission. However, I have also received photographs from many other sources, especially Kevin Clifford and Tim Walker, several of whose pictures appear; and there are some photographs from Simon Walker, Margery Russell, Nicky Butt, Chris Ball, Fred Buller, the Chub Study Group, John Searle and Steve Crawshaw. *Angling Times* gave me free run of their Walker files and some of their pictures have also been used. Many other people loaned pictures which, having so many to choose from, I did not need to use. To all of these I offer my grateful thanks. In all, I think that between us, Jon Ward-Allen and I examined about a thousand photographs.

Finally, I owe thanks to Wendy Green, who undertook the formidable task of typing the whole manuscript from my longhand.

I have listed at the back of this book the sources that I used to compile this biography. For those who wonder why a biography of Walker has not appeared before now, you may like to read this section first.

Contents

Foreword by Kevin Clifford *9*

Preface *11*

1. The boy Richard Stuart Walker 15
2. As a young man 23
3. First and last articles 31
4. Walker and the media 37
5. The Walker letters 45
6. The tackle trade 59
7. Tackle, techniques and photography 69
8. Carp fishing, 'that carp', and record fish 75
9. The Carp Catchers' Club 83
10. Redmire Pool 89
11. Philosophical matters 101
12. Perch and chub 109
13. Walker and pike 123
14. The roots of specimen hunting 129
15. On resistance and streamlining: battles lost 137
16. Dick Walker as a trout angler 147
17. Walker on match fishing 167
18. Bernard Venables v. Richard Walker 173
19. Richard Walker and Izaak Walton 179
20. The death of Dick Walker 185
21. A personal perspective by Patricia Marston Walker 191
22. In the final analysis 247

Personal recollections of Richard Walker *249*
Richard Walker by his mother, Elsie May Walker *289*
Richard Walker by his son, Simon Walker *292*

Appendix 1: *Walker family tree* *301*
Appendix 2: *Richard Walker's best fish* *302*
Appendix 3: *An article on the Inland Revenue* *304*
Appendix 4: *Richard Walker's Books* *310*

Endpiece *313*

Sources *314*
Index *316*

Foreword

It is extremely rare, if not unique, for a biographical book to be written about an individual angler. I can, in fact, think of only one other, and that was a recent publication written about Ivan Marks. I think it's fair to say that its availability was limited to sale through a handful of tackle shops, and it was born of a dedication by a friend rather than a comprehensive consideration of the life of an individual who many believe has been angling's greatest influence.

Notwithstanding this, and despite the premise that comparisons are odious, throughout his life Dick was often compared to other fine anglers: Tom Sails, Billy Lane, Jim Bazley, Jack Hilton and Ivan Marks, to name a few. As fish catchers in their prime, there probably wasn't much to choose between all of them, but as the complete angler Dick was in a different league altogether.

I should perhaps feel obliged to explain what I mean by 'complete angler', for that is the chasm that separates those who are adept at simply filling keepnets from those who can see far beyond pounds and ounces. But the pages that follow mine will do that far more comprehensively. I think you will understand what I mean when you've read the book.

Over the years, and perhaps more so since his death, Dick has had praise and criticism heaped upon him. As so often happens when someone in the public eye dies, 'good friends who knew him well' appear out of the woodwork with fanciful tales. I wouldn't dream of elevating myself to 'good friend' status. I corresponded with Dick on and off for ten years, fished with him a few times and had the good fortune to spend some unpressured leisure time in his company. I know we were friends, and I imagine he was fond of me, in a paternal sort of way, where a good many years sat between our ages. Dick's suggestion to David Hall in 1975 that I might be worth contacting as a potential writer for David's new coarse fishing magazine was simply based on a few letters I had written to him, and started me off on a journey I could never have imagined.

In the unthinking shallowness of youth I betrayed that pure kindness at least once. In the mid-1970s Dick believed, like most anglers and scientists, that coarse fish were relatively short-lived. He had often written such in *Angling Times* and didn't see a problem with killing a big fish, believing that it made room for smaller, younger fish to grow on and become big fish themselves.

I knew this to be incorrect, and could prove it. However, rather than write directly to Dick until the veracity of my argument convinced him, I relished the idea of proving the great man wrong in print, and did it on his home ground in the *Angling Times*. Later, older and wiser, I became a little ashamed of my motives. Yet my transgression appeared to go unnoticed by Dick; he never mentioned it and it didn't affect his continual encouragement, help and kindness. It is perhaps that, as much as anything else, that Dick has left me with to admire and live up to.

Nevertheless, there is no doubt in my mind that Dick did have a few failings. He wouldn't have been human if he didn't, and greatness with a few warts is always far more interesting. For example, he had some prejudices against pike. He didn't understand or care much for them - and to a similar degree the same applied to bream. He occasionally slipped down to the level of the rest of us and found it hard to admit that he was wrong. He could come across as arrogant. He could be dogmatic. He could talk the hind legs off a donkey. Most of his friends saw some or all of these traits in him at some time or other.

So why has Barrie Rickards chosen me to write this Foreword, when so many others have a greater claim? Perhaps Barrie sees in my perception of Dick Walker and his place in angling much that corresponds with his own. Yet in my reading of the book it is obvious that Barrie has unearthed so much about Dick Walker that was not previously in the public domain. In that knowing has there been disappointment? Well, the scientist's desire within Barrie Rickards, to dig deep and find the man inside angling's greatest angler, has left us with a truly fitting tribute - and in that knowing there has been no disappointment for me - both in the man and in the book. I think there will be very few who read on who will come to a different conclusion.

Kevin Clifford
Sandholme Grange, 2007

Preface

Picture this scene: we have a sitting-room in the Grange, Ellesmere, peopled by a small gathering of the directors of the Angling Collection (the body set up for the purpose of establishing a National Angling Museum). It is darkening outside, the day's work is done, and Jon Ward-Allen has poured out a glass, or two, for the participants, all of whom relax deeply in armchairs. As the drink is sipped, and a thin wisp from a small cigar hangs in the air, a silence reigns. No doubt each is thinking: how on earth will they raise a couple of million pounds to start on a new building for the growing collection? Then the quiet of the evening is broken when some fool asks, "Why is it that there has never been a biography of Richard Walker?" The fool was I. The question is followed by a long, long pause at the end of which Jon gently murmurs, "I think a few people have wanted to . . . from time to time . . . and I can tell you this much: we'd willingly publish a biography." There is a further, ruminative, reflective pause, and then Fred Buller leans forward in his chair, jabs an index finger in my direction and says to all and sundry, "And there's the very man for the job." That's how this book started. Personally I would have thought Fred himself better placed than I, but I learned that he was very deeply involved in writing other books and also felt a little unsure of dealing with some areas of Walker's great breadth of involvement in angling. Don't we all. I asked Jon for a few days' grace to think things over; and in that time I prepared what amounted to a chapter plan, laying out the various spheres of angling I would need to cover in order to give proper recognition to his achievements. At that stage I realised I could do the job, but that I would need help.

As you will see shortly from the sources section and the acknowledgements, I did get help, in very many cases quite unstinting, generous, overwhelming help with no strings attached. It simply showed that Dick Walker is held in admiration and affection by so many anglers. I think many people appreciate that he, and some colleagues, transformed angling as never before.

I determined, after working for some time, that the biography would be about Walker the angler and his contributions to angling. All great people have a polymathic tendency and there are facets to Dick that I shall not cover in this book, for example his writing for children, his poetry, his comic writing, his interests in genetics and rabbit breeding, his love of cats, and his thoughts on palaeoanthropological matters. Much of this is unpublished and may never be so, but the appraisal of it, or publication of it should be left to others better qualified. (Ernest Benn's were, at one stage, thinking of publishing Dick's children's stories and verse, but it didn't happen. However, Pam Ayres used one of Dick's limericks 'Jimmy Johnson caught a stoat' on her TV show.) Nor shall I deal with his career as an engineer at Lloyds & Co., the firm in which his mother rose from being a secretary to being Managing Director and in which Dick spent most of his adult working life.

Dick Walker was not a professional angler in the way so many of the best modern anglers are. But it would have been interesting indeed to have seen how he would have thrived in today's more receptive environment for professional anglers, offering as it does a much greater range of video, DVD, columns, magazines and other publication outlets than in the past. I suspect he would have been in the forefront, as he always was.

Because of his wide non-angling interests he also had an unusually large circle of friends and contacts outside angling. Again, I shall deal with none of this unless it actually impinges on angling in some relevant fashion. These matters will be for others to chronicle in different contexts.

Returning now to angling matters, it has become abundantly clear to me, as the work has progressed, that future editions of this book may be necessary. This is because information for inclusion arrives in a steady stream and shows no sign of abating. Yet I have to draw a line somewhere! So I would invite anyone who feels they have a contribution to make, having read this work, to get in touch with me. This might be to offer new information, to correct what I have written, to provide a telling anecdote, to lend letters I have not unearthed so far, and so on. Do not hesitate. I do not claim that this is the last word on Dick Walker!

Having said that, it is intriguing that so many of the recent items I have come across actually fit into various threads and patterns of his behaviour, some of which were established very early in his life. So I have now seen and read enough to be able to examine and analyse at least some of the sides of Dick Walker that pertain to angling. Take his reputation for generosity as an example. Had I just a few instances to report then it would have been interesting certainly, but hardly of major significance. However, generosity is perhaps the most commonly mentioned facet of his character, with letter after letter referring to some extraordinarily generous acts. And these were no publicity stunts; only the recipients knew of them, and the recipients themselves were often quite unknown and insignificant in the world of angling. I'll give you one example that I came across myself, almost forty years ago. It alerted me even then to this side of Dick.

The late Basil Chilvers was a friend of several of us who fished the Fens at the time. We fished not only for pike but also for tench and bream. Basil wrote to Dick to ask where he could obtain a Mk IV carp rod, because back then they were difficult to find (I think only J.B. Walker sold them). Dick replied by return of post, telling Basil to look no further, and that if he cared to drive to Dick's home in Hitchin, he could have one of Dick's own rods. Now, Dick didn't know Basil from Adam, and Basil himself was in no way a 'named' angler until much later. But he must have come across to Dick as keen. The story does not end there - although had it done so, it would have made my point easily enough. Basil drove over on Sunday morning, as arranged, and arrived at Dick's door. When he opened the door, Basil told me that Dick looked rather blank and withdrawn, but as soon as Basil explained hesitating-ly why he had come, Dick said, "Oh, yes! Well, here it is . . ." and reaching behind the door pulled out a superb Mk IV, in its bag, and handed it to Basil. He then excused himself and shut the door again! Basil wandered away from the house with mixed and rather odd feelings after such a brief encounter with the great man. It was only later in the week that Basil learnt from the newspapers that Dick's first wife, Ruth, had died - only the day before Basil had visited. Yet he still remembered to put out the rod for Basil and to have it ready for his arrival. It tells you a lot about the man.

Dick Walker's personal qualities were best known, of course, by his family and to a lesser extent by his closest friends. I knew Dick myself for many years, but although we spoke frequently on the phone and occasionally at meetings, I did not fish with him. Nor could I claim to know him really well. He was always very supportive of what I did in angling; and, of course, I had some dealings with him when I wrote a chapter (on zander) for his book *Still-Water Angling*, and when he contributed to the Pike Anglers' Club or the National Association of Specimen Groups' gatherings in Chelsea. The family have not pressurised me in any way to write this book with a particular slant. Pat, in particular, was concerned that I write a 'warts and all' account, something I was prepared to do, at least within the sphere of angling itself. Thus I have not ignored the very serious dispute that Dick had with Dr Terry Coulson, a dis-pute that I think Dick lost, one of his few defeats. Not, I should perhaps add, that Dick regarded debates and disputes in angling as matters of winning and losing at all, but rather ways of advancing knowledge. I am sure that Pat, and Dick's sons, would *prefer* a positive appraisal, which is both natural and under-standable, but I can state categorically that they have not tried to influence me other than to make corrections. Pat has read the whole manuscript, but she did so after writing her own chapter. She may or may not agree with it all, but the responsibility for the ideas contained are mine alone and she should not be judged as either approving or disapproving them. I needed a free hand and that I have had.

As you can imagine, putting a book like this together is very difficult indeed, not least because of the breadth of the subject matter. Many coarse anglers are aware of Dick's contribution to carp fishing but how many of those understand his huge input into trout fishing - or vice-versa? Similarly his role in the tackle trade can hardly be appreciated until you have read the vast files that he kept on his dealings with the trade. Nor can his direct contributions to individual anglers be understood without burning the midnight oil to sift through thousands of his letters. And let me put this question to you: how many anglers are alive today who read his weekly column in *Angling Times* from its beginning to its end, over thirty years later? Of course, there have been publications about Dick already - for example, Peter Maskell's excellent compilations of some of his articles, stories about Redmire Pool, and so on - but I suspect that it is the breadth of research required that has deterred would-be biographers of the past.

This book is not arranged in exact chronological order although it begins with Dick Walker as a youngster and young man; and it ends by attempting to appraise his relative importance with respect to one of the great stalwarts of the twentieth century, Bernard Venables, and with respect to one of the greatest anglers of all time, Izaak Walton. I shall not reveal, at this point, what I have concluded. In between are analyses of Dick's involvement with carp fishing and with Redmire Pool; with pike, perch, chub and trout; with match-fishing and specimen-hunting; with the tackle trade and the media; and assessments of those all-important matters of his personal philosophies pertaining to angling. Whilst these chapters attempt to analyse and appraise, I hope with anecdotes enough, Pat Walker's personal perspective in Chapter 21 paints a more homely picture and gives us a glimpse of Walker the family man, the friend and the husband. For the end of the book it seemed to me that a bibliography of Dick's published work should be attempted so that people could identify books that they may previously have missed. There is also a family tree as a reference for the earlier chapters and Chapter 21. In addition Dick's best fish are listed, some unpublished works are revealed, and personal views are given of him by his mother and son Simon. There is also an appreciation of Dick by some of the great anglers of the last half century. These contributions were obtained by Pat some time after Dick's death.

Barrie Rickards,
Cambridge, May 2007

Chapter 1

The boy Richard Stuart Walker

RICHARD STUART WALKER was born on 29th May, 1918, at Fishponds Road, Hitchin, Hertfordshire. It has been pointed out many times in connection with his birth that 29th May is Oak Apple Day, but I have never seen more made of this point. *Is* there any point? Is not 29th May just the same as any other day in our present context? Well, not quite. Oak Apple Day is the anniversary of the Restoration (1660), and people wore, or perhaps wear, oak apples or leaves to commemorate the Boscobel Oak in which Charles II hid after his defeat at the Battle of Worcester. Dick was a great admirer of Charles II, knew a great deal about him and often spoke about him or quoted things about him. A favourite, for example, was 'Methinks the more you stir a turd, the worse it stinks'. But there is a little more: it seems possible, his family think, that there is a line of succession leading back to Charles II although, as Dick himself often said, whether it is a legitimate link remains uncertain. And Dick's second name is taken from the Stuarts. Pat gives more detail in Chapter 21, and tells us about his upbringing by a powerful mother and two sets of very supportive grandparents.

At the age of five Richard attended school for the first time at what today we would call his primary school, in this case, Miss Darby's School, close to his home in Hitchin. He could already read well, having been taught by his mother, and so was involved in helping to teach others to read. It may be only a romantic thought, but perhaps the teaching and communication skills that remained with him to the end of his life may have been nurtured at that early stage, in primary school. I suggest this because it seems true of others I know who have become unusually good teachers as adults.

Dick was already fishing at this age, with one of his grandfathers, having first been taken fishing by his mother.

In September 1928 at ten years old he was sent as a boarder to the Friends'

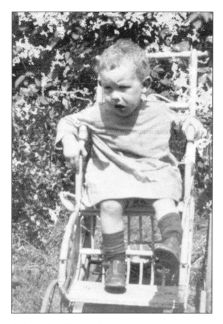

Baby Dick, eight months.

Lecturing! Aged fifteen months.

Dick aged seven.

And with an early mechanical engineering problem!

School, Saffron Walden, a Quaker School where he remained until finishing his General Certificate of Education in July 1934. Although initially unhappy and bullied, he did survive well and was very successful academically. Pat Walker, in her personal perspective in Chapter 21, gives further details of both this and his primary school which derive from Dick's own tapes.

Having finished at the the Friends' School, aged sixteen, Dick was too young to go to university, so the family enrolled him at St Christopher School, Letchworth, where he stayed from the autumn of 1934 until the summer of 1936. In contrast to his previous school, this one had relatively few rules and displayed what we would today term a 'laid-back' attitude. Ian Ogilvie, who was at St Christopher School at the same time as Dick, points out that the school was regarded as a 'progressive' school, with a flavour of Quakerism, vegetarianism, pacifism, left-wing politics and an atmosphere of 'ordered freedom'. Certainly the 'ordered freedom' would have suited Dick, but it is likely that some of the other elements did not, and Ian confirms that Dick 'did not seem to fit closely into that pattern'. As a new boy, Dick seemed to resent the discrimination that prevented him from addressing teachers by their first names, as all the other pupils did. His stay there was relatively short so it would have been less easy to settle in, and difficult to develop friendships amongst groups that had been there for some years.

This situation may have strengthened Dick Walker's rather independent spirit, a spirit probably imbued in him initially by his mother. We know, for instance, that he did not join the Old Scholars' Association of the Friends School, as confirmed by their current archivist, Roger Buss. Nor did he have anything to do with the St Christopher Club after leaving the school. Beric Wright helped organise that club for old members both locally to Letchworth and in London, and he has no recollection of Dick ever going back.

Beric Wright also says of Richard that he was 'a day-boy who arrived by car and was older and more mature than the rest of us. This slightly remote relationship with the school was accentuated by his height and maturity. In retrospect he seemed to be a young adult. He was very good at games but I don't think much involved in the life of the school . . . He seemed remote.' Of course, in those days, there was much less integration between boarders and day-boys, a point made by several of my correspondents.

Hugh Ross was Head Boy at St Christopher School in Richard Walker's time there and he told me that though he was not close to R.W. he had 'a clear image of him still . . . I recall him as tall, very outgoing, very likeable, good at activities such as sport. I do not recall how his studies got him to Cambridge - which was quite difficult then.' (There is more on this in the next chapter.)

R.W. was a little older than Ian Ogilvie when they were at St Christopher

Vitaï Lampada.

There's a breathless hush on the close tonight —
Ten to make and the match to win —
A bumping pitch and a blinding light,
An hour to play and the last man in.
And it's not for the sake of a ribboned coat,
Or the selfish hope of a season's fame,

School, but he has some interesting comments to make: 'He always seemed to me a boy of some mystery, not in terms of his personality, but because I thought it odd that he came so late to St Christopher.' This was because his family wanted him to continue in education, in a good school, until he became old enough to sit the Cambridge Entrance Exam, something he could not do post-GCE at the Friends' School. Ian goes on to say:

So far as I know, he had no origins in Letchworth, and he did not seem to share much of the outlook of the typical 'Chris' family background . . . Richard, in my memory, did not seem to fit closely into the [St Christopher] pattern . . . but I do not wish to imply in any way that he appeared a 'loner'. On the contrary . . . I recall him as sociable and popular, and he was as self-confident and assertive as any other boy near the top of the school . . . A couple of odd features which I recall are first, in a school where uniform was not rigidly enforced, and most middle to senior boys wore a jersey or sports jacket (occasionally a blazer) with grey flannel trousers, I always recall Richard wearing a suit, either dark grey or dark navy blue. I do not think he was in the least self-conscious about it. The other trifling thing is that he was prematurely grey . . . with noticeable streaks of grey in his otherwise dark hair. By the way, he was always 'Richard' and never 'Dick' or 'Dickie'.

Later in life we know that R.W. preferred to be called 'Dick'. But what is really important in these remembrances of his peers is the picture of a tall, confident, assertive, suited person, clearly self-contained and yet sociable. We also see that he did not readily join societies, was not clubbable in the modern sense, yet seemed to take part, and that he preferred, for many years at least, to wear a suit (when not fishing!). All these attributes we shall see time and again in the story that follows.

What of sport, and hobbies? There are two main sources, apart from the family ones, that provide information: one is the letters from his peers; the other the *St Christopher Magazine* of the time, kindly supplied by David Cursons of the St Christopher Club.

The July 1935 edition of the magazine has a report by R. S. Walker, Secretary of the Camera Club, which had been formed that term. This will prove of interest to many anglers because Dick Walker became a fine angling photographer and wrote on photography on numerous occasions; and here he was, actively involved at an early age, getting his basic training so to speak. Later that year, in December, he was in the winning photographic team of an Inter-Schools Challenge (run by Lilley & Skinner) and also won second prize in the holiday photographs' section of the school competition.

Dick appears again in the July 1935 edition, in the cricket reports. Under the heading of 'team criticisms' R. Walker has the following entry: 'On occasions has done some brisk and helpful hitting, but his strokes are usually uncertain, as he does not watch the ball. His fielding is rather weak but he throws in well.' He had a strong arm as an adult; and the comments on his batting agree closely with Dick's own recollections, which appear in Chapter 21.

In 1936 evidence of his soccer credentials is given in the football report: 'Richard Walker (Centre Forward [Striker these days]). At times he has put his best into the game and has been most useful, as he possesses a straight and powerful shot, but at the other has not put in the sustained plucky play which one ought to expect.' Such a comment will come as no surprise to those that knew him: Dick was not particularly interested in *competing*; he got a much greater enjoyment out of taking part and in doing his best whilst doing so. This explains why match fishing was never for him, although he did take part in the occasional social or charitable event. This assessment of his football ability gels with Dick's own (given in Chapter 21) and shows that although friends and family of R. W. have sometimes wondered whether he was a bit of a romancer when it came to stories of his activities there is, in fact, evidence to support many of them.

A lino-cut that appeared in the Friends' School magazine, The Avenue.

Dick at school, aged fourteen.

Aged sixteen years.

Now what of angling or, as it was universally known in those days, fishing? Ian Ogilvie has a telling paragraph in one of his letters to me:

Now, finally, his angling (at the time, always referred to by me as 'fishing' - the term 'angling' would have been very unfamiliar). I can assert confidently that by the time he came to Chris (ie, St Christopher School) he was already a keen and indeed dedicated fresh-water angler. I can illustrate this with an anecdote from perhaps 1935, more likely 1936. During a family holiday near Weymouth at that time I became rather interested in the idea of sea fishing, and I remember even going so far as to buy a hook and line, and dangling it off the pier at Weymouth (without success!). But sustained by this introduction, I have a very clear memory of approaching Richard on my return, and with bravado - and a good deal of 'cheek' to a more senior boy - telling him that sea fishing was a far more interesting and rewarding pastime than mere fresh-water fishing. He very properly gave me a prompt and loud ticking-off for my ignorance and presumption - but it illustrates that he was already established as an authority in that direction. If at any time either then or later, someone had said, "An old scholar from your school is a famous angler," I would have immediately said, "Richard Walker, of course," and later, in the 1980s I think, I used to read with interest a series about him in the *Weekend Telegraph.*

It is interesting to have evidence of Dick's interest in fishing, but also to see at what an early stage he formed his views of sea fishing. Many years later he would be regarded as, at best, rather neutral towards it - an attitude that was strengthened by some of his wartime experiences.

At St Christopher School it seems that Dick kept a relatively low profile, apart from being Secretary of the Camera Club. The school minutes make no mention of him - neither for taking positions of authority, nor for getting into trouble. He did his own thing, as he was to continue to do for the rest of his life. Those facets of his character that were so much a feature of his adult life - his independence of spirit and his rejection of positions of authority - were already becoming well established.

In academic terms, however, he was singled out. The *St Christopher Magazine* of April 1936 states: 'We congratulate the following on their academic successes: Richard Walker - Entrance Examination to Gonville and Caius College, Cambridge.' Hugh Ross, the Head Boy is also on the list, going for the same Tripos as Dick, the Mechanical Sciences Tripos (ie, Engineering in modern parlance); rather than Caius, however, Hugh Ross headed to Emmanuel College.

Royal Life Saving Society Award gained while at the Friends' School, Saffron Walden.

Chapter 2

As a young man

GETTING INTO Cambridge in those days was not easy: for many, there were funding problems and the competition was fierce. Dick had passed his GCE well, but probably did not do the Higher School Certificate; instead he tackled the Cambridge Entrance Examination. Passing that was no mean feat academically because the exam tested not only knowledge but also the aptitude to tackle problems the candidate would be unfamiliar with. That last aspect must have suited Dick perfectly because, as we now know as anglers, he spent his life solving problems. And, as we've seen, he was already mature and developing a strong independence. These were qualities that would be brought out by the examination at Gonville and Caius College (usually referred to as Caius College, and pronounced 'keys'). They would also be the qualities that then, as now, would have impressed the staff in the faculty and proved to them that he could stay the course.

Dick was fortunate in that his university fees were paid by his supportive family; but he still had to earn money to live. During his time at Cambridge he worked as a car washer, waiter, kitchen hand and in factories, but still found time to do his work and go fishing. In one letter Dick records that he lived off baked beans and faggots! In those days many of the students were very well off and this could have made life socially difficult for him had he not already been imbued with a high level of maturity and confidence.

At Caius, it seems, he lead quite an active social and sporting life, even spending a little time rowing. But he was more involved in fishing and would canoe up the Cam to what are today the more pleasant reaches around Grantchester and above, as well as fishing downstream of the town towards Milton (where I once lived). He once pointed out to me a swim from which, on fly, he'd caught a one-pound dace and a two-pound roach in a single session - I *think* on successive casts. Today that section of the river yields

A young Dick with a carp from Bearton Pond.

only tiddlers, and the big roach and dace are long gone.

There is a revealing comment in a letter to me from Hugh Ross, Dick's Head Boy at St Christopher's. He says, 'nor do I remember him amongst the rather few other Christophians . . .' in Cambridge. And, remember, Hugh was in the same faculty as Dick. Clearly Dick had already gone his own way. In fact, the college seems to have little record of Dick's activities and they have been unable to find photographs of him in college. They do, however, have his examination results, and these are interesting. In June 1937, at the end of his first year of university study he was given Second Class Honours marks. At that time there was no sub-division of Honours awards and there seems to be no record as to whether it was a good Second or not. In June 1938, at the end of his second year of study, he had slipped somewhat and was given Third Class marks. This must have set alarm bells ringing, not only amongst his tutors in college and the faculty staff, but with Richard too. Third Class marks put you in the relegation zone, for in Cambridge there is a black void below a Third: go below a Third and you have failed, with no 'resits' and no safety net of a 'pass' degree which exists in other universities. Dick did nine terms, which would have taken him to the summer of his third year, but he did not graduate, possibly did not take the exams.

The year 1939 saw the onset of the Second World War, into which Richard was rapidly drawn as a researcher in radar. Did this save his academic bacon? We shall never know for sure but it does seem that Dick may have been losing the balance between social life and work, or that he may have been finding the work itself difficult. Students usually do rather *better* in their second year than their first as the first year is always logistically difficult and the subject less focused. It is possible that he was getting behind with work, especially given the speed with which the Cambridge courses run, particularly in engineering where students have to keep up, week by week, with a whole series of mathematical exercises. Dick's academic track record to that date might make it seem unlikely that he couldn't keep up with the studying, but it could have been the case. His later debate with Dr Terry Coulson (see Chapter 15) reveals that he had not fully taken on board his engineering principles. It seems likely that Dick *was* losing it academically, probably because of the amount of time he had to spend earning money to survive, and possibly because of the time he spent doing other things, including fishing.

In any event, he did not complete the third year of study necessary to obtain a degree, so he did not graduate. It is not quite clear how he then became an Admiralty 'boffin'. Before being called for interview by the Admiralty he was working for Murphy Radio at Welwyn (where they realised he knew about transmitters) but whether this was after he had left university, or whether it

Dick as a radio ham, a pastime later abondoned according to Alan Brown.

A 2lb roach and a 1lb dace from the river Cam on fly.

was a means of earning money to fund his studies whilst still at university is not clear. After the war he did not return to finish his studies, but went from Farnborough into the family firm of Lloyds & Co.

The war years clearly brought out some of the best in Richard Walker and although I had intended a special chapter on the subject, Pat has covered it so well in Chapter 21 that an additional chapter seemed unnecessary.

Dick married Ruth Burdett-Holcroft on 21st May, 1940, and after the war their first child, Richard, was born on 21st July, 1946, and the twins Simon and Tim on 7th April, 1950. They lived in the family home, 11 Bearton Avenue, Hitchin, a house built by Dick's mother and an address well known to hundreds of anglers who wrote to him there over the years. Ruth was a great support to Dick during those crucial years when he was becoming famous.

It was also a house well known to the legendary angler and rod builder Alan Brown. Alan was eleven-years-old when he got to know Dick. Alan was (fishing) friendly with Brian Collins whose mother cleaned Dick's house. The two of them managed to get Dick to take them fishing and they went to the Ouse at Offord for some chub fishing. Alan also began to visit Dick at his house where a very large fishing shed reposed in the garden. (It is an interesting aside that I received a telephone call from a man who was a neighbour of the Walkers at the time, and whose property overlooked theirs. He tells me that Dick painted the shed a subdued shade of environmentally friendly green! It seems in keeping with Dick somehow.) Alan's visits to Dick's fishing shed were rather special. Not only was the interior always full of tackle and things being made, but Dick actively encouraged Alan in his fishing in a rather unique way. Each week he would give Alan a chapter to read from a famous book such as a Bickerdyke, and the following week he would test Alan on the contents. He was actually marked, given points, and when he reached a certain total was rewarded with an item of fishing tackle such as floats or, as on one occasion, a Mitchell reel. This little story brings out several things about Dick that will run as threads through the chapters of this book: firstly, the generosity he always showed to young and old alike; secondly, his commitment to teaching about the sport; and thirdly his not-so-widely-appreciated support of youngsters. The last of these he rarely wrote about or mentioned but it has become increasingly clear to me that, quietly, he often went out of his way to help young people. You will read of other instances later on.

At an early stage of planning for this book I came across a story that typifies Dick's kindness to ordinary adult anglers too. Derek Lewis was a parcel-deliveryman and regularly dropped off at Lloyds & Co. On one occasion he got talking to the man on the door at Lloyds and the subject of angling came up (Derek Lewis used to fish Southill Park in the 1960s, as I did myself).

Dick at university.

With first wife Ruth, mother of Richard, Simon and Tim.

Dick with Edwin Halford at Lloyds, the family firm where he worked after the war, and for all his working life.

He couldn't believe it when the man offered to introduce him to the now quite famous Dick Walker who was at work in his office. But he duly did, and Dick gave him a lot of time, and suggested he fished a section of the Ouse at Willington for big barbel (and this in the 1960s). Another friend of Derek's was Wally Prior who later taught Ruth Walker to drive: Wally had an invitation to fish Dick's section of the Upper Ouse and took Derek along with him. All these were private, kind acts by Dick, but they also agree with the public image we have of him.

Dick was not so popular everywhere, though, and there was evidence of some jealousy after he had caught quite a lot of good fish and won prizes. With the exception of a few individuals, this jealousy did not extend to the national scale, but at a local level it was quite pronounced and Dick found himself banned from several local clubs. All this animosity disappeared when Dick was older and his reputation by then quite unassailable.

Another aspect of Dick's character that is self-evident in the account of Alan Brown is the high value that Dick placed on *reading* about the sport. Very little got Dick angry, but one thing was anathema to him and that was the phrase 'You'll learn nowt about angling from reading books'. (It is true that he often adopted a northern accent when quoting this statement!) Like all intelligent people he considered reading up on a subject, sooner rather than later, as crucial to moving forward. 'We all stand on the shoulders of giants' he would say.

These might have been the last days that Dick was involved in amateur radio, an interest which had begun in his teens and which he had been involved with at the beginning of the war. Alan recalls that radio equipment 'littered' the household for a time but later disappeared, along with the Flemish giant rabbits which had for so long been part of Dick's life.

Alan was encouraged in tackle making and, as we know, later became one of the best rod makers in the UK, winning both national and international awards. He attributes the very roots of his success as an angler and as a rod maker directly to Richard Walker. This is not to say that all was always sweetness and light between them, of course. There were times when Alan spent most evenings in the shed, except at weekends when he was banned by Dick's wife Ruth: Dick would be away fishing as often as not anyway, which seems to have given rise to some tension in the household. Of all the anglers Alan has known in his life he considers Dick perhaps the most fanatical (in the best way, of course) - every waking minute seems to have been consumed with matters angling. It is worth reminding ourselves that Alan Brown knew Dick at a time when the latter was in his most inventive and revolutionary period, when the discourse with Maurice Ingham was taking place, when the Carp Catchers' Club was formed, when *Still-Water Angling* was stirring in Walker's mind.

Dick fishing on the Tweed.

Chapter 3

First and last articles

ALTHOUGH Dick Walker wrote some short fishing stories as a small child, they have not survived for us to read. His first *published* fishing article was written at school and appeared in the Friends' School magazine (*The Avenue*, 1932). His first professional article, according to Dick himself, was for the *Fishing Gazette*, in 1936. However, having carefully searched every issue of *FG* from 1935 to January 1939 I can find no record of this (even under possible pseudonyms) or even of any letter by R.W. His first commercially published article was therefore probably in the *Anglers' News* in 1938. This, together with *The Avenue* article and Dick's very last article for *Angling Times* (13th July, 1983) are produced below.

A FISHING EXPERIENCE
by R. S. Walker
(*The Avenue*, 1932)

I sat, rod in hand, contemplating the placid lake with its yellow water-lilies floating on the murky green water, its blue dragonflies disporting themselves over its surface, and birds twittering in the willow trees at its edge; and here and there I heard a splash as some small fish leaped to seize the insect his piscine little soul loved. As I watched the red-topped float I heard a rustle beside me, and turning my head, I saw a tiny field-mouse trying to drag away my bait, which consisted of bread and bran. The little creature was pulling with all its might, but it could not move the large lump of bread.

As I watched, I was conscious of a faint vibration of the line which I held between my thumb and forefinger and, turning, I saw the float give one or two preliminary bobs and then suddenly disappear as if a clutching hand had seized it and drawn it down into the depths of the lake.

My hand shook with excitement as I watched yard after yard of line slip from the reel, in little jerks; then, when I judged the fish had had enough, I put in the check of the reel, tightened the line, and struck. I felt a heavy jerk; then the line went slack, and I thought the fish had gone. Then a remarkable thing happened. Far out on the surface of the lake the water burst with a splash, and out shot a great copper-coloured fish. He did not get all the way out of the water, but when he fell back he made the water roar.

Frantically I wound in the line; it tightened, and heavy and strong came the weight. Again the fish leaped, tearing out line. He darted off in a series of leaps similar to his first, five in all. The reel screamed; the line sang. The rod, which I had thought stiff as a tree, bent like a willow wand. The reel began to get hot, and a wisp of blue smoke streamed out of the oil-hole.

When at length the fish foundered he had taken off over a hundred yards of line.

The next thing that happened was that the fish began to plug away and hit the line with his tail. He was trying to get in among the water-lily stems where he could lie up and break the line, while I leaned back on the rod and tried to stop him. At length he turned and swam towards me, while I quickly wound in the line. I knew he must be tiring, so I increased the pressure and led him nearer. But as soon as he was near enough to see me he made another powerful rush and took off a lot more line. At the end of this run he leaped again; but it was only the ghost of his former efforts, a slow, weary rise, clearly showing that he was almost played out. So I led him to the shore and, placing the wide-mouthed landing-net beneath him, I lifted him in.

As he lay in the landing-net, with the bright sun shining down upon him, he gave a convulsive jerk, opened his mouth wide, shivered, and died. He was a carp weighing six pounds.

Some people think of an angler as a person who sits for hours dangling a line in the water, seldom getting a bite. I hope that what I have written will convince them otherwise.

A NOVEL METHOD OF FISHING FOR CARP
by R. S .Walker
(*Anglers' News*, 11th June, 1938)

The method I am about to describe is eminently suited to very weedy waters, and to hot weather, when carp are to be seen basking on the surface of the water or lazily swimming about with their dorsal fins breaking the surface. At such times ordinary bottom-fishing methods are almost useless; even float fishing at a shallow depth being unproductive, as carp are suspicious creatures and will seldom take a bait if they can see a float and lead above it. In weedy waters, also, the fish may be seen on such days as I have described basking in small openings in the weed-beds, where they are out of reach of float or leger tackle.

The equipment required under such circumstances is rather specialised. A fixed-spool reel of large size, such as the Felton Crosswind or the no. 3 Altex, is a prime convenience, as long casts have to be made, and in weedy water a heavy line must be used. My own reel is a home-made affair, consisting of an ordinary wooden Nottingham reel adapted to turn on its seat and face up the rod. It is capable at times of producing the most involved and complicated tangles that it has been my misfortune to see. The rod should be chosen according to the size of the fish and the nature of the water; generally speaking, a light split-cane pike rod with wide porcelain rings will be found most useful. Mine is six feet long and weighs about ten ounces. The line should be of plaited silk, about 15lb b.s., and should be steeped in melted paraffin wax to make it float. Sixty yards at least must be on the reel; I have known a 9lb mirror carp to take that amount in one straight run.

A cast made of gut-substitute, with a breaking strain similar to that of the line, should be spliced to the end of the line, as a splice does not catch on water lily roots and the like in the same way as a knot is apt to do. Two yards is long enough for the cast. A size 4 hook is used, of the TDE variety, as ordinary hooks to gut are apt to straighten and tear out.

The bait consists of breadcrust and honey. A loaf two days old is cut into pieces the size of a golfball, crust on one side and crumb on the other. One such lump is impaled on the hook and dipped into the honey for about three minutes.

The water is now approached as quietly as possible, and the bait cast among the carp on the surface. They will at once disappear, frightened by the splash, but in ten minutes or less will be back, and after approaching and retreating from the bait a few times one will take it, go off with a rush and hook himself. It is hardly ever necessary to strike. The fish is then played in the usual way.

This floating bread method is one of the most likely that I know to produce either a carp or heart failure, as the bait is taken in full view of the angler by what usually seems an immense fish.

As long a cast as possible should be made, and care must be taken not to show oneself to the fish. Any available cover should be taken advantage of, and the rod is best placed at rest, not held in the hand, for, as I have said, the fish almost always hook themselves. It is wise to sit within reach of the rod, however, to save it from being pulled in.

Groundbaiting, if it is thought necessary, is done by throwing one or two pieces of bread similar to hookbait. This should be done very sparingly.

The size of bait which I recommend may seem preposterously large, but the bread very soon becomes pulpy in the water, and is easily sucked in by the average carp. I once caught a 14-pounder with half a cottage loaf as bait; it was only by using an extra large and heavy bait that I was able to cast far enough to reach the fish. So do not be afraid of using a big bait, it enables one to fish far off, the secret of success with this method.

The following is Dick's last article for *Angling Times*, a column that ran weekly for thirty years.

THE VOICE OF ANGLING
(*Angling Times*, 13th July, 1983)

When I began this column, I would have been amazed if I had been told I'd continue to do it every week for thirty years. That's what has happened - but it is with great regret I have to tell you that this is my last regular contribution.

The decision is entirely my own and I think I owe it to you, the readers, to explain the reason for it.

To begin with, I have now reached the age of sixty-five and although I still do a good deal of fishing, I can't do as much as I think a regular weekly contributor ought to be doing if he is to provide a proper service to his readers. I can't anymore put in a twelve-hour stint on a trout reservoir, or two successive nights on the bank of a carp lake. Your readers deserve someone who can, and there is no shortage of younger men who not only can do it, but who can write intelligently about it.

In addition, for some reason I don't understand, the correspondence that my writing has produced has risen enormously over the past three years, and frankly, it has now gone beyond what I can cope with, if I am to serve faithfully the company for which I work.

So, from now on, I must regretfully decline to answer readers' letters, though of course I hope to stay in touch with those with whom I have already had correspondence.

The others won't suffer because John Crossman's information service in *Angling Times* is excellent. I've known John for a long time. He doesn't know everything about fishing, any more than I do, but whenever he doesn't know the answer, he'll scurry about until he finds someone who does. As you may guess, I'm feeling very sentimental about ending my regular column, especially because writing it has brought me so many good friends, few of which I would have met otherwise. To me, good friends are the most important part of fishing - I'd rather have a blank day with them, than a big catch in uncongenial company.

I'm not going to list all the good friends that writing this column has brought me, because there simply is not enough room - but there is room enough for me to thank them all for the great kindness they have always extended to me. I must also thank a vast number of readers who, over the years, have given me, either intentionally or otherwise, ideas for subjects for this column. I don't think I could have kept it going without them. Writing a thousand words is easy when your head is buzzing with a good subject, but there is nothing in journalism worse than sitting wondering what to write about. Time after time when I have been in that position, a timely letter from a reader has arrived that has started my pen running happily over the paper.

I must also thank the succession of editors and editorial staff with whom I've worked over these last thirty years. Without exception, they have left me free to say exactly what I liked, and there has never - no, not once - been the least suspicion of a quarrel or ill feeling with any of them. I suspect this is because they have all been, and still are, keen anglers and very few anglers are anything but nice people.

It has always amazed me to see how generous anglers can be when approached personally for a contribution for a good cause - perhaps a fellow club member who has suffered some misfortune - but how, at a meeting from club to NFA or NAC level, any proposal to increase contributions by as little as the cost of a few pints will inevitably be voted down. I need say no more about it - you've heard it all before from me, but you will not hear it from me again. Perhaps on the day when you find you have nowhere to fish, some of you will remember, and say: "Old Dick Walker warned us enough times didn't he?"

Looking back over sixty years of fishing, forty-seven years of writing about it, and thirty years of producing weekly columns, not only for *Angling Times*, but at intervals, years of doing it for national newspapers as well, brings me back a host of memories, nearly all of them pleasant ones. Oddly enough, although I have caught some big fish, their captures do not shine as brightly in reminiscence as you might think. I think more of the happy times spent with good companions and what they have said. Fred Taylor, sitting fishing with icy sleet blowing almost horizontally into his face. "How are you doing Fred?" I asked. "Oh Dick," he said, "I will be glad when I've had enough of this!"

Then there were days when I fished with my old friend 'BB'. We used to keep our eyes on the time in the evening, and when a certain time arrived, we would begin to recite, in unison, a passage from H.T. Sheringham that we knew by heart: 'At a little after half-past eight, this tip trembled and then disappeared. My first thought was a mild wonder as to why it did that . . .' And so on. Once, when we were reciting it, the float tip did tremble and then disappear. A 4lb tench was responsible.

Then there was the day when Pete Thomas foul-hooked a huge carp, at least forty pounds, by its rear end. He played it skilfully for some fifteen minutes, and then said: "It must be pretty firmly hooked!" Whereupon the hook instantly came away. There was also the day when we pulled a bullock out of Redmire pool - but I could go on and on, and that's the very thing I've decided not to do.

So it's goodbye and good fishing from yours sincerely,

Dick Walker

Chapter 4

Walker and the media

I HAVE often heard it said that Dick Walker *used* the media. In the crudest sense this is, of course, correct, but those people making the comments are using them in a derogatory sense and have in mind the frequency with which Dick appeared in the press and on TV. In reality Dick worked *with* the media. When the cameras or microphones were there he produced results, whether of fish or knowledgeable comment. So the media *wanted* him. Magazine editors liked him because he was not only controversial but he produced his copy on time, well prepared, of the right number of words, and with good photographs for illustration. They could expect a response from their readers and they became fully aware that Dick normally kept some ammunition in reserve and he frequently led antagonists, by the nose, into traps. His opening gambit, as it were, often sounded so outrageous that readers would fire off a hasty and heated reply, only for Walker to calmly shoot their heads off in the next issue.

Dick, as we've seen, was an excellent teacher, partly, if not wholly, as a result of his upbringing and early schooling. Not surprisingly, therefore, he had a clarity of style in writing that lent itself to the publication of articles and books, and a clarity of expression in speaking (if sometimes rather verbose) that suited him so well to radio and TV.

Colin Willock writing in the *Shooting Times and Country Magazine* (19th December, 1974) wrote that Dick Walker was, '. . . the happy possessor of a prose pen that is almost Churchillian in its lucidity and directness'. Dick also wrote under pen-names: in his early years, 'Water Rail'; and, occasionally in later years 'L. O. Mycock'.

But Dick was not only a competent presenter, he was also a very experienced and knowledgeable angler. The combination of attributes enabled him to communicate his angling knowledge to a wide range of the public. And because he wrote in journals other than angling ones, as well as appearing on TV and radio, he also reached an extensive non-angling audience. It's not surprising that the media wanted him. Proof of this is to be found in the many letters from editors, producers, and publishers, the authors of which became life-long friends.

Dick's competence when faced with a camera crew was nowhere better exemplified than in the *Philpott File* series of the early 1970s. The series dealt with contentious issues and one of these was angling (probably in response to the anti-angling noises of the time). Trevor Philpott wanted angling to be shown in its various forms, and two of the programmes covered chub fishing on the Great Ouse with Dick and friends (Peter Thomas if I recall), and pike fishing on Loch Lomond with myself, amongst others (Eric Allen, Eric Hodson and Mike Prorok). When the series was actually televised most anglers, myself included, were horrified: thanks to the poor filming and editing, anglers were made out to be idiots who spent huge amounts of money on tackle and didn't catch anything anyway.

My programme really was dreadful. We were shown doing anything but catching fish, and that was despite the fact that, in front of the camera, I had produced three very good pike on lure with a great deal of airborne action from the fish and action in the boat from me. We'd had other good fish and plenty of action, plus lots of good discussions and bank-side tackle analysis. Philpott himself had not deigned to come to Scotland, but his dogsbody had seemed very pleased with the filming and had really got quite excited. However, in the editing room all the good stuff ended up on the floor and the result was a complete misrepresentation of what pike angling - indeed angling - was about.

You might think that the same thing would have happened to Dick's programme, but to Dick's credit, it did not: the crucial difference was that Dick discoursed direct to the camera and the interviewer, which meant that the producer had to make the programme *around* him. The force of his arguments was so strong that to edit things out would have shown up strange gaps. A good television programme *needs* that strong personality (look at John Wilson today).

Dick also contributed to the Jack Hargreaves *Out of Town* series, a very popular programme for country lovers, as well as for anglers. On one occasion Dick used a superb match rod and centre-pin reel combination with which he had taken some very big roach. Jack Hargreaves greatly admired the outfit and, quite typically, Dick simply made him a present of the rod and the reel. There's an interesting philosophical angle to this - Dick's natural generosity aside, what angler gives away the most important, and clearly very favoured,

Assembled for Jack Hargreaves' Out of Town *programme, covering a match which Dick's protégé won. Peter Wheat is also in the picture, third from left.*

tools of his trade? Dick gave away cherished rods and reels on many occasions. At a later stage Jack Hargreaves sold the rod and reel (which, given the circumstances, seems a little puzzling) but, as it happens, they went to a good home: Nick Butt became aware of the sale and he, being a Walker fan, purchased them and used them, and gets a great deal of pleasure out of their use. I reckon Dick would have been happy with that outcome.

Dick seemed completely at home on TV, but he was also just as assured on radio. Radio, some might say, is easier - less sensationalism is involved, less prejudice, perhaps, from the producer. (Even I have done some reasonable radio . . .) Dick did quite a lot of radio broadcasting and was excellent value. In fact he was, and remains to this day, the only angler to have been interviewed on *Desert Island Discs* - as an angler that is (plenty of people have been on *Desert Island Discs* who happen to fish but were there for other reasons). Dick was interviewed by Roy Plomley, and it *was* a good programme, with Dick giving his choices of operatic pieces (one of his other real loves in life).

Another marvellous radio programme was broadcast by the BBC Midlands' Home Service in 1953, in which Dick caught a nice carp. Photographs of the action have appeared in several books, showing Bill Latto clutching a microphone, going live to the listeners. Bernard Venables provided the technical commentary. It was dramatic stuff at the time, more particularly so because Dick, having fished since midnight, caught a good fish 'to order', just before a 6am deadline. (Maurice Ingham gives a full description of this incident in his book, *Woldale*.)

Radio action: Dick plays a good carp, whilst Maurice Ingham waits with the net.

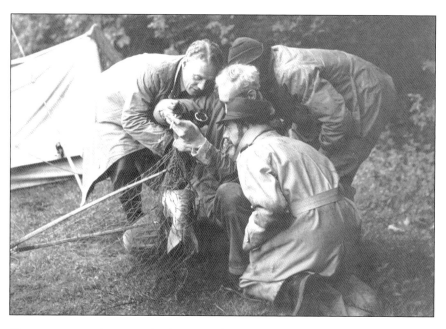

The same programme: the moment of truth as a 16 1/4 lb carp is weighed.

This ability to catch to order characterised his media forays and was one very good reason for the media's love of him. This is not to say that Dick did not prepare very thoroughly because he certainly did. His correspondence with Peter Stone show that he caught 'insurance fish' the day before, and kept them overnight just in case . . . These fish were to be shown to the camera, but not rehooked of course. (I remember Bob Church and I doing exactly the same for a pike fishing TV programme produced by Terry Thomas.)

That Dick had the gift of the gab I have mentioned elsewhere in its more negative context, but when it came to radio or TV it was, naturally, an advantage for the star to be fluent, unstoppable - and knowledgeable. One of the tricks in presenting is to use not only your voice, but your hands: if your hands are used in French-style gesticulation, especially if they come up anywhere near your face, then editing out a section of the run is very, very difficult. Dick did not blatantly engineer this, but his delivery was so expressive that cutting him out was always going to be tricky. He was forceful, competent and engaging, and the programme-makers loved him.

It is interesting to hear of an insider's experience of Dick's television persona, as recounted by his son Tim:

In the past a number of people have attached labels to Dick Walker - 'arrogant', 'immature', 'a showman'. Well, he was all of these things, and none of them. If you stay at that level of analysis you miss the complexity of the man beneath the façade. Let me explain.

When you're a child you tend to take whatever your home environment is as the norm and accept what you are told as fact writ in stone. I knew my father was famous, I guess, but it made very little impact upon me. Wasn't *everyone's* home life like that? If I didn't see my father for weeks on end, well, wasn't that the same for everybody? It was not until I was sixteen that my perceptions of my father changed and I realised there was far more to the man than I had assumed.

In 1965, one Thursday, Dick told me that he was travelling down to Hampshire the following day to do a TV broadcast and would be away for the weekend. Before I knew I'd said it, I asked, "Can I come?" To my amazement he said yes, providing I asked my headmaster if it was all right to take the day off school. And he said yes, too!

The next morning we set off for Hampshire. Dick kept a slightly dilapidated caravan in Ibsley, just the other side of the road to the river Avon. The broadcast was to be from Two Lakes, Alex Behrendt's water, with Jack Hargreaves. We met with Colonel Stanley Crow, who was also to be involved, along with Captain Oliver Kite and Colonel 'Tiger Rags' Locke. The cameraman was Stanley Brehoe.

It was a wonderful day. Mention has been made elsewhere of a 'joyous crew' and that day it was a joyous crew indeed! The true highlight was when Colonel Crow was made to walk behind Dick as he was casting. Dick said, "Don't walk behind me, Crow!" He did, and got the hook of Dick's fly through his ear. It was, "I say, Walker, that's a bit much!" and, "I told you not to walk behind me!" Dick had a pair of wire cutters and cut the point and barb off the hook to allow it to be drawn out backwards. Dick told Colonel Crow, "Well, I don't want to waste the feathers!"

The side I saw of Dick during the filming was at total variance to the man I knew as a father. He was in showman mode. His voice was louder than usual, full of self-confidence and every gesture exaggerated. I caught my first trout that day, and was filmed doing so. When Dick congratulated me he slapped me roundly on the back, which nearly knocked me over. To me, this seemed out of character.

When it was all over and we were alone, he relaxed and became his normal self again. We talked about this and Dick told me that he considered his public persona needed to be larger than life and it was clear he donned it quite deliberately.

Dick's book publications are fairly well known, and are listed for reference on page 310. What is not so well known is the fact that he was involved in the publication of many other angling books, often contributing forewords or chapters, and that he also acted as a consultant for publishers of fishing titles. We learn from *The Stone-Walker Letters* that Dick acted as a (positive) referee for one of Peter Stone's books. Peter knew nothing about it until after he'd had the good news from the publisher. It is also evident from the files of publisher Ernest Benn that Dick offered publishers his advice and helped authors with their book proposals. As I said at the beginning of the chapter, he did not *use* the media, but worked with it. Nothing was ever too much trouble, and his input was always highly regarded.

Dick's public speaking skills were also put to good use in the lectures that he gave all over the country (at no charge other than expenses). He spoke fluently and engagingly but never spoke for too long and always stopped in time for questions: and there always were questions!

Being on the public stage in these various guises suited Dick's confident personality well. It allowed him to dominate without opposition (until question time). This is not to say that Dick had a 'domineering' personality. Brian Clarke puts it better when he says of Dick that, when he entered a room, his *presence* immediately dominated what was going on: he may not have intended this, and may not have intended in any way to be theatrical, but this was, in reality, the exact consequence. The next chapter reveals aspects of Walker that point to a much greater modesty than his media persona implies.

From the left: Jack Hargreaves, Capt. Oliver Kite, Col. Crow, Dick and Tim Walker, at Two Lakes.

Dick instructing a young angler.

Dick and Pat, Russell Hole (then Angling Times*) and Robin Miller at the George Hotel, Stamford:
a presentation to Dick from* Angling Times *in recognition of his long years with the paper.*

Dick demonstrating fly casting with Terry Thomas commentating.

Chapter 5

The Walker letters

I DON'T think anyone can really appreciate the sheer scale of the literary contribution of Walker's correspondence: there are *hundreds* of letters, those sent to him coming from all over the country, and from anglers of all disciplines in all walks of life. A huge file of letters is held by Pat Walker; Kevin Clifford holds many; there is a Berth-Jones set; a Maurice Ingham set; Fred J. Taylor and Chris Yates letters; and the Stone-Walker letters that have recently been published in book form, incorporating most of Dick's letters to Peter Stone. Dick did not keep a record himself of his own letters and articles, but many recipients have kept and treasured the correspondence they received from him.

The letters to Dick came from a wide range of people: schoolboys, raw beginners, experienced anglers, famous anglers - at times, it seemed, almost every well known angler in the land - club officials, politicians of all rank from Council to Cabinet, environmental buffs, anti-anglers, pro-swan fanatics and an enormous number from publishers, editors and the tackle trade. Some of the files in connection with an individual or a company are quite extensive and reflect analyses of on-going questions or problems. He must have received at least ten letters a day, for years, and as far as we know he answered them *all*. His early letters were all written in his famed copper-plate handwriting, but latterly, perhaps because he had so many, he turned to dictating his replies so that they could be typed by his secretary at Lloyds, Dorothy Johnson, and then Karen Dymock. Replying to letters was a task that Dick never complained about and he seemed to have replied with relish rather than resignation. Indeed, his enthusiasm is consistently evident in his replies. Often they were lengthy, as he always answered every single question asked of him, and they were always incredibly helpful (many recipients have emphasised this time and again to me and, having now read near on a thousand letters, I can confirm that this is correct). Another feature of his letters is that he never talked either up or down to people: each letter is measured, basically friendly, never rude in adversity, and always, always informative. Quite often he would give names, addresses and telephone numbers of further contacts that the letter-writer might need in order to obtain an item of tackle or a fishing permit. If he knew someone who could help the writer in better fashion than he could, then Dick would tell him or her. For example, although he had some ideas about water and fish management, he often referred people to Eric Birch for a more professional opinion.

The letters are often well illustrated too, with anything from very beautiful thumb-nail sketches to large plans of waters. And he very frequently sketched tackle to clarify a point. Of course, some of the best of his writing is seen in the book *Drop Me A Line* (a name suggested by Dick's mother) where he and Maurice Ingham exchanged letters on all manner of angling subjects from a beginner's route to fly fishing and fly tying, to stuffing fish and carp fishing. It is one of the conundrums of angling that this quite splendid book (which I have read with pleasure several times) was never a best-seller.

Dick's manner of answering the many letters he received, taking care to answer all the questions asked of him, was quite exceptional. One of the great letter-writers of the time was a good friend of mine, Ray Webb. Ray wrote a great many letters to a great many people in his attempts to obtain information about fish and fishing. At one time he kept a record of the responses he received and his analysis was interesting: at least 60% of the people he wrote to didn't bother to reply at all, in spite of the enclosed SAE (Ray reckoned they steamed off the stamps!); with the exception of Dick, of those that replied hardly any answered the questions they had been asked (Ray always carefully enumerated his questions). All this serves to emphasise what a remarkable attitude Dick had towards helping people at his own expense and in his own time.

Dick's letters to editors and publishers have quite fascinating slants to them at times. In complete contrast to Dick, these are not people generally noted for their efficiency and yet he remained unfailingly courteous in dealing with them. Many editors have a creative streak, which, whilst entirely necessary for the production and publication of attractive publications, is sometimes at odds with the organisational skills required for safe filing of a writer's slides and copy. (In later years I suspect Dick was treated more carefully than most.)

Another aspect that is apparent in his dealings with the trade and the media, is his attitude to payments. It's fairly obvious from his letters that he did a great deal for the trade without payment or sponsorship of any kind. I'm sure that tackle came his way regularly in consequence of his efforts, but he often gave this away should anyone show an interest in it. He was especially helpful towards small companies, or inventors of tackle items. His early involvement with Intrepid and Ken Morritt is well known, but the files show dozens of firms asking for his advice and their letters make it very clear just how much help they received from him. Only occasionally is there any mention of payment. This is particularly ironic when one considers the advice he would give to new writers. He was always keen to make sure that they behaved professionally, providing good copy and pictures, but he also stressed that they should be treated well financially by the magazines or publishers. He clearly felt that if the workman was worthy of his labour he should be paid. Yet he did not seem to apply the rule to himself!

There is one final point to be made about Dick's letters: this is that they were quite astonishingly consistent. Opinions and ideas held early in his career may have evolved or been honed in later years, but there is little in the later letters that contradicts what he has written years before. Given that he kept no record of his work, either letters or articles, it does give further evidence of the strength of his convictions.

The following letters are a few examples which show just how thoroughly Dick dealt with his correspondence. In places you can also see just how seriously he took attacks on angling, or cases where angling was dealt with in an unfair manner with respect to other sports. The last letter (to me) clearly demonstrates the mixture of practical commonsense, humour and helpfulness that was so typical of his correspondence.

Colin Booty, Esq.
Wildlife Officer,
RSPCA,
Causeway,
Horsham, West Sussex.
RH12 1HG

> 37 Ivel Gardens,
> Biggleswade, Beds.
> 11th May, 1983

Dear Mr Booty,
Let my say at once that I would much prefer private discussion about swan deaths, or indeed about any other matters of a similar nature in respect of wildlife that the RSPCA, the NCC or the RSPB may wish to initiate, either with individual journalists like me, or with representative angling organisations, or both.

Unfortunately, no such course has been followed. The result has been that statements, many of them either unsubstantiated or exaggerated, have been issued to the media, who have still further exaggerated them and, in many cases, used them to attack angling.

To take some examples, a figure of 500 tons of lead lost in our waters has been freely quoted. You know and I know that this figure is an exaggeration of at least ten times.

It has been projected into an estimate that states as a fact that there are two split shot for every foot of riverbank in Britain, and this has been widely publicised. It is, of course, quite ridiculous, if for no other reason than the fact that shot cover a great range of sizes from LG down to dust shot!

We have also been presented with another figure, used by the media as if it were fact, that 3,000 swans are killed by anglers' shot every year. Do you really believe this? I don't! Not many anglers spend more time at the waterside than I do, and I can't remember when I last saw a dead swan.

I can find no evidence of any significant decrease in swan population for the United Kingdom, though one source postulated a decrease of 5% over the last ten years. That is half a per cent a year; if 4% equals 3,000 swans, then the total population must be 600,000! Surely you must agree that there has to be a glaring error somewhere.

Forgive me for correcting you, but I have not in fact questioned whether lead poisoning in swans is due to lead shot. Indeed, I think this is the most likely cause; but before statements are made to the effect that it is the proven cause, and the only cause, there are other possibilities that should have been investigated. I have been involved in more than one scientific investigation, in which it transpired that the most obvious answer was not in fact the correct one. I shall not describe these instances here, unless you tell me that you would like to hear about them. One, incidentally, involved the deaths of thousands of tame rabbits.

I am interested to hear from you something that I didn't know before, namely that in those rather limited areas from which the vast majority of lead-poisoned swans have been recovered, only a proportion of the swans so suffer; other birds on the same waters have normal levels of lead in their blood. Nobody seems to have asked why. Do some swans acquire a positive liking for lead shot? Or do the tamer swans, who get the most bread thrown in by the public, in quantities much greater than is generally supposed, need more grit to break down concentrated carbohydrates? Or is there some other explanation?

Some years ago, not only was there serious slaughter of New Forest ponies in car collisions, but not a few motorists were killed and injured. This was almost entirely due to motorists stopping to feed the ponies, which assumed that if they could stop cars, they would be fed. A combination of severe penalties for feeding the ponies, and extension of fencing, has virtually eliminated these collisions. Has any experimental work been done to discover the effects upon swans of being fed with large amounts of bread, as many are in urban areas? If not, why not? This seems to me a pertinent question, as yet not answered, specially in view of the fact that the vast majority of swan deaths due to lead poisoning, whether by ingestion of shot or any other cause, have occurred in predominantly urban areas, and/or in areas where very large numbers of powered pleasure craft are in constant use.

Many of these are hired craft, especially on the Norfolk Broads, and consequently tend to be operated by less responsible, less well-informed people than privately-owned craft. Excessive speeds are commonly seen.

Regardless of whether lead compounds are emitted by the exhausts of these craft, it cannot be denied that their wash stirs up bottom mud, washes material from the banks - including shot that has been accidentally spilled - and, in addition, swamps nests of a variety of waterfowl, including swans. This is why I asked whether the alleged reduction in swan population on the Thames is paralleled by a similar reduction in coots, moorhens, dabchicks and mallard.

As for finding a non-toxic substitute for lead shot, it takes but a simple check on a list of specific gravities of metals, and some other characteristics such as melting points and ductility, to discover that there is no acceptable substitute for lead. Our proper course is to ensure, as far as possible, that as little lead as possible is lost in our waters or on their banks. Shot dispensers have already been devised that release one shot at a time, and do not spill their entire contents if accidentally dropped or tipped over, and I hope very much that all angling organisations will, as soon as possible, ban all other shot receptacles. Unfortunately, while this fruitless search continues for lead substitutes, there is less incentive to press on with means for avoiding spillage.

We do, however, face another problem. As I have said repeatedly, anglers have been using lead for some four hundred years, probably much longer. There must be a good deal of it already in our rivers and I think we should be considering possible ways of getting at least some of it out. Unfortunately, it is non-magnetic, but it is metallic and, therefore, detectable, and it is also, like gold, of high specific gravity, so that it could be readily separated from silt, sand or gravel.

I think it likely that it may be found in concentrations, rather than evenly distributed, so that extraction might be easier. Given the apparatus, probably ornithologists, anglers and conservationists in general would volunteer their services without payment. If there is indeed as much lead in our waters as is claimed, the sale of such as might be recovered would help to defray costs.

Even if anglers ceased using lead tomorrow, the problem of poisoning by lead already in the water would remain for very many years to come, unless means for removing at least a considerable percentage can be found.

I hope very much that means can be found by which ingestion of anglers' leads by swans can be at least minimised, but I repeat, there is no satisfactory substitute for lead and I think it much more practical to address ourselves to means for avoiding the loss of shot, rather than to a fruitless search for alternatives. I repeat, while people continue to pursue the impossible, there is far less incentive to consider the practical.

On the question of water pipes, I assure you that copper replaced lead simply because it is less expensive. It needs none of the skills of the old-fashioned plumber with his melted lead or solder, and ability to 'wipe a joint', and it can be used with far thinner wall thickness than lead. I have to chuckle a little when I read about the dangers of lead plumbing, since I was born in a house so plumbed, spent ten years there, then eight more in boarding schools with lead plumbing, followed by all the years up to 1971 in houses or establishments where the plumbing was lead, What a genius I might have been, if only those pipes had been copper!

Which leads to another point - are the waters from which the dead swans have come, acid or alkaline?

You mention the Royal Commission on Environmental Pollution's Ninth Report. Where does it recommend the banning of anglers' lead shot?

What strikes me forcibly is the attitude of the RSPCA towards conservation in general. Numbers of creatures that were common when I was a boy are now relegated to rarities. I can remember when corncrakes were so noisy that they kept me awake on summer evenings. There were plenty of nightjars, and I could have shown you two nests of the red-backed shrike within two miles of Hitchin town centre. Not now! Yet I have never heard a word of protest from the RSPCA about this. Such birds are not well known to the urban public and, no doubt, the RSPCA thinks there is little or no emotive mileage to be gained from their demise. Everyone knows swans, however, so they can be used to mount attacks on angling via the gutter press, with good chances of success, which has already been achieved in some areas where angling has been banned.

The RSPCA appears to be quite oblivious of the fact that it is angling organisations alone that have fought pollution over the years. If it succeeds in having angling made illegal, can it take over the anti-pollution role itself?

Yours sincerely,
Richard Walker

If you found that rather heavy going you might like to read the following letter and poem from a pen swan in Devon, one Suzanne Sally Swan (Hon. Sec. Swan Egg Control Society), after she had read a letter of Dick's in the *Daily Telegraph*.

Dear Sir,

Chancing to observe a fragment of yesterday's *Daily Telegraph* floating in my home river, I read your letter, which inspired me to pen the following comment (I am a pen swan).

> I'm a swan from the Witham, and one of my tricks
> is to search for split shot, which I swallow for kicks.
> My town friends, per contras, are poisoned by lead
> in their grit and their salad, and forced to beg bread.
> I look down upon any relation who begs
> and suggest they'd do better to lay fewer eggs!

The following was written to angler Vic Bellars.

Vic Bellars, Esq.
Fritton,
Great Yarmouth,
Norfolk.

37 Ivel Gardens,
Biggleswade, Beds.
22nd April, 1983

Dear Vic,

I'm glad you are happy with the contribution to your perch book. Ken Taylor suggests that he should have added to his piece, the following:

'In slow, rush-lined swims, the B.B. shot nearest the hook can be replaced by a smaller shot or, when using big lobworms, it is sometimes better to dispense with this lower shot altogether.'

The firm that makes the 'Valley' disgorger also makes a very good version of my Flipstick; I'll get them to send you one. I think they'd appreciate a mention of their products in your column, provided, of course, that you approve.

One point I neglected to mention in those 'notes' was that perch have a remarkable sense of smell. Many years ago, I kept two little perch in a large aquarium, for three or four years. I found that if I put a few worms in a jam jar full of water, a single drop of that water put into the aquarium made the little perch dash about frantically, looking for worms.

It has occurred to me since that a suitably-sized bottle, filled with 'wormy' water, with a small hole in its cap to allow the contents to disperse slowly, could be cast out on a separate rod, or alternatively used in lieu of a swim-feeder, and might prove very effective in attracting perch.

Are you familiar with Francis Francis's classic description of the behaviour of cautious perch? If not, I'll have it photostatted and send it you - it really should go into your book; no problem, it's years out of copyright. It's in *A Book on Angling*. There is also a lovely little account in the same author's *Sporting Sketches* about how a juvenile negro servant extracted a couple of big perch from the Thames, using live minnows.

And, of course, the account in the earliest known fishing book in English, *The Arte of Angling*, by Samuels, long preceding Walton, of catching a big perch. This book was published many, many years before Walton. In fact, a short chapter full of quotes from the literary history of fishing, that apply to perch, would enhance your book, I think. There's Col. Thornton's account of catching a 7lb perch from Loch Lomond; whether true or not, it is not beyond the bounds of possibility. I've had more than one 2-pounder there, without even trying to catch perch!

I'm afraid this is rather a rambling letter; the reason is that I'm becoming more and more excited about your book. Anything I can do to help, I will!

Just remembered another thing about Arlesey perch, which was a contributory factor in the decision Bob Rutland and I made to stop fishing for them. I told you that now and then, we pulled up a perch of about 1lb from the 40-foot holes; well, every one of these came up with its guts blown out of its mouth, through the change of pressure. It didn't happen with the fish over $2\frac{1}{2}$lb or so, probably because it took longer to bring them up and consequently they had more time to adapt to the pressure change. There may well have been enough damage done, all the same, to kill even the big ones, though when released, they swam off and down. I doubt if any of the pounders survived, though. I think that when fishing very deep water, anglers ought to take lots of time in bringing perch to the surface. The change of pressure is about 14lb per square inch for every 32 foot of water and that is considerable. Fred Taylor and I have dived as deep as 20 foot and, although avoiding serious 'bends', we have felt pretty grotty afterwards! Headaches and lassitude, mainly. You can't take your time about surfacing when you do it without breathing apparatus, as we, perhaps foolishly, did. About two minutes underwater was our limit.

If I were back in the big-perch days at Arlesey, and hooked a big perch, I'd bring it up slowly over at least ten, preferably fifteen minutes, checked by a watch, not guessed.

If I were asked what is the maximum possible size that perch can reach in Britain, I'd guess at around 8lb. I once saw a perch of 3lb 2oz at Arlesey, attached to a line, grabbed by the nape of its neck by a much bigger perch, and carried off. The attacker eventually let go. I think it must have been in the region of 7 or 8lb, but that'd only be a rough guess. Certainly in those days, we lost fish that were much stronger than any we landed, though, of course, we can't be sure they were in fact perch; could have been pike or big eels; but to judge from the characteristic thumps, I still think outsize perch are the most likely to have been responsible. There was all sorts of rubbish at the bottom of Arlesey Lake, including rusty steel hawsers, corrugated iron sheds, and tipper trucks on narrow gauge railways, left over from the days when the pits were worked, and if, after connecting with a perch, you failed to apply a degree of heave-ho, the chances were that your fish would get round or into some of this rubbish and snag you solid. The fish we lost did this despite the heave-ho! One can only guess that they were considerably bigger. They felt like it, anyway!

However, despite all the perch I've caught over 3lb, I still regard a 1-pounder as a nice fish and a 2-pounder as a really big one! How many of our two million coarse-fish anglers have even seen a 2lb perch, let alone caught one?

One nice thing about big perch; no other fish does so well in perpetuating the legend of the boy with the bent pin and stick who catches the big fish when all the expensively-equipped experts have failed.

Another point - I devised a formula for calculating the approximate weights of various fish from the dimensions. It says, 'weight in pounds = length x girth x girth (all in inches) + 806'. It fails with fish that are comparatively deep in body but thin from side to side, like roach, rudd and bream, but it is astonishingly accurate for pike, trout, salmon, chub, dace, barbel, carp - and perch.

Example: my biggest perch was 19 inches long and had a girth of $14^{1}/_{4}$ inches, which by the formula gives a weight of 4lb $12^{1}/_{2}$oz! When you realise that length and girth measurements are seldom nearer than plus or minus $^{1}/_{8}$ inch, the accuracy of the formula seems to me quite remarkable. However, all I claim for it is an accuracy of plus or minus 10%; the girth of a fish doesn't increase in direct proportion to the fullness of its stomach, and this could introduce error - though so far, I've encountered no errors as great as 5%.

I expect you will warn your readers that they cannot only get pricked by perch dorsals; the edges of the gill covers can inflict nasty cuts if the fish is being held behind them, and kicks.

I'm enclosing a print of the opercula bone of a 3lb 6oz female perch from Arlesey, which appears to have been in its eighth year when caught. There was great difference in growth rates at Arlesey; my biggest fish was in its seventh year (4lb 13oz). What I find interesting is the evidence of variations in growth between the annual (winter) bands. It would seem that food supplies varied greatly throughout the feeding period, or possibly changes of temperature affected feeding activities - or both factors may have applied. Whatever the cause, it is clear that growth throughout each year fluctuated considerably. One might assume from this that perch reared artificially in a water of constant, suitable temperature, might reach sizes of from $1^{1}/_{2}$ to 2 times heavier!

Despite the fact that most of my big perch were caught on worms, I am sure that fast growth and large ultimate size in perch are dependent on dense populations of small fish, preferably in comparatively clear water.

Stirring up mud may often attract perch - in gravel pits still being worked, you find these fish all around the dredger, as you do when rivers are dredged. I've never caught big ones in such areas, but fish up to 1 or $1^{1}/_{2}$lb are often taken within a few yards of where the dredger is actually working, despite the enormous disturbance.

One more thing - on no account allow the name of an illustrator (which includes a photographer) to appear on the title page of your book! As I have just discovered, to my cost, this virtually eliminates any claims for Public Lending Rights.

Yours sincerely,
Richard Walker

Sir John Lang, GCB
Department of Education and Science,
Richmond Terrace,
Whitehall.
London SW1

11, Bearton Avenue,
Hitchin, Herts
31st May, 1967

Dear Sir John,
Thank you very much for your letter of May 30th.

Perhaps I failed to make myself clear when I first raised the subject of rates payable to Local Authorities in respect of fishing rights.

I do not think that any angler or angling organisation complains about fishing rights being liable to rates. What we consider to be unjust is the fact that, although as I understand it, Local Authorities have the power to reduce or altogether waive payment of rates in respect of non-profit-making recreational facilities and indeed do so in the case of every other sport, they never do so in respect of angling.

As you may know, some recreational facilities need no concessions of this kind and it would be wrong for concessions to be made, and these include some angling waters which are run on a commercial basis and from which considerable profits accrue.

We have on the other hand angling waters that are not so run and it seems to me quite wrong that there should be discrimination against these by Public Authorities who are not only willing to waive rate demands in respect of other non-profit-making facilities, but who in most cases subsidise these facilities out of public funds.

In the case of angling, the situation is aggravated by the increasing shortage of angling waters brought about primarily by the activities of Local Authorities, Water Undertakings and nationalised industries. As you are well aware, these organisations are now destroying angling waters at a most alarming rate, by sewage effluent, tipping of domestic refuse, using wet pits for the deposition of fly ash, and by source abstraction. The result is that the law of supply and demand operates and the rents asked for fishing rights rise rapidly. Naturally rate assessments will rise in step.

The only weapon the angler has against the destruction of his waters is to proceed at law against those engaged in destroying them, and this can only be done where waters are either owned by an angling organisation or leased under seal. The lodgement of a lease under seal renders the angling organisation liable to rate assessment, so that in order to place themselves in a position where they have some legal rights, anglers render themselves liable to this very heavy taxation.

It is ironic that a situation has arisen where those largely responsible for pollution and tipping, namely the Public Authorities, are in a position to levy a tax on ordinary citizens, should they take steps to obtain legal protection against damage to their interests and in some cases to their property.

I hope very much that this situation in regard to angling, which notwithstanding the liability of other sports to rate assessments, is unique in the respects I have stated, will become a subject for early discussion and positive action by the Sports Council.

Yours sincerely,
Richard Walker

The following letter to me shows how helpful Dick could be to other authors. In this instance, he discusses the issue of Public Lending Rights - the system that entitles authors to a return on the books that are borrowed from a public library.

Dr B. Rickards,
Pike Anglers' Club,
Milton,
Nr Cambridge

37 Ivel Gardens,
Biggleswade, Beds.
20th May, 1983

Dear Barrie,
I wonder if I could trouble you to fill in the enclosed Public Lending Right application? I also enclose a letter (please return this) from the PLR people, which will explain why this is necessary.

Unless you want to claim a share in the PLR for the fourth edition of *Still-Water Angling*, all you need do is complete sections A and D on the back of the form.

If you do want a share, which, from what I can gather, might amount to about 10% of £5 a year, less tax, it will be necessary to fill in the form in full and get your application duly signed and witnessed by a solicitor or a notary public, which will cost you more than you'd get from PLR!

The only reason for my applying for PLR at all is that with ten titles, there might just be enough to come from it to justify the bloody paper-work involved.

Take warning - never allow the name of an illustrator or contributor to appear on the title-page of any books you write in future! Not that you or I would grudge either a share in the paltry proceeds; but if your contrib-utor or illustrator should die, your PLR, it seems, dies with him! So guard your health, mate!

Have you applied for PLR for your own books? If not, what I have enclosed will show you how to go about it and whom to apply to for the necessary forms.

I have abandoned my claim for PLR in respect of *No Need to Lie*, because to the best of my knowledge, the illustrator, Reg. Cooke, is seriously ill, and also for *Dick Walker's Modern Fly Dressings*, because the edition was only a thousand copies and I'm not going to bother Taff Price, who took the photographs, about the matter, since the PLR will in any case be too trivial to bother about. *Still-Water Angling* is different; lots of libraries have copies, otherwise I wouldn't have troubled you in the matter.

In the very unlikely event of any worthwhile emoluments accruing from PLR, I promise to send you a fair share!

Yours sincerely,
Richard Walker

PS   I have some spare PLR forms. If you want one to claim for your own books, just let me know.

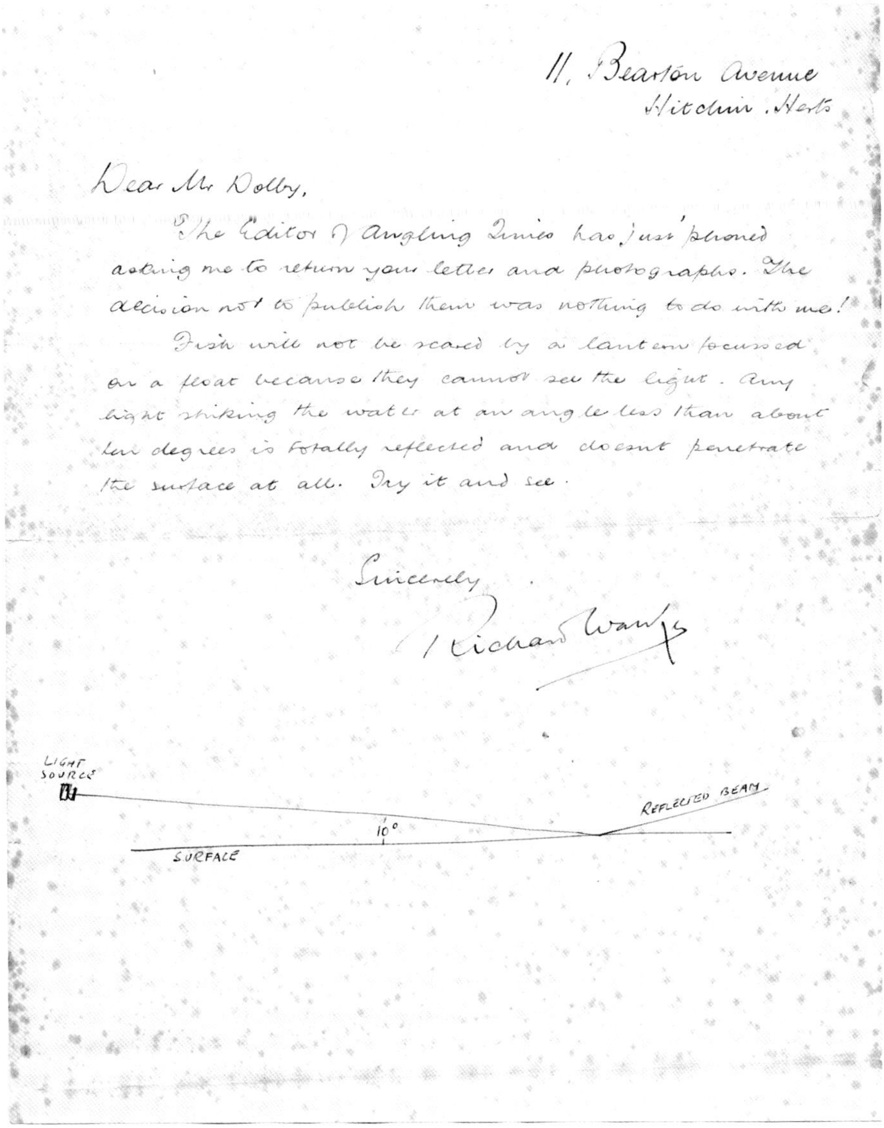

11, Bearton Avenue
Hitchin. Herts

Dear Mr Dolby,

The Editor of Angling Times has just phoned asking me to return your letter and photographs. The decision not to publish them was nothing to do with me!

Fish will not be scared by a lantern focussed on a float because they cannot see the light. Any light striking the water at an angle less than about ten degrees is totally reflected and doesn't penetrate the surface at all. Try it and see.

Sincerely.

Richard Walker

LIGHT SOURCE · SURFACE · 10° · REFLECTED BEAM

A typical Walker letter to an angler. Even when giving the writer bad news about the publication of his letter, he still manages to be positive and helpful!

Chapter 6

The tackle trade

MANY ANGLERS are fully aware of Dick Walker's inventiveness with tackle - his rod-building (about which he wrote a book) and his development of bite-alarms and so on - but I do not think they have any idea of the depth of his involvement with the tackle trade itself. A browse through the files of correspondence is quite mind-boggling: there could hardly have been a tackle firm, in his day, that he did not help and advise, often quite without payment.

One of his more famous connections was with the tackle giant Hardy's. He worked primarily with Jim Hardy, initially on his own but later with Leslie Moncrieff, the sea angler, Fred Buller and Fred J. Taylor of the Moncrieff Rod Development Company Ltd (a division of the Angling Technical and Advisory Group). At one stage Leslie had a boat rod and a beach rod with Hardy's, Fred Buller a couple of rods, Fred Taylor one too, and Dick some trout rods.

At first the rods they worked on were of glass but later carbon-fibre was used, and Walker and friends must be credited with its introduction to the fishing-tackle industry. Dick, as we know, had wartime connections with Farnborough and after the war the Ministry of Defence had been investigating the use of carbon-fibre in its work there. Dick and Jim Hardy drove to Farnborough to meet another friend of Dick's, Leslie Phillips, who was then working on the carbon-fibre. It was produced in ribbons up to three-quarters of an inch wide, and they took some of it back with them to Alnwick. There they decided to try some of it using the old fibreglass mandrels but the resulting rod was far too stiff. They immediately devised a smaller mandrel, which they deemed more suitable for carbon-fibre. The prototype, stiff rod stayed with Fred Buller for years, and is awaiting a permanent home in a national angling museum.

Dick had calculated that the carbon percentage should be no more than 20%. This small amount would result in a far lighter, narrower rod for the

From the left: Peter Thomas, Fred Buller, Frank Moir, Dick Walker, Bill and Jim Hardy at Hardy's.

Fred Buller, Dick, Fred J. Taylor and Leslie Moncrieff - the Moncrieff Rod Development Company assembled.

Piscatorial supper and sing-song at Dick's mother's house, Scudamore. From the left: Fred Buller, Dick, Dick's mother Elsie, Fred J. Taylor, Maurice Wiggin, Jack Thorndike (Ed. Angling Times), Leslie Moncrieff, Ken Sutton and Elsa (Mrs Walker's housekeeper).

same power than was possible with glass. As a result of this research a patent was taken out under the joint names of the Ministry of Defence, Hardy's and Dick Walker. But, in fact, Hardy's did not begin carbon-fibre rod production immediately because they wanted to see how the market would react. Other companies who did begin production ran into quite a few problems, producing rods that were too stiff or too brittle. Some, such as Fenwicks, had trouble with the spigots. Other companies used glass spigots in carbon-fibre blanks for a while.

Although Dick did not go into immediate production with Hardy's, he did write about carbon rods in his column, with great enthusiasm, and not surprisingly, it led to a considerable debate on the subject of carbon versus glass. Carbon won, of course, and when you think of it, glass as a rod-building material must have had one of the shortest runs in rod-making history. That is not to say that glass rods were all poor - good glass rods still survive today. In fact, it was because Dick was so concerned about early glass rods - they did not use compound tapers and the hollow build was initially poor - that he pressed for their improvement and they became just about right as the carbon boom hit.

So what we have in Dick Walker is a man who not only resurrected the use of split cane as a result of his Mk IV series of designs, making cane much more popular again, but who was involved in the birth of glass rods (especially their improvement after solid glass) and who was then instrumental in the birth of the carbon-fibre rod industry, today a billion pound industry. These are not small achievements. Of course, split cane was already in use in fly rods and some match rods, but it was as a result of his designs that the actual building specification of cane improved - it was his idea, for example to retain the outer, stronger skin of the cane on the best rods. These rods would have not a flatly hexagonal shape, but a *very slightly* rounded hexagonal cross-section. One could also argue that carbon-fibre rods might have happened in due course anyway, but the fact is that he was there, and he instigated it.

The following three letters from Leslie Phillips at the Royal Aircraft Establishment to Dick and Bill Hardy reveal the efforts that they went to in order to perfect those earliest carbon rods. And at this stage they had been working on the rods for almost nine years, as they began in 1968 - much earlier than most people think.

Mr R Walker,
Flitwick,
Beds.

Procurement Executive, Ministry of Defence,
Royal Aircraft Establishment,
Materials Department,
Farnborough,
Hants .

5th November, 1976

Dear Dick,

HYBRID RODS

I do love this three-cornered correspondence - your letter to Bill Hardy coming to hand at an appropriate moment as you will see below.

The stiffness at the extreme tip of a carbon-fibre rod has been bothering me for some time. We have been discussing your staggered layers idea and even gone beyond it to the extent of making the last few inches in glass.

Inevitably, with a tapered rod, the volume fraction of carbon-fibre rises and in the end, at the end, we become too stiff just when deflections are largest.

If one cuts the amount of carbon the tip rod becomes too weak as you say.

Now to the remedy!

We have now received the very long light alloy mould and in a few days will be able to turn out many different sorts of blank.

We will try the 3/2/1 layers idea and also 3/2/1/0 leaving a glass end. I have no doubt that if it makes a better rod we can 'sell it' using the magic word 'hybrid'.

Had a heavenly end of season day with Dermot Wilson and caught TROUT. Oh, I do thank the day when you visited RAE!

Sincerely,
L. N. PHILLIPS
cc Mr W. F. Hardy, Hardy Bros

Mr W. F. Hardy,
Vice-chairman,
The House of Hardy,
Willowburn,
Alnwick.

Materials Department
15th June, 1977

Dear Bill,

Many thanks for the letter of June. Answering your two points:

1. Yes, by all means, we shall make some more blanks for experiment (see below) and send them off to you. Also, to be getting along with, some pieces of heavy and medium Rohacell which should be machined into the normal triangular sections and returned for weighing and glueing.

2. I agree the carbon/Rohacell should be a little lighter, as well as cast further than, the cane. At the moment we do not have a weight breakdown and this is the next step, ie, we must find out what percentage of the weight is due to skins, to core and to glue-line.

If the glue-line is excessively heavy, we can seal the Rohacell and reduce its absorbency.

If the core is too heavy we can go to a lighter grade - but perhaps lose a little strength as well!

If the skins are too thick, then fewer layers or a lighter cloth is called for.

I should also add that the unidirectional glass-cloth that we added was quite a heavy and substantial layer, as you will see from the sample enclosed. I am confident we could lighten this considerably.

If you can return to me the machined samples of Rohacell in two separate marked envelopes we will weigh them accurately. Then, if we have the final weight of a length of rod we can get the weight of the glue-line by difference and present you with the complete weight break-down.

As you will gather from all the above, there is a lot more work to be done before we have all the answers.

I remain optimistic that we may be able to have our cake and eat it as compared with cane!

Sincerely,
L.N. Phillips
Cc Mr Richard Walker

Mr W. F. Hardy,
Vice-chairman,
The House of Hardy,
Willowburn,
Alnwick.

Materials Department
27th July, 1977

Dear Bill,

Many thanks for the letter of 15th July and for the machined samples of core which arrived separately.

I certainly did not intend you to go to a great deal of trouble, in the circumstances you have done miracles of machining! We shall, as you say, work backwards from the nominal densities. It is already clear that the 'Rohacell gepresset' is much denser than Rohacell Grade 70 but is still comparatively light.

Much of the extra weight of which you complained lies in that third all glass layer, also I am making up some blanks with two layers in each, both in the lighter and heavier forms.

One of the layers of reinforcement will be carbon, the other one will be carbon in the butt and glass at the tip. When made into a rod this will be about half-and-half at the tip which you thought looked more interesting.

I shall also be recommending a new adhesive, DLS 468, which has been giving us greater strength and rigidity under test.

The whole combination should begin to come down below the weight of the cane competitor.

Looking ahead a little, I have been experimenting with a quicker way of making the blanks. If we use a hot setting system instead of a cold setting and make two skins at a time back to back, this could more than double production. Enclosed please find a sample made from a hybrid cloth which happened to be handy. It will give you the idea!

Sincerely,
L.N.Phillips
Cc Mr Richard Walker

Dick's involvement with reels was less hands-on than his work with rods. With reels he was concerned with certain aspects of reel design that could be improved to the angler's benefit, and he made serious suggestions to manufacturers. Some of his suggestions were derived from his engineering background, such as the matter of roller pick-ups in fixed-spool reels. He pointed out that the friction over a fixed bearing in the reel pick-up head was much greater than if a roller bearing was in place, leading to loss of 'feel' when playing fish. Ken Morritt of Intrepid reels responded positively to this idea and introduced a roller pick-up in the Intrepid Elite reel. This was not a deluxe reel by any means, but anyone who played a fish on one of these reels and on a Mitchell (until then the market leader) could feel the difference in moments. Roller bearings are fairly common these days, in fact they were almost universal until fairly recently. And their introduction was a direct result of Dick's influence and persuasiveness. We all benefit from that today.

Dick played a similar, if smaller role in the improvements to slipping clutches on fixed-spool reels. Prior to the 1960s these were rather erratic and snatchy in performance and many anglers, myself included, resorted to backwinding with the slipping clutch set so hard that it only operated in a dire emergency.

It was his critical analyses of reels and their performance that seemed to produce a new mind-set amongst manufacturers. This resulted in numerous changes including, of course, the increased availability of left-hand wind (or ambidextrous) reels for right-handed anglers. There were at that time a few ambidextrous reels of quality, such as the Ambidex range, but the wide availability today of reels to suit either is, again, a direct result of Dick's input.

Another project that Dick was involved with from its early beginnings was the fly flotant Permaflote. Dick and a chemist friend, Arnold Neve, experimented with a combination of candle wax, dimethicone, and carbon tetrachloride to produce a flotant that worked far better than earlier products. Some modifications were later required, as carbon tetrachloride is both a dangerous substance and supposedly damaging to the ozone layer, and dimethicone was problematic. Hardy's adopted it for a while and sold it in their shops in Pall Mall and Edinburgh, but they gave it up eventually and it resumed sale from Chubb's of Edgware, where it is still sold.

Dick is probably best known for his involvement in development of the electric bite alarm. The early Heron alarms that he had a hand in were a great improvement on dough bobbins or silver paper. They had a long antenna which, when pulled across by the line during a bite, made a contact, set off a buzzer and lit up a small bulb. They registered drop-back bites as well as runs, but they were not 100% reliable in cases other than full-blown runs. However, they did allow one's mind to wander a little during the hours of darkness.

These alarms were very controversial at the time, being labelled, as it seems all new inventions are, as 'unsporting'. Dick always used to point out that it is the angler who is sporting - or not - not his equipment. In any event, there was no going back. Better models than the Heron were brought out, based on the same principles, and we used to make home-made versions in which all vital parts were contained in a small tobacco tin. Dick liked these! Later, other people incorporated their own inventions - rollers were introduced, over which the line ran, and LEDs that were rather better than the old lights arrived. Today electronic bite-alarms sell by the million - another major piece of angling equipment which might have been decades in the coming, were it not for the drive of R.W. He did not actually invent the Heron, but he helped and then pushed the principle.

I cannot finish this chapter without mentioning firstly the bivvy, which is covered at greater length elsewhere in the book, and secondly baits. Walker and friends bivouacked on their carp fishing weekends. From this was born the brolly camp, a good wrap over for a brolly (I used one for years) and finally the modern bivvy, which in commercial terms has resulted in a turnover of megamillions. It is easy to see from where the inspiration came.

Now, baits. How can you invent baits for Heaven's sake? Well, Fred Wilton did, inspired by the Carp Catchers' Club's use of large, fry-safe baits. And from his Walker-inspired invention sprouted yet another billion-dollar industry. They didn't knight Dick Walker, but Fred Wilton should be so honoured. Read now about Fred's boilies.

FRED WILTON'S BOILIES

Elsewhere in this book (Chapter 11) I refer to the fact that Dick may have underrated the value of baits in his quite relentless, and surely correct insistence that anglers should not spook the fish. Somehow this demotes the bait, and it seems that, in Dick's eyes, the bait itself *was* the least important of his list of big fish hunting criteria. Having said that, he was insistent about the importance of big baits for catching carp - a conviction that is clearly evident in the letters of the Carp Catchers' Club. Several times the members suggested moving on to what we now call particle baits, but were dissuaded by the force of Dick's argument. (The consequences of this I have outlined in the chapter on Redmire Pool).

He reasoned that large baits avoided the attentions of small fish, enabled a free-lined bait to be cast some distance and allowed more productive pre-baiting - the small fish would not eat the freebies and the large carp would get used to them as food items. Small, parboiled potatoes fitted the bill perfectly - even though, as it happens, they were not, and are not, good carp baits.

Nonetheless, the principle of large, 'pheasant's egg sized' baits prevailed, and, amongst the many who adopted it there was a certain newcomer, one Fred Wilton. Fred, a docker living in south-east London's dockland, had come relatively late to fishing, taking it up in his late twenties while instructing his nephew - equally a beginner. Their water was Keston Ponds in Kent, and it was here that Fred saw a large fish he couldn't at first identify - a carp of around six pounds as he discovered later. Being a persistent soul, Fred went to the local library and almost the first book he picked up was Dick's *Still-Water Angling*. Although he'd only been fishing for about a year Fred got into pre-baiting, and for hook baits he went for large lumps of paste. Not knowing how big a pheasant's egg was, he had to turn to the library for that too! He told me that pheasants were not exactly abundant in the docklands of his youth! His first balls of paste were of mashed potato, mixed in with Dick's groundbait, called 'Pomenteg', plus wholemeal flour. However, after reading about rabbits in Australia which obtained their required mineral supplements by chewing wooden stakes soaked in preservative minerals, he became more aware of the importance of the food content. He, therefore, modified his paste to mashed potato, wholemeal flour, Pomenteg, PYM (Phillips' Yeast Mixture) and Lowe's bar (dehydrated meat for dogs).

Not long after this, he adapted and simplified the recipe again, this time to wholemeal flour, Pomenteg, and PYM *mixed with eggs, rolled into balls, and boiled.* Thus were boilies born. Later still he modified the contents again so that they really did become high-nutritive-value baits - and the carp loved them. Note, though, that his development of boilies *began* with Dick's principles of bait. Now reflect on the enormous impact boilies have had, not just in the UK, but in Europe and, increasingly, in other parts of the world. (I saw some for sale in Australia not so long ago.) A whole generation of carp fishers know of no other bait. Millions are made and sold. Millionaires have been made, and yet Fred followed Dick's principle of not seeking monetary gain from his inventiveness. I know this for a fact because I was involved with Martin Gay in testing Fred's baits. Fred himself bought all the ingredients, often by the sack load, ordering them via his dockland contacts. We were then given bags of the deep-frozen baits to test: they had a 'smell' which was simply an identifier that the carp used to recognise good food. I have used his simple system on one lake for the last eighteen years and it still produces good carp regularly with no drop off in takes or results. No badly designed or shelf-life baits have gone into that lake at all, no inferior products, and the carp have not tired of the bait, or become finicky. In effect Fred's baits have taken Walker's principles to their zenith. And, of course, boilies have spread far beyond carp fishing, and far beyond Britain's shores.

Dick demonstrating double-haul fly casting.

Dick with four new Hardy rods for trials; products of the Moncrieff Rod Development Company.

Chapter 7

Tackle, techniques and photography

DICK WALKER, as we've seen, was deeply involved in helping, inspiring and cajoling the tackle trade. In so doing, he became closely associated with big business and with major tackle items, ultimately involving trade worth millions of pounds. However, he was also interested in the ordinary angler and provided that vital link between the trade and the angler, acting as a conduit for ideas going in both directions.

Walker was not only concerned with the major tackle items. He had a real interest in the small items too; the things that made life easier for the common man. Take the humble rod-rest. Nothing is more useful to the coarse angler, of whatever persuasion, than the rod-rest - something that can take the minimalist form of a forked stick or the complexity of an Apollo launch pad. And when was the rod-rest produced on a commercial basis? With the introduction of the Heron bite-alarm. When the bite-alarm was in use the rod rested on a V-shaped slit, with a narrower vertical slit below the V which enabled the line to run quite free of the resting rod. If it does not run free then the line becomes trapped and the bite is aborted or otherwise fouled up. So the rod-rest was fundamental to the success of the bite-alarm. At about the time when the Heron bite-alarm was introduced, Walker and others were using a simple rod-rest, made essentially of bent wire. When the rod was in place, the line ran freely just below it, not in a slit but a circular bend of wire. The drawback to this was that on the strike (except when carp fishing when the rod is picked up slowly before the strike) the line can easily catch on the neck of the circular part. One of these styles of rod-rest was made commercially for Dick, but instead of a wire frame it had a moulded rubber head - still with the circular hole below. (One of these was kindly given to me some years ago by Alan Vare, and although the rubber head is excellent on the rod it does suffer from the drawback I have just mentioned.) The question is: who modified the Heron rest so successfully? I have been unable to find out, but I must assume Walker had a part in it even though it would represent a marked improvement from the one he described to Maurice Ingham in *Drop Me A Line.*

Since the Heron alarm all electrical or electronic buzzer alarms have had a rest position similar to the one in the later Heron indicators. And yet, even in 1981, when Ken Whitehead and I wrote our book *Fishing Tackle,* ordinary rod-rest tops of this superior design were not readily available. It was only after we featured the preferred design in our book that they began to arrive in the shops from a variety of manufacturers. But the original thinking on this subject came from Dick Walker, and possibly his colleagues, and has been used by specimen hunters ever since.

Bite indication is a critical matter in all fishing and especially so in carp and pike fishing. The free-line fishing technique advocated by Dick is, today, properly open to criticism: in carp fishing it can lead to bite-offs and in pike fishing it can lead to deep hooking. In other fishing, too, it is not generally an effective strategy and it has now been largely abandoned. But in the 1950s and early 1960s most anglers would use a drop-back indicator at the rod butt with or without an electric alarm on the front rod-rest. Dick recommended that the drop-back be silver paper or a 'dough bobbin'. The silver paper was often simply left on the ground, but such a method would *not* register a drop-back and a bite-off could result if the carp swallowed the bait deeply. The necessity for a hanging bobbin became widely recognised and a whole variety of things were invented. Many worked quite well, but the simple bobbin of bread or silver paper, or a ball clipped on the line and attached by a cord to the back rest, took some beating. Eventually electronic drop-backs were devised (such as those by E. T. Tackle) and also monkey climbers, in which the bobbin ran up a steel rod. The latter flipped off the top of the steel rod in the event of a strike, and the rod itself prevented the wind flap which most of the simpler versions suffered from. Dick was never far from the forefront of developments and in 1980 he was in long correspondence with B. W. Barnaby about the LED indicator systems that the latter was making. (I didn't see the end result of this but the proposals looked good!) So the drop-back indicator began its life with the pioneer carpers, whose observations led them to look for something to help them detect a carp bite when the carp swam slowly towards the rod. And from those humble beginnings it has metamorphosed, with ever more improvements, into the sophisticated, commercially produced, equipment of today. Here is evidence, yet again, that it is the experienced anglers, technically 'amateurs', who precede the professionals in any invention of tackle.

Dick used to discuss bite indication in his *Angling Times* column. He once described a method of clipping up the line to the reel spool so that it did not blow about in the wind, and so that it helped the drop-back facility to work properly. This trick was very simple: it required two matchsticks held together on the spool by coils of the reel line. The line was then pulled between the abutting matches so that it became trapped but would easily release in the event of a run. It's a technique that works well and I often use it today. Dick did not say where he had got the idea from, though neither did he claim to have invented it; which is just as well because it first appears in Izaak Walton's *Compleat Angler*! Walton used bits of stick.

However, and this is where it gets interesting, Dick's method of line clipping was taken up commercially and line clips of plastic were produced by the million! John Roberts' version saved anglers a lot of time because the two matchsticks method *was* fiddly. Now you simply tape them or clip them to the appropriate part of the rod handle or rod butt piece and they remain, inconspicuously, in position. So for hundreds of years an invention lay dormant waiting for a man such as Walker to bring it to life. As Dick so often stated, it pays, in angling, to be well read!

There is one aspect of Dick's treatment of lines that I have never been able to fathom and that is Dick's idea of dying nylon monofilament with silver nitrate. It has simply never worked for me and I know others have had a similar experience. Dick had a debate on this subject with Tony Perrin of Abu, and whilst Tony did not appear to dispute the colour imparted, he did dispute the claim that silver nitrate protected nylon from degradation by sunlight. According to Tony, silver nitrate *does* penetrate the nylon, makes it heavier, makes it more rigid and impairs the knot strengths. I'm afraid I don't believe any of this: either Tony Perrin or Dick Walker. It's all nonsense.

However . . . with landing-nets Dick really did know what he was talking about. Before the big fish movement, before the Carp Catchers' Club, proper landing-nets simply were not available, had not been dreamt of. In pike fishing gaffs were used (and in carp fishing in some quarters!) so inventiveness could not come from that quarter. It came from the carp fishers. It came from Dick Walker primarily, and is well documented in *Drop Me A Line* and *Still-Water Angling*. The triangular net frame was born, either collapsible or not; and the nets themselves were originally of wide mesh and knotted and, later, of micromesh. Neither of these features are suitable for pike nets but that is not at issue here; the Walker-style landing-net is admirably suitable for most other forms of fishing where you need a big net to enmesh a big fish. In any tackle shop today you will find big, triangular carp nets very little different, certainly in principle, than the ones built by Dick all those years ago. And what has been the commercial spin-off of his endeavours? It's difficult to quantify isn't it? 'Rather phenomenal' might be one way of putting it.

The famous Arlesey Bomb.

STILL-WATER ANGLING
RICHARD WALKER

Now let's look briefly at rucksacks. There are famous pictures of Dick striding along with an old canvas A-frame rucksack which, in his published articles, he claimed was far better for fishing than the box or basket (or creel) traditionally used. So all the specimen hunters, myself included, invested in rucksacks and, low and behold, Dick was right. You could carry them miles, tackle fitted into them more easily, and when plonked on the bank you could use them as a back-rest. And so the rucksack industry for anglers was born. Now the firms produce angler-friendly rucksacks of mega proportions, some almost big enough to sleep in. Once again it's a million-dollar industry, and anglers have benefited from it.

Dick had such an extensive input into modern-day angling equipment, including floats (of which more in Chapter 15) that it is difficult to cover it all here and do justice to it. So let's look now at his techniques.

Walker's angling philosophy and methods are well covered in *Still-Water Angling* so I do not want to dwell too long on the subject here, but it is obvious from the foregoing that all his tackle designs and inventions were developed by him to allow him to fish in particular styles. The Arlesey Bomb, for example, was developed for long-range legering with the Mk IV carp rod and Mk IV Avon. When he wanted to roach fish he came up with a rod to suit. He became a species-specialist angler: not for him the one-rod-for-all or the multi-tip rod of the old days. For legering he was keen on Peter Stone's 'Legerstrike' or rods very similar or with similar tips. For long-trotting for dace he'd use a longer, more slender wand that, as you will read elsewhere, he gave away to Jack Hargreaves the TV star of *Out of Town*. And so it goes on. This is not the approach taken by all anglers, just the specialist anglers. We choose the rod and reel to suit the target.

Walker used all kinds of reels but tended to favour the fixed-spool reels even for long-trotting. In his column he strongly advocated long-trotting with a fixed-spool as opposed to a centre-pin, raising the hackles of many centre-pin fanatics who quickly took him to task. I don't think anyone won the arguments because both reels have advantages and disadvantages for long-trotting. One reel he might have used was the closed-face reel, but he came out quite strongly against these explaining that when the line enters the spool centre hole it has to go through about three right-angles before it reaches the spool lay position. There's a lot of resistance in this and Dick dismissed them for anything other than small fish. In long-trotting they work well, of course, as any match angler can tell you, but possibly not so well if you are playing a big fish. It's interesting that their use has declined in the last decade, and maybe that's why match anglers are catching so many big fish!

What is true of rods and reels applies also to all the other tackle developed by Dick: it was developed for a particular technique. For example, the electric bite-alarms were for carp fishing, initially with free-lined large baits. The free-running rod-rests, mentioned earlier, were devised for general specimen hunting; big landing-nets were originally for carp. In trout fishing he invented many flies, but he was not as inventive generally with trout fishing, confining himself to altering knots, leaders and line trays, and devising good shooting head systems (although, of course, the rods he was serious about, hence his work on carbon with Hardy's as explained earlier).

One final piece of equipment that Dick was rarely without was his camera. From an early age he was a photographer, even a prizewinner, and he was at the forefront in persuading anglers to photograph their catch before releasing it. Dick grew up in the stuffed-fish era and he himself became a skilled taxidermist, setting up considerable numbers of fish. But it was for his photographic skills that he became known. In the 1950s there were not many good angling photographers around, not amateurs anyway, and he often devoted his column or part of it, to explaining how to get the good shots - which film to use, which lens for an SLR 35mm camera, how to focus, how to get the films processed and so on. His articles were supplied to editors with batches of photographs. He also supplied many photographs to other anglers, for the illustration of their own articles, and for this he made no charge, arguing that in the long term things would even themselves out.

His own photographs were often outstanding although, like many perfectionists, he was rarely fully satisfied with them. Dick's approach to camera work is covered in some detail, for those who want to read further, in *Drop Me A Line,* where he discussed photographic problems with Maurice Ingham, and in *The Stone-Walker Letters* (of more recent vintage than the Ingham-Walker book). Photography, though, may be the one area where Dick's work will have declining impact, simply because of the massive change brought about by digital cameras. I suspect that, had they been around at the time, Dick would have gone for a digital SLR of high calibre. (When I make the change myself, which will be by the time you read this, that is what I shall do.)

An early photo by Dick of his first wife Ruth in the garden, demonstrating the curve of a Mk IV. In previously published versions of this photograph, Ruth was cropped out!

"The best photograph I ever took."

The snapper snapped!

Chapter 8

Carp fishing, 'that carp', and record fish

THERE IS a sad irony in the fact that Dick Walker is probably most famous as a carp angler and yet today's young carp anglers seem hardly to have heard of him. They use tackle, techniques and baits that, although not actually used by Dick, have developed, as we've seen, as a direct result of his innovation. One can blame the passage of time, of course, and also perhaps the fact that Dick did not really write very much on carp fishing - there was no book specifically on carp, for example, although he wrote a great deal on other angling subjects. In fact, and this may surprise some, he did not fish for carp for very long after the Carp Catchers' Club was formed: just for the duration of the club from 1951-1957, and thereafter only sporadically. But *before* the formation of the CCC, before the 1950s, he was an exceptional carp angler. This was a period when a carp of more than ten pounds was extremely rare: there were not many around and very few were caught, *except* by Dick. He caught large numbers of them, often using his margin-fished floating-crust technique, and mainly from a small lake near Hitchin. He wrote about these catches in the *Fishing Gazette*, but it was clear that some readers thought such catches were impossible - that Dick was, therefore, a liar. In fact, Dick, and Pete Thomas caught more than ninety in excess of ten pounds between them and it wasn't long before the critics had to eat their words.

By the time the CCC was formed in 1951 Dick was already a very experienced and successful carp angler and had written authoritatively on the subject. What followed within the CCC - the identifying of waters with big carp, the catching of them, and the showing that it was possible to catch them - is now the stuff of history. But it is easy to see how Dick was ready for the challenge, having so much carp-catching experience already under his belt. Some of the other anglers involved in the Club were nothing like as accomplished, and it was probably Dick's ability to inspire, and his knowledge of

One of the nicest pictures of Dick with his record 44lb carp from Redmire Pool.

carp, that led to the successes of the members. The Club's achievements have been well documented in Kevin Clifford's *A History of Carp Fishing*, and Clifford and Arbury's *Redmire Pool*, so I do not wish to reiterate them all here. I do, however, want to make some brief comments on the carp of 44lb - the record fish.

'THAT CARP'

I have long argued that a single point in time marked the revolution, the change in angling from a very ordinary past to the modern sport we have now. That moment was when Richard Walker, fishing in the early hours at Bernithan Pool ('Redmire'), had a bite, which resulted in his capture of the 44lb carp. Others have put it more eloquently, notably Brian Clarke writing in *The Times* (12th May, 2001) when he wrote, 'In a sport such as angling there are few instances where a seminal shift can be pinpointed. But one can. Angling's float watching, worm-drowning, hazy-day ethos changed forever shortly before 5am on 13th September, 1952. That was the moment when a length of fishing line was drawn out from between two metal contacts and a buzzer sounded through a Bible-black night.'

The capture has been detailed many, many times, but it is the impact of the catch that I want to focus on here. Initially the news was met with disbelief: some sections of the press really did not believe that such a huge fish could exist, let alone be captured. It was only when the photographs began to appear that the critics were silenced.

Pete Thomas netted the fish and it was weighed in the dark first of all, on a balance that went up to 32lb. The marker shot down to the stop with a clunk, proving that the fish was well over 32lb. The next morning, having sacked up the carp, they borrowed from a farmer another balance, which went up to 16lb, and using the two (and allowing for the weight of the sack) registered a weight of not less than 41lb - possibly even half a pound more. It is perfectly easy to weigh a fish using two balances, as you can test for yourselves in five minutes, but the two must be used apart and the pull on them must be clean and vertical. The weight of the sack or netting was never stated in anything I have read but it would be

FISHING, September 10, 1965 13

It's Clarissa again!
You've met Clarissa the carp before, no doubt, perhaps only in picture form, but very likely through the glass of her tank at the London Zoo Aquarium . . . Yes, this is Richard Walker's 44 lb. record-breaker, captured 13 years ago next Monday from Redmire Pool, and photographed just a few weeks ago by 'Fishing' contributor Steve Crawshaw. Unhappily, although she still seems in the best of health, Clarissa isn't quite the fish she was, for at her last weigh-in she could tip the scales at only 38½ lb. But, then, perhaps, she's just been watching her figure . . .

Pat Walker with Fred Buller and Peter Stone holding up Walker's cased 44lb fish, years after its capture.

perfectly straightforward to weigh it separately and deduct it from the gross weight. I'm sure they did this as a matter of course.

Dick then rang London Zoo and offered them the fish. At first they thought he said *fourteen* pounds and were not really interested, and he had to make it clear he was talking of *forty* pounds, not fourteen. One can readily imagine the confusion in the excitement, over the telephone line! The zoo official thought, at first, that it was a hoax call and Dick had to tell him that if London Zoo didn't want it, then Bristol Zoo certainly would. From that day on Dick always referred to his 'forty-pound' carp, not his 44lb carp and it is well known that he regarded the true weight as 41lb. The weight of 44lb came from London Zoo, the officials of which weighed it accurately upon arrival. Furthermore, Ken Sutton (later of ACA fame, then of the *Daily Mirror*), together with a Weights and Measures Inspector, and Bernard Venables, attended London Zoo shortly after the arrival of the carp and had all the details confirmed. The carp weight of 44lb did *not* include the weight of the sack, something that had worried Dick when he first heard the weight from the zoo. It was a tremendous fish, which, like its captor, became a legend in itself.

There can be no doubt at all that the fish weighed 44lb at the zoo; and that it was weighed at the lake at about 41$\frac{1}{2}$lb. I have no information as to the accuracy of the two balances used by Peter Thomas and Dick Walker, although the 32lb one was known to be accurate.

As well as the amendment to the weight at the zoo there was also a rapid name change! Peter and Richard had called the carp 'Ravioli' (after the food they had been eating during the trip) but the zoo named it 'Clarissa', a name under which it became very famous indeed. And just to add to the confusion that can so often reign at the time of capture of a big fish, the *Fishing Gazette* in 1953 printed the weight of Dick's fish as 44½lb, correcting it to 44lb in an editorial comment at the end of the letter concerned.

It is important to re-visit these events, if only to prove that there really can be no doubt about the weight of the fish or about the thoroughness with which the anglers and others went about authenticating both the capture and the weight. It is true that in one photograph, and one photograph only (see *Redmire Pool* by Kevin Clifford and Len Arbury, p. 20) the fish does not look all that exceptional, but in all other pictures it is staggeringly impressive, especially one in the same book on page 21 where the fish is held by Peter Thomas: here the great thickness of the fish is visible. Not long after its capture, the carp could be visited at the zoo. I went along to see it myself and on two further occasions! It was in a tank with several fish, including a pike of 20lb. Now, I know a thing or two about 20lb pike and this certainly was one. It was completely dwarfed by Dick's carp which was so obviously twice as big. The huge girth of the carp was clearly visible, as it is, indeed, in an excellent video of Pat's.

I do not doubt that Dick's capture of such a fish resulted in some jealousies. In fact, elsewhere in this volume I deal with one specific example, but in the 1990s another maggot of a complaint reached the skin of what most regarded as a very rosy apple. Unfortunately, this complaint reached the public domain in *Carpworld* ('Face to Face', pp 71-75). During Tim Paisley's interview with Fred J. Taylor it was revealed that Fred J. had received a letter suggesting that the carp wasn't all it was claimed to be. Fred J. drew the line at naming the individual but made his feelings about the man quite plain.

In 1981 Dick tried to get his 44lb record removed from the British Record list, because he felt Chris Yates' fish was the record. The National Anglers' Council refused to remove the fish even though Dick had never claimed it and had not, in fact, complied with the Record list rules anyway.

RECORD FISH

Dick caught a record carp, but what of his other record fish? And did he really see fish the size that he claimed to see? I have to tread carefully here and what follows is a personal opinion. It always seemed to me that Dick *exaggerated* the size of the fish he saw in various waters and on which he reported in his articles. I do not want to belittle Dick's actual achievements in this respect in any way. He did, after all, catch the record carp, and the record rainbow trout at the time. I should also make clear that if he *did* exaggerate, it was not for any personal gain: he was not obsessed by big fish, neither did he want the glory of catching them, as evidenced by his failure to actually *claim* the record carp or the record rainbow; that he had caught them was enough. So what was behind it?

Dick certainly did see bigger fish in waters than other people. In terms of carp this applies to his observations at Mapperly, Bernithan Pool (Redmire), and Arlesey. His observations at Redmire were partially confirmed, but even here he saw fish up to eighty pounds, which were not caught. Having said that, there are those better qualified than I who think Dick was right, namely Chris Yates, Maurice Ingham and Fred Taylor, all of whom saw a great carp there, and there are also the famous Eddie Price photographs.

So what of the other species? On more than once occasion Dick reported seeing huge chub on the middle reaches of the Great Ouse at Beachampton where he rented the fishing. Fish of over eight pounds, even ten pounds, were mentioned. They were never caught. Today chub of that size have been caught, elsewhere, but this does not make Dick right. Was he simply trying to stir up interest, to be sensational? Others have suggested this; but there is nothing in his private correspondence to suggest that he was reporting anything other than what he believed he saw.

Or take tench. There is more than one account of a lily-infested lake that he and Fred J. Taylor fished where Dick said there were numbers of tench in excess of ten pounds - a staggering claim at the time. They hooked these fish, but lost them each time in a tangle of roots. None of these veritable giants was landed, which does seem rather odd when you think about it. Surely a bit of very careful swim clearance, a choice of robust tackle, a bit of persistence, a bit of luck, would have paid off, especially as they had the convenience of a boat? Were the fish really there at those weights? Or was he just trying to inspire anglers into having a go?

Dick also saw perch bigger than have ever been caught. In a letter to Vic Bellars (22nd April, 1983; see Chapter 5) he said he thought perch might reach eight pounds, and that he'd seen one in Arlesey Lake which he estimated at seven or eight pounds - a fish that had grabbed, by the nape of its neck, a perch of 3lb 2oz that was being played. Such a fish would be very impressive, of course, but here we are, nearly a quarter of a century later, and a perch of eight pounds still hasn't been caught, despite the fact that all species of fish are now growing much bigger than they did in the early 1980s.

A young Dick in classic old-fashioned pose with two double-figure carp.

Good carp safely netted in one of the revolutionary triangular landing-nets.

Woldale September 1957 - a family outing. On the left: Peter and Pat Thomas with children Jane and Paul in front. On the right is the Russell family, Pat and Margery with Shaun and Jeannie in front. In the centre is young Richard Walker with Tim and their mother Ruth. In front sits Dick and Simon.

Dick with his 33lb Redmire carp in the punt.

Then there are the giant barbel in the Hampshire Avon, at Avon Tyrrell I think. Here again he saw, and fished for, barbel which he claimed were well over the record. To an extent this was a very reasonable claim because from time to time salmon anglers reported barbel over the then record. Walker had in mind barbel that might go to twenty pounds. None were caught anything near that. In fact most of the really big fish they caught were in low double figures. There's no doubt that, with barbel, he really was trying to get anglers to have a serious go at the record which he believed could be broken. But I think he was in error in this estimation of the size. Others who fished the same stretches of water at the time agree.

I have left until last the saga of the giant pike lost by Fred Buller on Loch Lomond which Dick, in private, estimated at 65lb with a length of five feet and a width across the back of ten inches. Dick and pike are covered more thoroughly in Chapter 13, but suffice it to say here that although I think Dick genuinely believed the fish to be so big (having discussed it with him myself), I do not think he was in a position to estimate it correctly. He was not experienced enough with big pike. However, he *did* want anglers to go to Loch Lomond and have a crack at breaking the record. Go they did. Break the record they did not.

Dick may well have believed in all these giant fish of the time, or perhaps he deluded himself. Both scenarios are possible. However, my own view, which I think much more likely, is that he was trying to encourage anglers to go out there and do it and at the same time raise awareness of angling amongst the non-angling public, as every record fish capture does.

Dick with Pat Russell, inspecting 27lb Redmire fish caught by Pat.

A young Dick with good common carp.

Chapter 9

The Carp Catchers' Club

THE CCC is one of the most famous angling clubs in the history of the sport though it lasted barely seven years. The club had neither rules nor a subscription, an arrangement happily agreed to by all the members, although, had they not, Dick Walker, who disliked rules and regulations, would have insisted upon it. Any costs sustained were to be shared out appropriately amongst the members. It operated through a rotary letter system but the members fished together on occasions in various small groupings on a variety of carp waters which they thought had potential. The CCC provided the template for the later big fish groups (specimen groups) but I think it is fair to say that only a few of these latter groups were imbued with the same spirit of friendly cooperation, and once subscriptions and rules and reporting forms were introduced they tended not to last very long (see Chapter 14 on the roots of specimen hunting). From time to time the CCC rotary letter ran into circulation difficulties, as such letters always do when one individual hangs on to it for longer than necessary - or for longer than the others hope for! Its movement finally ground to a halt seven years after it began.

In one sense none of the above is important: what really matters is that the group of people involved, beginning with the founders Denys Watkins-Pitchford ('BB', whose idea it was), Dick Walker and Maurice Ingham, started a movement, a philosophy, which transformed the whole of angling. They added members fairly quickly - people who had already had some success with the then very difficult carp: Harry Grief, John Norman, Jack Smith, Bob Richards, Peter Thomas, Bernard Venables, Gerry Berth-Jones and Dick Kefford. At a later date they were joined by Fred J. Taylor, Bob Reynolds and May Berth-Jones. Only one person ever resigned, namely Bernard Venables, and that was towards the end of the Club's life, as I shall explain later. I do not think Bob Reynolds actually took any part in the club: apart from his

Dick playing a big fish at Redmire Pool.

acceptance letter, there seems to be nothing else on written record. He was certainly a very successful carp angler at the time though. May Berth-Jones had been involved, through Gerry, from an early stage and latterly the Club members clearly decided that she should be accorded full membership status. I have not seen written confirmation that she accepted this. Today I think only Peter Thomas, Fred J. Taylor and Bob Reynolds are alive. I have no recent knowledge of Bob Reynolds, but Peter Thomas and Fred J. Taylor are amongst the most revered names of living anglers.

The way in which these anglers transformed angling was by setting out to catch carp deliberately in order to disprove the common assumption that they were uncatchable; and to ensure success, they devised special tackle and techniques and adopted a focused, logical and scientific approach that was new to angling. And yet they did this in a manner that they thoroughly enjoyed. They were never overly serious. They had a President - 'BB' - and a Secretary in Dick Walker, but there were no formal meetings; they simply put down their experiences and ideas on paper, in letters, and circulated them.

In the late 1990s all the letters were published for the first time (1998, The Medlar Press), in a huge volume put together by Maurice Ingham and Peter Rogers. The book had a short foreword by Chris Yates, an introduction by Maurice Ingham, and a scene-setting piece by Bernard Venables, which dealt with the history of carp fishing, and the problems of carp fishing that were gradually resolved by the CCC members. After that there are the letters, including Bernard Venables' resignation letter in 1957. The end of the letters is signified by one from Richard Walker and an unfinished and unsent letter from Maurice Ingham dated 25th January, 1958; thereafter there is a summing up by Maurice Ingham dated May 1998. The volume is one of the most captivating reads in angling, not least because the writing is blunt and frank - they were written for private, not public consumption, of course.

So what exactly was Walker's role in the CCC? It wasn't his idea (we've seen before that he didn't particularly like the concept of clubs), but he became its Secretary, generally kept it organised and, most strikingly, he dominated the body. In the letters themselves there is actually some discussion of his 'arrogance', but although he was dominant, I do not think this was arrogance on his part: Walker *did* listen to people, learn from people, and was able to adapt to the ideas of others on occasion. We see more arrogance displayed in some of the other letters: those by 'BB' and Bernard Venables, for example, which is surprising given their public personas. Walker could be forceful in argument and he pushed free-line tackle, large baits and large hooks, sometimes against arguments to the contrary. But his inspiration certainly kept the CCC going, and contributed enormously to the eventual cracking of the carp problem.

Maurice Ingham with a good catch of carp from Woldale in August 1950. Note the night fishing lamp.

His 44lb fish helped a great deal in this respect, of course (see Chapter 8) but lots of other good carp were also caught and enabled a general philosophy to be developed: first, find your carp, (this meant being ruthless about waters that held only small carp); then put some time in (often camping over a weekend) without, as we say today, 'spooking' the fish (this might involve some pre-baiting or putting in of free offerings). Never before had this kind of wholehearted approach been taken and it is that approach itself which yielded dividends, rather than just the tackle and baits.

The techniques they succeeded with and the baits they used have long been abandoned (more or less) by today's much more successful carp anglers. Now don't get me wrong: post-Walker successful carpers owe almost everything to Walker and the CCC. But post-Walker, successful carpers come in two phases: there are those who *immediately* followed the CCC and fished places like Redmire Pool, including Jack Hilton and Kevin Clifford; and then there is the later, present day angler whose success stems, in no small measure, from the wider availability of big carp waters. The first of these groups fairly quickly abandoned the techniques used by the CCC and adopted the methods and baits which Walker had resisted. For example, if you follow the CCC arguments in the rotary letters, you will see that small baits are discussed, and then rejected (see pp. 36, 179, 181, 183, 303, 334, 394, and 398 of *The Carp Catchers' Club*). Walker and friends were 'into' particle baits, as in chub and tench fishing. In these letters, John Norman actually suggests using sweetcorn, although this was not tried until several years later. Fred J. Taylor planned to take a sack of maize to Redmire, as we know from Kevin Clifford's book *Redmire,* but in the end took chipped potatoes. And that wasn't such a bad idea, was it, given the preoccupation of carp anglers in those days with the use of potato as bait? But maize was a better idea, as we now know.

It's easy to be critical in retrospect, with all that we know now, but at the time, their approach and philosophy were completely new - they really were the pioneers in carp fishing and the inspiration to anglers of carp and other species. They were also way ahead of their time in many smaller matters: bite-alarms, first-ever back leads, foreign carp fisheries (they spotted France in 1952), barbless hooks (Bob Richards in 1952), soft hook links (Jack Smith, 1952), and so on. But it was the approach they brought to fishing that was their major contribution: always questioning, always trying new things, always trying to apply observations of fish behaviour, common sense, logic, and some science. If this approach *had* been taken prior to the CCC then it had made no impact.

So why did the CCC come to an end? In part it is likely that its members were moving on to other things. Bernard Venables' resignation may have been

For the author, this is the most evocative view of Redmire Pool ever published, September 1955.

On a farm gate. From the left: Dick, Pete Thomas and Pat Russell, September 1955.

One of the anglers who knew Redmire Pool from an early stage in the Fifties was Dick Kefford, of the Carp Catchers' Club, so it was with great interest that I heard of an article that he'd written on Redmire that was apparently unpublished. Collector Dave Ivey came across it, recognised the handwriting and checked it with Dick. Dick confirmed that it was his but couldn't recall writing it! He gave Dave permission to do what he wanted with it, and Dave then rewrote it carefully (because Dick's handwriting was almost indecipherable - vets being, presumably, like doctors) and edited it slightly, so that I could reproduce it here:

CONCERNING REDMIRE POOL BY DICK KEFFORD

Redmire Pool received that name in 1952 as a pseudonym to hide its real identity from too curious an angling world. For in the autumn of 1951 the late Bob Richards, carp fishing this very private pool, secured the then record, a mirror carp of $31\frac{1}{4}$lb.

The history of this near three-acre lake, which lies at the top of a valley in the Welsh Border Hills, is wrapped in mystery. One thing is quite clear however: the lake was man-made by damming up the valley against a small stream. Standing at the base of the twenty-foot high dam one can only wonder at the magnitude of the work that was undertaken, at least centuries ago.

The mind may also turn to the somewhat frightening thought that with the firing of a few sticks of gelignite the lake would be emptied within a matter of minutes. Maybe the pool was made in connection with the old iron industry, which flourished, in mediaeval times in the Forest of Dean. The lake is triangular in shape as one might expect, and its long point leads in a north-westerly direction. Here the stream enters - nowadays as a mud-filled ditch, its water seeping rather than flowing over the layers of silt laid down in the long course of time.

When conditions are suitable, the carp work right up in the mud of these shallows finding a sense of security in the tree branches, which winter gales have distributed about the lake floor. A once-cultivated osier bed flanks the north-western bank. This, for many years now, has grown unattended, making the angler's progress through it, as John Nixon once said, 'Like going on safari in darkest Africa'! Proceeding with difficulty along a hidden pathway skirting the boundary hedge, you come suddenly upon a clearing which is known as the 'Stile Pitch', scene of the capture of Eddy Price's 40-pounder, and then one is at the famous 'Willow' - four in five of the weeping variety now, in 1967, almost dead. I am told that the length of life of these artificially induced trees only amounts to some fifty years. Here in a sheltered nook is the site, the very spot where on 18th September, 1952, Dick Walker with

Early morning at Redmire Pool, a fish leaping.

Dick Walker gazing out over a water at which he made history.

his companion Peter Thomas landed the record carp, which weighed 44lb.

You then climb over a wooden fence, which to my knowledge has not been renewed since that momentous occasion. Now you are on the farm track way, which tops the dam, and leads up to the big house - a William and Mary residence. The eastern bank is thinly lined with ancient trees, oak, holly and scrub where stood the old boat house, now only revealed by a few rotting timbers.

Standing sentinel over Pitchford's Pitch are twin balsam poplars from which the summer night wind wafts fragrant scent about the lake. A series of old, gnarled pollarded willows set in the bank along a stretch of low-lying meadow completes the environs of the pool. As one would expect, the bed of the lake is trough-like, following the contours of the original valley floor, but the inflow of silt brought down by the stream has shallowed the northern end of the lake somewhat.

The deepest area, up to fifteen feet, is from the middle of the dam to a point opposite the stile and Pitchford's Pitch. In the early years of the present century the lake was stocked with trout, but with apparently little success. Then in 1934 the water was so badly choked with weed that the filters connecting the water-supply to local dwelling houses became blocked. Advice was sought and fifty king carp obtained from Haslemere were introduced. As far as is known, this was the earliest occasion that the lake had held carp. How well they have thrived is now well known.

There appear to be two main sources of almost limitless nourishment for the carp in the pool. By far the most important is the astonishingly high concentration of daphnia - minute crustaceans, which under stable conditions of environment and weather, multiply at a phenomenal rate. To obtain this nourishment the carp, for much of the summer, need barely to move, for they are at all times swimming in a highly nourishing 'soup'. Secondary in important food value are bloodworms, which in some summers occur in great numbers in the shallow areas at the northern end of the pool and around the area of the Stile Pitch. One can tell at a glance when the carp are busy with the bloodworms, which are mud dwellers, because the water takes on an opacity resembling milky tea, due to the mud disturbed by the carp.

My own personal experience is that this gives the least likely conditions to the angler hoping for a fish, for the carp appear to be completely preoccupied; and also the opacity of the water masks bread baits. If one could develop suitable tackle to deal with large carp, baiting with bloodworms, the angler would still be at a disadvantage for, as one writer stated, it would be akin to 'angling for a cow in a summer field, baiting with a blade of grass'! The general movement of the carp in average conditions of summers is similar to that in all waters, ie, they move with the sun. Soon after the sun has topped the eastern trees, dispelling the mist, the carp may be expected to move out of the deep water either directly up the lake centre towards the northern shallows, or to fan out towards the western bank.

If on a warm sunny morning one moves very cautiously along the western bank which is shielded from direct view by the osier thicket, you may well see the carp, some of prodigious size, moving in the more sheltered bays which receive the early sun. In the afternoon some carp begin a very leisurely movement up the eastern shore towards the dam, furtively pushing their way into the bankside shallows. If the night is warm many of the carp stay in the shallows. Some of the carp, at least, spawn practically every year, usually at the first prolonged spell of warm weather in May. Were it not for this, the natural ecology in the pool would most likely lend itself to a lot of smallish carp. Fortunately, or more often than not (and unfortunately for the carp angler using worm baits), the lake holds plenty of eels. Not only do they mop up much of the carp spawn but they no doubt take carp fry as well.

Years ago, before winter frosts reduced their numbers dramatically, kingfishers were always at the pool fishing industriously and doing much better numerically than I have done. Waterfowl, if present, also help the eels with the spawn, and I recall one year when the lack of weed caused the carp to spawn amid the trailing fronds of the willows and a pair of swans was much attracted to the spot. Waterweeds can be a great nuisance to the angler. In the summer of 1953 the lake was almost filled and covered with a mixture of common and crinkled pond weed. Not a carp was caught that year at Redmire. There is no doubt that in some years conditions suit the growth of water plants better than others. The presence of wild fowl can make a big difference. Swans, I feel, especially, will keep the weed growth within reasonable proportions. Unfortunately, the wild fowl have their own troubles at Redmire in the form of foxes, which abound. It only requires a frost severe enough to allow these nocturnal marauders a safe footing on the ice and the fowl are either devoured or scattered.

The lake bed grows a thick mantle of polyzoa and 'blanket weed' most summers. Often, in a spell of hot weather, this weed, assisted by gaseous formation in the underlying mud, rises to the surface in great clots. The accumulation drifts on the surface, moved by the prevailing wind, causing incessant trouble to the angler. All one can hope for then is a drenching thunderstorm, and they are not infrequent, which breaks up the stuff and sinks it. Angling pitches at Redmire are well known to the habitués and several with constant usage have been named, eg, the Willows Pitch, Pitchford's Pitch, and the Stile Pitch. Most of these are self explanatory as to their position. No single one is better or worse than another for it depends on where the carp are, and more important, their inclination to feed at any given time. Actually, the Willow Pitch has yielded more 20lb-plus carp than any other pitch, primarily because more blokes have had a rod or rods doing duty there than anywhere else. The fact that the record leather was here extracted no doubt lends enchantment to the scene!

What of carp baits at Redmire? The main trouble is to present any bait which may interest a fish, which is already super-fat and food-satiated with natural food of minute size and of mass quantity. Worms may attract them as they did for Roger Bowskill last year, but with much greater certainty will they attract eels. A very intensive pre-season baiting-up with potato was undertaken a few years ago. This accounted for at least one carp, if not a lot of fish for their efforts, but as far as I know nobody has ever caught a carp on potato bait at Redmire. Bread in some shape or form has accounted for almost all the big fish taken since 1951. Occasionally floating crust has been accepted but bread flake or stale bread paste fished on the bottom have done best. Bread baits are very occasionally set upon by carp fry or by gudgeon that later also occur of specimen size. The angler gets the usual indications of what is going on, eg, quivering of the line and intermittent drawings away through the rod rings, an inch or so at a time.

Often paste baits remain untouched for hours, gradually disseminating into amorphous shapes. At such times foul-hooking of a large carp has occurred. Due to the configuration of the lake bottom with deeper water falling away from the shallows, a patrolling carp may glide under the reel-line. The dorsal fin, subsequently acting as a fulcrum, may well contact the line which, with the movement of the fish, draws the line and hook. The angler on the bank receives the impression of a normal run and strikes accordingly: a flank-hooked fish may well be the result. There are occasions, very few and far between, when the carp at Redmire, as elsewhere, lose all inhibition, sense and readily accept bread baits, and it happened for me on a warm still night in July 1963. Fishing from the osiers I had three good runs between 9.40 and 10.30pm, but for one reason or another failed to land a carp. I hasten to add that it hasn't always been so, but know this, Redmire carp are very far from being 'easy meat'.

This article sets the scene so well, describing as it does, in some detail, the key features of the lake and the methods of fishing it. Some of the questions that Dick Kefford raises here were, in fact, later answered in the book Kevin Clifford wrote with Ken Arbury, *Redmire Pool*. So what further is there to say about Redmire Pool and the goings on there? Well it would be interesting to

Dick demonstrating the casting action of a Mk IV, retail version carp rod, from the dam at Redmire Pool.

look at the use of free-line tackle, large hooks, large baits, and the Mk IV carp rod in the 1950's Redmire scene. And here we're referring to the activities of the Carp Catchers' Club, again.

Dick was a strong advocate of free-lining, adding a (running) lead only when some greater distance was needed. The Mk IV carp rod casts relatively light baits quite well, but casts more easily the large baits proposed by Dick for carp - small, parboiled potatoes, large balls of paste (walnut-plus size) and large paste/crust balancers. Leads were, therefore, not necessary on Redmire.

The large baits needed large hooks, and it is worth remembering that this was decades before bolt-rigs and hair-rigs. The problem with large hooks, especially with the barbs of those days, is that a considerable force is needed to set the hook over the barb. Quite a high proportion of Redmire fish 'fell off' during playing and the most likely cause seems to have been a failure to set the hook.

Many of the feeding fish were reported as being suspicious of the baits, hence the view that carp were crafty - a view that explains Dick's insistence on using free-lined tackle because the drag of a lead, he believed, would alert the carp to problems. Ironically, we have now learnt that carp are *not* really crafty or suspicious, although they may learn more readily than some other species, and the drag of a lead does not alert a carp to problems (see Chapter 15).

In fact, you know, I don't think the carp *were* suspicious of parboiled potatoes and very large balls of paste. I think they were *puzzled*. This was not the kind of thing they expected as food and they took a bit of persuading that it actually *was* good to eat. The amount of groundbaiting and pre-baiting in those days was probably insufficiently frequent or bulky enough to actually turn them on to the baits. Not only that, but I wonder if the Mk IV carp rod, in the event of a good run after what was very often a long wait, was man enough to set the hook at more than ten or fifteen yards - or even at that range. This sounds irreverent but it is based on my own experience of carp on the Mk IV: I've had plenty of double-figure carp but no 20-pounders; and on the Mk IV Avon, on which Chris Yates took his 50-pounder, only one 20-pounder. I did not feel that the rods were really *powerful* enough and the baits I used were quite small (as were the ones that Chris Yates used too). However, it is true that the Mk IV steels up under real pressure and providing the carp is still partially attached perhaps this was the moment when the hook was actually set. The Mk III carp rod was also a good rod, and was given to Chris Ball in 1970; Dick had planned to bin it. Chris refurbished the rod and has caught some nice carp on it.

The Mk III was built in the winter of 1949/50 and the Mk IV No. 1 in the winter of 1950/51. The latter was bought by Chris Ball in 1989 and he still has it. It is difficult to know how many Mk IVs Dick made, but in one of his letters he said that he probably made around a hundred or more - many of which will have been given away. Each of these rods, if the origin can be authenticated, is now worth a few thousand pounds. Chris Ball had some interesting observations to make on the subject of Dick's Mk IV carp rod range. The following comes from a letter he sent to me during the research for this book.

Though I only met Dick in comparatively recent times (1971) I had seen him earlier at the National Angling Shows held at the Royal Horticultural Hall, Westminster, London, in the late 1960s. However, I went a number of times to the house in Water Lane, Flitwick and it was here that Dick gave me a number of items which I still have today.

I mentioned about browsing through his bookcase once and finding a copy of *Be Quiet and Go a-Angling* which I'd been trying to find for a number of years, he immediately said, "Take it, don't worry, there are a number of copies here." Though I protested he wouldn't budge. It was only when I got home and I sat down and opened it at the beginning that suddenly I was confronted with the personal dedication. I rang him straightway saying that I couldn't possibly have the book; he interrupted quickly with, "Why, has it got some pages missing?" When I explained that it was the copy he gave to his mother, he still wouldn't hear of having it back.

It was the same with the Mk III carp rod. On another visit I was examining an old umbrella stand in his study which was stuffed full of broken bits of rods. I spotted a piece of cane; it was a top section of a rod, and holding it against my body it seemed around five feet in length . . . Was the butt section around? Sure enough I found it amongst the tangle of rods. Then Dick came into the room, "What you got there?" "It's a cane rod," I replied. "Oh," said Dick, "I must throw all that lot away, they're no good."

Immediately I mentioned I'd like to refurbish it back to new. Then Dick took more notice; it transpired that it was his Mk III carp rod, a weapon made in the winter 1949/50 which was the only carp rod he personally made that was 'double built', the immediate predecessor to the famous Mk IV. He used the Mk III extensively in the 1950s and landed, amongst others, the Redmire 31^1/$_4$lb (34lb) common at the start of the 1954 season.

It took my spare time during the winter to strip the rod down (carefully keeping all the old green silk whippings in the tin) and I then finished it off with new rings and generally brought it back up to scratch.

I have used this rod a number of times (Golden Scale Club fish-ins, etc.) and landed a few carp of around six pounds in weight.

Mk IV No. 1, the rod Dick used to catch Clarissa, I bought from the late Mike Oyez in 1982. He was in prison and his eighteen-year-old son was left to dispose of his tackle and accessories. The authenticity letter from Dick Kefford explains what happened to the rod. Mike Oyez became friendly through fishery work he did for Dick Kefford in the late 1970s. By chance I saw this rod at Mike Oyez's house a year or two before I bought it, when I became a member of his syndicate water near Heathrow airport. His son knowing of my interest in the rod, fortunately rang me (and a number of other interested parties at the time); I bid the most.

This truly historic rod has only been used twice in the last twenty-five years, both times by Chris Yates. The first was the thirty-second anniversary of Walker's capture of his record carp (13th September) in 1984 and Chris landed a 20lb common! The second time was, of course, in the *Passion for Angling*, 'Redmire Legends' episode. There is little doubt that Chris was the right person to take the rod back to Redmire and fish for those remarkable carp. A personal thrill for me was when Chris caught a 20lb-plus common off the top of the rod with chum mixer. . . what a magical weapon.

I discussed the two points about setting hooks with Kevin Clifford and he told me I was wrong. He was too polite to put it more strongly or to suggest that I didn't have the experience to comment but he would have had some justification had he done so. But I still wonder . . . !

After the 1950s - in the post-Walker-at-Redmire era - the young Turks came with particle baits such as sweetcorn and it has to be said that their catches far exceeded those of the pioneers. It may be that in total they fished there more often, prebaited more frequently, and got the carp feeding on the kinds of bait they were using. Certainly, also, the nature of the water had changed and was receiving far less in the way of nutrients from the farmland, something that, in the past, had led to masses of daphnia and other food at intervals. These modern anglers eventually abandoned free-line fishing for the most part and concentrated on modern rigs and tackle. As I've already mentioned, though, several members of the Carp Catchers' Club *did* question what they themselves were doing and they *nearly* opted for particle baits, *nearly* went for small hooks, and *nearly* stepped up the power of the rods. In hindsight I reckon they got things wrong to some extent. But then pioneers always do.

Although Redmire Pool became more regularly available to many more anglers, often fishing on a rotation basis, its atmosphere and the pull it exerts on anglers has never waned, many regular fishers professing to be deeply moved as they arrive at the waterside. The role it has played in angling, with

Dick and friends, is probably incalculable, and vastly greater than its nearly three acres of fishing water would suggest. So great was the feeling for the place that, at one stage, when the fishing at Redmire seemed at risk, Dick even contemplated making an offer to buy the fishing rights outright. In the event, however, that wasn't necessary.

Peter Thomas demonstrating just how dangerous swans can be to an amused Dick and youthful assistant. Redmire Pool on Dick's first visit there.

Chapter 11

Philosophical matters

Y<small>OU CANNOT</small> have read this far without realising that Dick Walker was much more than an inventor, more than just someone who devised new bits of tackle like bite-alarms or improved upon others, such as rods. Improving tackle would not be enough on its own to cause a revolution. Even new baits could hardly do that unless one thinks of Fred Wilton's boilies, developed much later. Walker had to have an outlook, a *philosophy* of angling, something which underpinned all his successes and those of his friends. So let's look first at his approach to catching fish, and then at the way he saw fishing as part of the wider world.

Although he reiterated his fish-catching principles many times over the years, not least in his classic work *Still-Water Angling,* this list of important objectives comes from the tapes he made during the last year of his life for Pat. This is what he said:

1. **Find where they are**. You must locate the fish before you put your tackle together, if you don't your chances of catching them are poor.
2. **Having found them - don't scare them**. Or you are not going to catch them.
3. **Choose the right time**. The right time is when the fish are willing to feed, not when it is convenient for you.
4. **Choose the right tackle**. It is no good using tackle that is too strong, coarse and heavy so that the fish won't bite.
5. **Choose the right bait**. This is least important.

He added a rider to point five, saying, 'if you have got the first four essentials right, then you will be amazed at how catholic fish are in their taste about what bait they will take.' The last point is possibly the most contentious so let's look at the others first.

Dick in his library at Flitwick.

Dick accompanied by the Revd Edward Alston, previous holder of the tench and rudd records.

In his first point he didn't mean that you necessarily had to *see* the fish before setting up tackle - you might wait for ever on some pike waters where the first pike you see is in the landing-net. What he meant was that you should research the waters, using any and all means to do so, to find out which ones have fish of the size you seek. Then observe them if you can: carp or tench rolling, bubbling, pike striking (where they do so) and so on. Next, try to work out where they will be if you cannot see them and, most importantly where they will be when feeding, or when likely to feed if offered a bait. All of us make these decisions incorrectly from time to time and subsequent experience on a water often demonstrates forcibly just how time has been wasted! You can, of course, if you have time, use a trial and error technique, or the experience of friends to give a better idea of where to set up your tackle. This first major point of Dick's seems obvious to us now, but it was not so in the 1950s except to a few enlightened people. Many anglers then - and now (let's not mince words here) - simply wander down to a water and drop in their tackle. There's nothing at all wrong with this if you simply want a few hours in peace and quiet, observing nature, but if your concern is catching fish then it is time wasted. The very traditional, head-in-the-clouds types also tend to forget that you can commune with nature even whilst enjoying angling success!

His second major tenet again seems rather obvious, but it is one of the areas where so many anglers went wrong, and still do. I know one angler who hasn't quite managed to catch the giant pike he seeks, but if you fish with him you understand why: his footsteps on the bankside are those of a giant; the ground quakes on occasion. Any age-wise pike will be spooked if it's within fifty yards of him. Then there's the little matter of not letting the fish see you. Dick used to go on and on about anglers standing on the skyline in full view of the fish, wearing a Persil-white shirt. You can wear a white shirt if the background is snow, say, but in general dull clothes are better unless you are always very low to the skyline and well back from the bank. In his efforts to get his arguments across Dick would never compromise on white shirts! They were wrong he said. The strange thing is that fish are spooked by a human profile (and the profile of a heron incidentally) but ignore cattle. Long-term learning on the part of the fish is involved here. There can be no doubt that keeping low, dull and quiet is by far the best approach for the angler, and the importance of this increases with the age and the size of the fish. Dick always reckoned that chub 'came unscared' at about twenty minutes to the pound: two hours for a very big chub does seem about right, doesn't it? Sometimes you cannot get into casting position without scaring them and then you really do learn just how long it takes for them to 'come unscared'.

A joyous crew on the banks of the lake at Woburn Abbey. Includes Fred J. Taylor, Barrie Welham and John Goddard.

Hear no evil (Peter Thomas); see no evil (Dick); and speak no evil (Fred Buller) at Loch Lomond.

I think there was more debate about the third of Dick's principles than about any of the others, especially as it included debates about night fishing and night-fishing bans. Some averred that as fish fed easily at night it wasn't sporting to fish for them then, but that and other anti-night fishing arguments have long been scuppered thanks to Dick Walker and friends. Dick wrote often on the subject of how and when fish feed. It is usually easier to catch big fish when *they* are preparing to feed anyway, than it is to try to *bring them* to the feed, so it makes sense to find out when your quarry normally feeds. This can be by observation, as in the case of bubbling carp, tench or bream, or, again, it can be by trial and error, or experience. Quite often each water is different, and the big fish may well feed at a different time or in a different place to the small fish of the same species. As a general rule the best times are dawn and dusk, with night-time running a close second. Fish also change their feeding habits at night, for example big roach might run a mile at the sight of a big lobworm in daylight, but at night they often devour them avidly. Dick was aware of all these things, and much more, and had to simplify his principles into punchy phrases that captured the essence of what he wanted to say. As a consequence of this approach, he was often attacked on matters of detail, or on the exceptions to the rule that undoubtedly occur. But it was a general theory that Dick was attempting to build, not a fully comprehensive list of do's and don'ts and might be's.

'Rule' four says 'choose the right tackle'. Clearly the line and rod have to be chosen not only on the basis of the likely or hoped for size of fish, but also for the circumstances in which they would be caught. I remember once, getting a fair shellacking from Fred Carter at Garnafailagh, in Ireland, for catching tench just under six pounds using 11lb b.s. line. What he hadn't appreciated was that otters, hunting through the swims every early morning had forced the tench to live and feed in thick beds of bulrush. I had to pull them out of the rushes quickly, and as I couldn't have done it with 6lb b.s. line, I used my pike line. "QED," I would have said, but I don't think Fred was convinced. In the 1950s and 1960s the right tackle was not always available and this is why Dick set about making rods and why he urged the tackle trade to put roller bearings in the pick-up heads of fixed-spool reels. Other peripheral tackle had to be made too, such as rod-rests: there was little point in getting a carp run if the line jammed at the point where the rod lay on the rest!

His last point, about baits, was the most contentious because fish can be very, very finicky about the baits they will pick up. I remember once night-fishing for barbel on the Yorkshire Ouse with Ray Webb: we found that sausage paste worked superbly, but not *any* sausage - we'd tried half a dozen brands and only one of them worked. Dick's points 1-4 we had well under control, but we could have come unstuck on the fifth. This kind of situation is quite common. Everything Dick says in points 1-5 is true, and it is only in the last one that his 'buts' become big ones. But, as he says, it is points 1-3 that are the crucial ones; get these wrong and points 5 and 6 don't matter.

There was a rationality about Dick's philosophy that put off some of the traditionalists: they didn't *want* rules. Fishing was about enjoyment, they said. But Dick was not against enjoyment, and he would defend anyone's right to simply go and dangle if that is what they wanted to do. He didn't criticise the traditionalists unless they tried to tell him how to catch fish. Dick took a lot of very famous people fishing, people not famous for being anglers, and for the most part they were 'danglers'. What he did was to show them another side to angling, which often amazed them. And Dick and his companions were not averse to fun or to making sure their fishing *was* enjoyable as well. When camping they really made themselves as comfortable as possible given the camping constraints of the day - good bivouac, good food, even a guitar or two! 'Comfortable perseverance' could have been their motto. Dick never did believe in taking angling too seriously: as he once said, decisions you have to make whilst fishing are every bit as difficult as those a Prime Minister has to take, but they don't have the same consequences.

Of course, if you had to *live* from the fish you caught then that would be different: your decisions would mean you would starve, or not, and I'd like to bet you'd want to employ principles 1-5 in those circumstances. Dick had a deep interest in palaeoanthropology, and he always argued that fishing was engrained in the human psyche, that it was the nearest we came to fulfilling our hunting instinct. Man has hunted fish with lines, with or without a rod or hook for thousands of years, and until very recently, all the fish caught were used as food, and let's face it, food of very good quality if we are to believe today's nutritionists. You can try this for yourself. Go somewhere remote and live by the fish you catch. It does help put the hunting instinct in perspective. Jeremy Wade and I did this for a month on the Amazon and ate a wide variety of fish, including several species of catfish and piranha as well as peacock bass. You soon learn where your food is coming from, and you soon learn what is good eating - none of this nonsense about earthy tastes, believe me. Dick had this absolutely right: man was always a hunter and a fisher, and it is still in our genes. It is the most natural thing in the world for men to fish.

None of this means that they can't *enjoy* what they do. All hunters in primitive societies today not only worship their prey, to varying degrees, but they enjoy the hunt too, and ritualise it (providing the ritual does not impinge on the success too much). Dick was fully aware of all these matters related to angling and even though aspects of his philosophy had been used before, even in Izaak Walton, they had never before been put forward as a unified package, a total philosophy of the sport. It's my view that such a package could never have come from a game fisherman, and that's because the ritual of game fishing has possibly overridden objectivity; and it is also unlikely to have come from a sea fisherman because, for him, the catch is all (although I may be wrong about that). I think it had to come from a coarse fisherman and Dick Walker was the man of the time with the necessary breadth of knowledge and a background that gave him the wherewithal to convey it.

I'll end this chapter by dispensing with one little myth. Dick always said that there was no point in trying to solve a problem until you knew what the problem was, and that this was drilled into him as an engineer in Cambridge. The story goes that a lecturer in Cambridge would enter the lecture room, make this statement, and then walk out. The philosophy is certainly sound, but I think the story of its origins are less so: I have checked with Dick's engineering colleagues and none of them have any recollection of such an occurrence.

Principle number two. Having found them - don't scare them! Dick on a Test carrier stream.

The Walker way of perch fishing!

Chapter 12

Perch and chub

WHILST Dick is now best known for his carp fishing, it was his perch and chub fishing that first captured the imagination of anglers (most of whom, initially, had little interest in carp). In fact, Dick's early fame was due to his perch captures. These were, to start with, on Arlesey Lake, but later on he fished for perch on the middle reaches of the Great Ouse with the Taylors and often talked about their catches in *Angling Times*. How Dick would have enjoyed the twenty-first century with its big perch turning up everywhere. A lot of his chub fishing, too, was on that Beachampton stretch of the Great Ouse that he rented - of which more a little later.

The Arlesey perch were not discovered by Dick but by a local angler, Frank Belcher, who caught a 3lb-plus fish from 'the stumps' area of the lake. Good perch had occasionally been caught by accident at the lake and it became clear to Dick that they needed a targeted approach. First of all he went to the brick company and obtained a contour map of the lake! I'm not sure that anyone had ever before gone to the trouble of contouring a lake - although Dick did it by short cut, of course - but by the late 1950s we were *all* doing it! (Ray Webb and I spent many days plumbing the depths of rivers and lakes in which we had an interest.) Prior to this an angler would work out by trial and error, and over time, the deeps and shallows, and both match and pleasure anglers might plumb the depth (with a plummet) around their floats, but such thoroughness as Walker showed was to become the norm for specimen hunters.

Dick decided to fish the deeps of Arlesey because, in winter, that is where the warmest water should be. He explained this, with diagrams in *Still-Water Angling*. His first perch weighed in at 3lb 10oz: not a bad start! At this stage in the campaign he was using drilled bullets; in fact, that's all most of us used in those days, or we used coffin leads that lay flat on the bottom rather than rolling. However, Dick soon decided that a more streamlined casting weight

Dick with a fine chub from Beachampton . . .   *. . . and a 4lb perch from Little Brickhill.*

Happy campers. Dick with Peter Stone and Frank Guttfield (in foreground).

was needed and came up with what we now know as the Arlesey Bomb, taking its name from the lake for which it was devised. Dick didn't make the first one; it was made by Alan Brown, who was a young lad at the time. Dick had prepared the mould and the lead, and had left them ready in his garden fishing shed until he had time to run some off. Alan, on one of his many visits to the shed (which happened whether Dick was there or not) decided to speed up the proceedings, but unfortunately, he didn't get things quite right, possibly getting a little moisture in the mould: the whole caboodle exploded! Not to be deterred he had another go, and this time he succeeded, the explosion probably having dried out the mould. Quite what Dick thought of this adventurous boy is not known, but the Arlesey Bomb certainly had an explosive impact both literally and metaphorically: it took the angling world by storm. (I once made my own, with the same initial result as Alan Brown, although I didn't have the sense to do it in a garden shed, not having one anyway.)

Details of Dick's catches at Arlesey have been widely covered elsewhere so will not be repeated here. Suffice to say that the principles of common sense and logic that he used were exactly those described in the last chapter. These catches hit the headlines and resulted not only in prizes but in recognition from the likes of Bernard Venables, who was already famous, and others who were shortly to embark on the founding of *Angling Times*. B.V. covers this period in his second autobiography and makes it clear that they regarded Dick as an up-and-coming genius of angling with a striking track record with carp and perch. The Arlesey story somehow gripped anglers more than the carp story at that stage, and Dick was soon to be offered a column in *Angling Times*, when it was launched.

Dick considered perch to be one of the biggest of fishes. By that he meant that its pugnacious, bristling appearance, and its boldness at times, made it rather special and he remained fond of perch fishing all his life. His next phase of perch fishing was rather different, concentrating as it did on the perch in the Great Ouse at Beachampton. The catches made there were reported regularly in his column in *AT* or, more particularly, the techniques needed for their capture. I recall their experience that the float-fished worm tackle had to be within an inch or two of the massed bulrush stems before they could get a bite: the perch wouldn't take the bait in open water. However, I don't think the Great Ouse perch were scared, they were just cautious of open water, and there were big pike in those pools! I have successfully enjoyed both styles - open water and close to bulrushes - using Dick's Arlesey Bomb in deep gravel pits in East Yorkshire; and in North Yorkshire I've had large catches (of smallish perch) by fishing a slow-sinking, float-fished worm within an inch or two of the rush beds. Dick also noted from time to time how skilful the bigger perch

Building the fishing hut at Beachampton. Plan shown opposite.

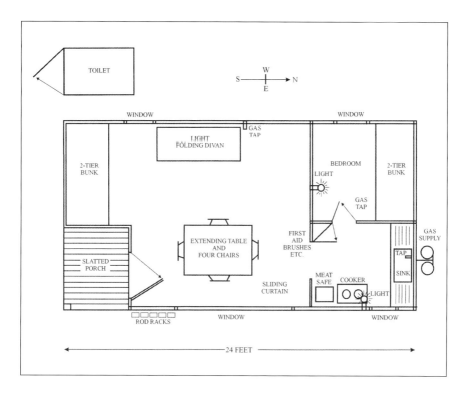

were at transferring the hook from mouth to reed stem: anyone who does much perch fishing will attest to that. At a later date Dick became President of the Perchfishers' Club.

The Beachampton stretch of the Great Ouse also led Dick to some serious chub fishing. Perhaps now is the time to say a word or two about that famous fishing hut at Beachampton (although the photographs perhaps say all that is necessary).

Permission for the ten-foot by twenty-foot hut was given by the landlords of the Beachampton water, the farmer Mr Marchant, and the Towcester RDC. It's interesting to read of Dick's plans in letters written to Peter Stone on 9th January, 1961, and 28th March, 1961:

> We aim to commence building the hut as soon as weather permits but it is necessary first to get planning permission from Towcester Rural District Council, and for this plans have to be submitted. All this side of the job is being handled by John French who is, as well as a very keen angler, employed

in the architects' department Louth Urban Council. Until he gives us the OK we cannot do anything, but I have no reason to suppose that we shall be unable to start work any later than about the beginning of April. I am anxious to get the whole job finished before June 16th and this I am sure we shall succeed in doing. The 'Clerk of Works' is Ken Taylor, and I will let him know that if he needs any additions to the labour force, we can drag you in!

The situation about this is that we have now all the necessary planning permissions and by-law approvals and it is only a matter of getting the job done. Ken Taylor is bossing the job and as far as I can see, it will mean doing the foundation digging next weekend, April 1st, and 2nd, and possibly Easter Monday as well; then we shall try and get all the concreting done during the following weekend, April 8th and 9th. If this proceeds according to plan, we will try and erect the hut the weekend after that, always supposing that its sections can be delivered to the site by then. This will depend to a large extent upon the condition of the ground, as it will be necessary to run a fairly heavy vehicle down to the site unless, of course, we can get the farmer to lend us a tractor and trailer. However I will keep you posted and as soon as I have had a bit of a conference with Ken, I will let you know whether you are earmarked for hole digging, concreting, shovelling or hammering nails!

One of Peter Stone's accounts of the building of the hut is equally instructive. It is clear that it was Dick who had the organisational skills and the drive; the others did the work:

During our conversation, Dick had mentioned the possibilities of building a hut and it was good news to hear that it was going ahead. Work duly started on time and it took Dick, the Taylors, Peter Drennan (whom I had roped in) and me every weekend of the close season to get the hut completed. It was hard work but we had a lot of fun too. One weekend we went home with the floor in place, which meant that the following weekend we could start decorating the interior. We arrived the following Saturday, decided what had to be done first, then after refreshments started work.

Or at least, five of us did. Dick had bought several bottles of Lucozade, plus an armchair, and he plonked himself down into it and had the occasional drink while the rest of us slaved away. He spoke now and again, "Yes, that looks right!" - "No, I don't think it should be there!" - "I suggest it goes better there!", and so on. And he was sitting right in the middle of the working area, which meant that we were constantly skirting round him and the array of emptying bottles, unable to walk in a straight, sensible line.

After an hour or so I could see that Fred was getting somewhat cross. Then

Stone and Walker relaxing.

Dick rose from his chair and walked across the room. In a flash, Fred grabbed the chair and threw it out of the door.

"If you're going to sit there all morning," shouted Fred, "get outside and let us get on with it!" at the same time throwing the bottles outside too. What did Dick do? He went out and sat down outside without uttering a word!

That hut made a big difference to our fishing. It was nice in summer to fish until dark and then retire for the night; then up again at dawn with the gear already assembled and the bait waiting. In winter, the comfort of being able to stop fishing at midday, retire to the hut and cook a meal, then fish again until it was time to go home, was very nice, and much better than eating sandwiches while sitting under a brolly in the cold and wet.

Visitors to the fishery were given a key for use during their stay. Dick never charged anyone for the privilege - and it was a privilege - instead he had an Anglers' Cooperative Association box inside for donations. [Note that, at a later stage, Dick had to introduce a charge, to cover silly abuse by some of the guests.]

'Walker's Hut' became famous and over the years many well-known names enjoyed its comforts. It became a meeting place and in winter it was not unusual for us to stop fishing at midday, cook a meal, then sit and yarn until it was time to go home.

It was by all accounts a comfortable, beautifully designed hut, and it was built by a team of Dick's friends. Initially, it was made readily available to anyone, with no charges; all that was asked was that people left it as they found it, replacing any long-life stores that succeeding inhabitants might need. Many famous anglers stayed there and fished for roach, bream, perch and chub, with occasional pike. At a later stage the facility was run by Ian Howcroft, and eventually the rental was given up by Dick and his friends, but only after a long tradition was built up and many famous catches made. Lots of the letters in Dick's files refer to the fishing here and there are many words of thanks for Dick for allowing them to fish a wonderful water. This aspect of Dick's generosity was much more public than his many other acts of kindness to people, but it is nonetheless typical of the man. Maurice Ingham once said that the word which immediately sprang to mind when he thought of Walker was the word 'generosity'. His Beachampton hut is perhaps what we think of when we think of Walker now. The rules for the hut, and instructions for its use, were carefully thought out, and extraordinarily comprehensive:

The fishing hut at Little Hill Farm was built so that Fred Taylor and I could not only enjoy its facilities ourselves, but offer them to our friends who live all over the country.

It can accommodate four persons in comfort, and two more by bringing into use as a bed the convertible divan. Two bunks are in a separate room, so that ladies can be accommodated.

It is situated only 40 yards from the river and is cool in summer, warm in winter, dry, and out of reach of floods. A calor gas supply provides lighting and heating, and there is piped water.

No charge is made for using it; all we ask is that you read the attached information, act upon it, and enjoy yourself.

Little Hill Farm is situated about 3¼ miles along the A422 (Stony Stratford - Buckingham) road, from its junction with the A422 road at the northern end of Stony Stratford. The entrance is on the left-hand side, when coming from Stony Stratford, over a cattle-grid leading to an avenue of lime-trees. Two alternative routes lead from the farm to the hut; unless otherwise informed, ask Mr Marchant at the farm, which you should take.

The slatted porch is provided so that you can stand under cover to remove muddy footwear, wet waterproofs, etc., and deposit muddy baskets and wet nets, before entering the hut. Please use it as intended

A dustbin is provided for burnable refuse. Don't light rubbish fires yourself, leave it to me. My old man isn't a dustman and neither am I, so don't put empty tins, bottles, or waste food in the dustbin. Take them away with you. If you are staying long, you can bury waste food, well away from the hut. We are getting niggly about this. The next visitor to leave a dustbin full of unburnable rubbish will have paid his last visit. Don't leave perishable food-stuffs, or milk, in the hut. It may be some time before the next visitors arrive, and they don't want to find either a stink of decayed food or a colony of rats, attracted thereby.

The sink wastepipe leads to a soakaway, not a sewer. Don't put tea-leaves or other solids down this pipe. It is a plastic sink; don't use abrasive cleaners, like 'Vim', on it. Water is laid on. There is a tap on the sink and a gate-valve underneath the hut below the sink. Open on arrival, close on departure.

Breakages. I shan't mind if you accidentally break a plate or a cup, but I'll be dead niggled if you go away leaving a lot of dirty crockery, cutlery or cooking utensils.

Cleaning. In spite of every care, some dirt and dust does find its way inside the hut. Brushes and dustpans are provided and I'd be obliged if you would sweep up, shake out the mats, and dust the place before you leave. If everyone does his share, the place will stay reasonably clean.

Toilet. The key to the toilet is kept on a hook behind the hut door. The Elsan closet may need emptying, in which case dig a hole along the hedgerow, well away from the hut. Refill the closet with Elsan fluid and water as per directions on the cans. Don't empty the closet into the river. Lock the toilet door and replace the key on its hook before leaving.

The gas supply comes from cylinders at the rear of the hut, which must be turned on when you arrive, and off when you leave. Please don't forget this.

The Chub Study Group poster (by John Searl), with Walker and Stone at the centre.

Fred J. Taylor and Peter Stone fish spotting, circa 1960.

Anglers who were mediocre chub anglers, such as myself, were enthralled at Dick's activities on the Ouse and his tales of giant fish. We lapped up all the stories of using crayfish as deadbaits, something one is not allowed to do today, of course; of stepping down the legered crust size in really cold conditions; of varying the length of the hook link to find the taking length on the day; and the neat manner of fixing swan-shots to a wrap-over of line above a stop shot, in order to get the exact casting or holding weight (a Fred J. Taylor invention, I think). It was the way he wrote about it all that captured our imaginations - it wasn't just the fishing but the atmosphere that went with it. Dick and his friends also fished for big roach and bream, as well as chub, and one of the more humorous stories concerns bream. In an attempt to draw and hold bream, and get them feeding on maggots, they suspended a whole dead sheep in willow branches at the head of the swim. They were nothing if not thorough, but the result was a huge shoal of dace, not bream!

Peter Stone, of course, was a known angler in his own right. Dick once referred to him, in jest, as the 'Stone bream basher', a reference to his early success with that species. Later Peter became one of the greatest specimen hunters the nation has had, and he became particularly expert at chub, and that is one of the ways Dick and Peter crossed paths.

Peter and Dick corresponded and met as early as 1956. One of Dick's early letters to Peter discusses the fact that heavy leads cause chub to drop the bait, and Dick advocates leads that only just hold bottom so that on pick-up the chub feel minimal drag. Peter agreed with Dick on this one, but I do wonder if it is correct: perhaps some experienced chub angler will tell us, because if it *is* true, then chub are quite unlike most other species, which will tow a sizeable lead around quite readily. (I'll return to this a little later from a different perspective.)

The two of them spent a great deal of time discussing the merits of legering. Both were experts - Peter wrote a now classic book, *Legering*, in 1963 - and they debated the effects of current on thin and thick lines and the weights appropriate to hold bottom when chub fishing. Interestingly, Peter picked up on something of Dick's that has always puzzled me and that is Dick's use of shot as a stop. Like Peter, I found mine always slipped, usually on the strike, so I stopped using them. Presumably the invention of leger stops was a consequence of the shot failing. So why didn't it bother Dick? It's a real problem, because if the shot slips on the strike you invariably miss the bite. Another interesting comment in the Walker-Stone correspondence (*The Stone-Walker Letters*) is Peter's assertion that the Mk IV was not much of a rod-tip indicator rod, and he makes, quite correctly I feel, a negative comparison with today's carbon-fibre tips. Of course, the Mk IV was designed for casting and playing fish, not for registering minute cold-water chub bites. The matter of large leads may need looking at again, for chub too, as has happened with other species, because during the last two or three years chub anglers have been having considerable success with big chub on large, matchbox-sized, chunks of luncheon-meat attached to tackle featuring fixed leads up to five ounces in weight. This in conditions of high and coloured water and very fast flow, conditions which might, perhaps, have been ignored in the past. Time will tell on this one, but I should not be surprised to learn that chub will pull a big weight at *any* time. Of course, all Dick's chub fishing was pre-boilie: these are super chub baits as I know from my own experience. I wonder what Dick would have made of them.

The Walker-Stone letters cover many other issues aside from chub fishing, and towards the end of the series is one where Walker gets at Stoney over his liking for bream, writing, '. . . where I shan't be in any danger of hooking one of those beastly slimy breams . . . I hear that a glue factory is being started in the Oxford district by a couple of local chaps named Taylor and Stone who catch lots of bream, and scrape the slime off, for making this special brand of fish-glue.' Dick Walker could never remain serious for too long, and evidence of his humour crops up time and again, as you'll see also in the next chapter on pike.

Chapter 13

Walker and pike

P OSSIBLY the one area of angling in which Dick Walker trod with trepidation was pike angling. People very close to him tell me that he hated pike. Tim Walker, Dick's son, told me that, as far as he was aware, Dick knocked on the head every pike he caught. This is not literally the case because there were features in *Angling Times* that showed Dick unhooking pike at the side of the boat - without removing them from the water - and letting them slide back into the water. Even so, it would be fair to say that he was far from fond of pike.

His early piking was done under the guidance of his grandfather who was, understandably, a piker of the old school; one might almost say of the Dark Ages. Knowing that pike angling had been revolutionised in the later 1950s and 1960s by Fred J. Taylor, Bill Giles, and others, and that he was to a degree being left behind, Dick sent me a contribution to the Pike Anglers' Club magazine based upon the old piking. I was Editor at the time and he dared me to publish it. I did. The reaction, despite a cautionary postscript that I added to the article, was ferocious and predictable. The comments quite missed the point that it was tongue-in-cheek and intended to paint a picture of the piking past in which Dick still had one foot.

His article was entitled 'A Step Back into the Past'. That in itself ought to have warned readers. It began by reciting his grandfather's advice to him when he, Dick, was a boy: 'Never you offer to strike a pike, my boy, till that's had it for ten minutes - by your watch!' Dick then went on to say, 'This is very sound advice,' and advocated hooking the pike in the stomach which avoided the risk of hooks failing to penetrate the bony jaw of the pike . . . and so on in that vein. He also recommended use of a 38oz baseball bat; which you should practise with using a sandbag or the neighbours' alsatians! But he added a word of warning: 'A cricket bat is not an acceptable substitute for a baseball

Dick Walker beatified by Fred Buller, on Loch Lomond, using an inflatable inner tube (often used by boat anglers as cushions).

Oops!

bat; if it is brought down flat, two to four pounds per square inch are applied. Any attempt to use its edge leads to inaccuracy of aim since the cross-section is not aerodynamically symmetrical.' (I love that!) You can well imagine the reaction of PAC members to all this, especially those who couldn't see the joke. There are two things I particularly like in that last quote from his article: firstly, the implication that he had actually tried both methods of subduing a pike; and, secondly, the gentle poke of fun at his own reputation for having a thoroughly scientific approach to all angling's problems.

Here, also, we see some of the contradictions that were Dick Walker. He did not like pike; yet he was prepared to lend unstinting support to the PAC; and he did so on many occasions, often backing me, as Editor, behind the scenes when I needed help to further pike conservation and pike angling. He was concerned enough to ask me to read and check for him the pike chapter in *Still-Water Angling* in the third and fourth editions. If you browse through the pike chapter you will find little that harks back to the bad old days and he does say early on, 'I do not understand pike' and adds that he didn't like them. Nevertheless he applies his characteristic logic to argue that as pike get bigger they'd prefer a big, easy meal if they can get it, rather than one that needs a lot of chasing around, using energy. He backed up the thought by pointing out that the weight of a fish increases by the cube of its length, but the tail fin area only by the square of the fish length. Hence more energy is needed, in proportion, to move a big fish through the water than a small one.

Much of his writing on pike is thoroughly modern and quite a number of his ideas, then rather novel, are widely accepted today. There are areas, though, where he was quite wrong - and here I speak with some degree of expertise. For example, he states that deadbaits suspended off the bottom catch few pike when it is, in reality, a very successful technique, as we now know. His floats, and the streamlining of them were ahead of his time, and I made my own to his design, but his hook-rigs are, I believe, poor, and do not work as well as the modern snap-tackle rigs. He was wrong about the upper treble on snap tackles needing to be fixed: it works far better if sliding loose. I reckon he was also wrong about pike eating birds. This is exceedingly rare. His claim that, 'Most anglers at one time or another will have seen a moorhen vanish with an anguished cry . . .' is a figment of his and everyone else's imagination, not of reality. However, there is nothing in his *Still-Water* pike chapter that is not thoughtful and forward-looking - despite his dislike of the species.

At a later stage Dick became fond of stating that just using deadbaiting (rather than dead- and livebait) had not led to any deterioration of his pike catches. Such a statement does need to be treated with caution, not only because his pike catches were nothing to get excited about anyway, but because one *must* use the two techniques in tandem, trip after trip, to be able to judge the effectiveness of one and the other. I did this myself for many years, fishing deadbait on one rod and livebait on the other, in the same swim. There is no doubt whatsoever that livebait produces more fish, more of the time, and just as many big ones as deadbaiting. You'd only use deadbaits in preference if you *preferred* the method to livebaiting or if, like me, you are bone idle. So Dick, I think, got this quite wrong and deserved the criticisms he received.

At one stage Dick was concerned that pike anglers were not getting together as a body and they were not, in his view, targeting big pike, or rather, monstrous pike. Well, the first part of that statement was certainly true: although many specialist anglers were pike fishing in the 1960s with great success, often as members of specimen groups, there was no equivalent of the Carp Catchers' Club or the Tenchfishers. So Dick and Fred Buller called a meeting of notorious pike anglers at the White Horse pub in Milton, near Cambridge. The pub was about a hundred yards from my then home, and I think the choice of venue was influenced by the success of the Cambridgeshire Pike Anglers at the time. In addition, Norfolk wasn't so far away, and anglers from Bedfordshire, the Midlands or London wouldn't have too difficult a journey. As it happens, northerners also made the trip.

It was a full-day meeting, beginning after breakfast, breaking for a working (ie, talking) lunch which Dick and Fred laid on for everyone. There seemed to be two main objectives: firstly to encourage the formation of a national pike society of some kind; and, secondly, to encourage experienced pikers to head for Loch Lomond and its monstrous pike. Neither of these objectives was fulfilled in terms of definite commitment on the day, but the seeds were undoubtedly sown in people's minds.

The attendance list included some very special pike anglers, such as Bill Giles and Reg Sandys from Norfolk, Ray Webb from Sheffield, Hugh Reynolds and other Cambridgeshire Pike Anglers' members, Bill Chillingsworth and several others, including myself. The meeting did not go too well. In the first place it was difficult to convince those present that Loch Lomond was anything special; as a place, yes, but in terms of pike results it was far less productive than the Cambridgeshire Fens. That year the Cambridgeshire Pike Anglers had caught far more twenty-pound fish (and a couple of 30-pounders) than had been caught on Loch Lomond, and they simply did not believe that the anticipated numbers of Lomond 30-pounders, predicted by Dick, would actually materialise. They were right, of course, because big pike on Lomond proved just as difficult as anywhere else, perhaps more so.

Another problem with the meeting was summed up by Ray Webb, forthright as ever, as we broke up after the morning session and went out to stretch our legs. He said to me, "This man Walker has talked for 90% of the time this morning, and yet he knows less about pike than any man present. I'm not sure I'm going back in after lunch." He did have a point, of course, and what he said was quite literally correct. Ray wanted to listen to Fred Buller and Bill Giles, not R.W.! Others seemed equally disgruntled and yet I think most people realised that Dick was trying hard to sell two big ideas. Quite naturally, one of his selling points was the loss of a huge pike on Lomond by Fred Buller, which Dick (who saw the fish more closely than anyone else) rated at around fifty pounds. That was his *public* pronouncement at the time. Privately, he said sixty pounds or more. I didn't believe this myself, and I doubt if anyone else present did, for reasons which I'll go into elsewhere, but on that day it oversold his case and I think was instrumental in failing to get everyone galvanised towards Lomond and its piking.

The afternoon session was rather more rewarding in that other voices were raised more often and many pike angling matters were discussed, such as the value and practice of deadbaiting and so on. However, the idea of forming some kind of pike anglers' society was downplayed somewhat and the meeting ended quite inconclusively in this regard. The meeting did reveal a downside to Dick, namely his tendency to talk too much on occasion. Bernard Venables is reported as saying that Dick was the only man who could bore him on the subject of angling, although that seems a strange and unfair remark: at the meeting in question not one individual was bored, and subsequent discussions I had with the participants revealed that they had really enjoyed the day - and whilst they'd have liked R.W. to have talked a little less, they certainly did not find him boring! On the contrary, he raised a number of issues upon which they wanted to challenge him and they did so, both in the afternoon session and subsequently.

Whether it was an indirect result of this meeting or not, Eric Hodson (who was *not* present) formed the Pike Society. It is not the place to discuss this body here, but suffice it to say that it did not succeed; Fred Buller was its first President, and I, myself, the second! It was later replaced by the Pike Anglers' Club (PAC) which was, and is, a success; and this, as I've already mentioned, was backed by R.W., as well as by Fred Buller. And anglers *did* go to Lomond, in numbers, but it never produced the spectacular results predicted for it by Dick.

Walker's views on pike were remarkably similar to Izaak Walton's, as I discovered only recently. If you look in the first edition of Walton's *Compleat Angler* (p.143 *et seq.*) you will see that he regarded large pike as a menace to a fishery: 'All pikes that live long prove chargeable to their keepers, because their life is maintained by the death of so many other fish, even those of his owne kind . . .'

Yet, despite his anti-pike stance, Walker actually made significant contributions to pike angling. Once again, we have one of the contradictions that was Dick Walker. Many anglers today attribute to myself the recognition and promotion of the fact that if you destroy large pike then this invariably results in a water overrun with smaller pike which create ecological havoc. That is, they eat even more prey fish. It is true that I have done a lot of work in this area, yet is was Dick who came up with the idea before I did, and he pushed it hard from time to time, to the extent that I believe that in his later years he would not have killed big pike indiscriminately for this reason. In fact, this is why he supported the PAC.

Interestingly, I discovered an article written in the early 1900s in which the owner of a series of trout lakes and streams came to exactly the same conclusion and given that Dick was so well read, I would not be at all surprised if he had got his ideas from this source.

So there we have it. Even in this, his weakest area of freshwater fishing, Dick Walker had contributions to make, and he made it with his usual leading-from-the-front style - irritating people in part, but also coercing and inspiring them.

Dick Walker with a mixed bag, including pike, caught by himself and Peter Stone.

Chapter 14

The roots of specimen hunting

D ICK WALKER is often said to have been opposed to specimen hunting but, as we shall see, this is not really correct. It's true that there were elements, when the movement was young, that he did not like, particularly its competitive element and its tendency to be overly serious. Even Bernard Venables, in his autobiography, confessed that Dick would have been disturbed by some developments, and, remember, Bernard was anti-Walker and blamed him for the birth of the specimen hunting creed. But Walker and his friends *enjoyed* their fishing together, had fun, and, as a friend put it, had time to smell the flowers along the way. Fred J. Taylor memorably described them as a 'merry band' and five minutes talking to Dick would confirm this exactly. This is not to say that they were not 'serious' about solving problems - on the contrary, they used science, logic, commonsense and innovative approaches all the time - but they kept the seriousness in perspective.

Jim Gibbinson's superb book, *Modern Specimen Hunting* (1983, Beekay Publishers) provides a detailed background to the roots of specimen hunting, so what I'm looking at here is Dick Walker's involvement.There is no doubt at all that R.W. and friends inspired, and hence almost directly gave rise to, the specimen hunting movement. There were numerous role models. First of all there was the Carp Catchers' Club. Shortly after this came the first Tenchfishers. This first version was not, I think it is true to say, very successful in that it did not last long. The second Tenchfishers, formed not long after the demise of the first and led by Peter Jackson and friends, was an on-going success and is still with us today. I suspect that the very social nature of this club would have met with Dick's entire approval; and I fancy he would have liked their analytical and scientific approach too. They are a merry band and no mistake. If I might add a personal aside here, I was once a member of this group but I was eventually excommunicated because of my reluctance - nay, refusal - to disclose the details of one of my tench waters! Not, I hasten to add, that my results were anything to shout home about, but I had given a promise on accepting the fishing. Perhaps they had a short spell of being serious. Regardless of that, this is exactly the kind of club that R.W. would have endorsed wholeheartedly.

Following the original Tenchfishers came the first of the two Northern Specimen Groups which had as members none other than Dick Clegg and Tag Barnes. After that groups formed thick and fast, and disappeared almost as quickly. At one point there were probably sixty such clubs around the country, including more than one sea group. Today there are very few and, I feel, only those with a good social mix survive. Examples are the Herts/Chiltern Group and the Peterborough Specimen Group: the former is covered rather nicely in recent books by Bob Buteux; and the latter has Bob Church (see Chapter 16) as a founding and active member. I am sure from talking to Dick that he really approved of these not-so-serious and long-lived organisations. They have his spirit.

The specimen groups in the early 1960s were brought together in a single association largely by the efforts of the Northern Specimen Group member, Eric Hodson. In later years there was a dispute between Eric and others about who was actually responsible for the development of specimen hunting. I, personally, do not think there is any doubt at all about how it happened: Richard Walker *inspired* it; Eric Hodson *organised* it. It is clear in letters to me that Eric felt his role had not been recognised by the angling media and neo-gurus, but I am far from certain that this is true.

The National Association of Specimen Groups (NASG) later became the National Association of Specialist Anglers (NASA) - formed as specimen *groups* declined (and with myself as President) - and finally merged with the Special Anglers' Conservation Group (SACG, political wing associated with NASA) to become the Specialist Anglers' Association (SAA, with myself as President). I feel R.W. would have been rather proud of the SAA because it really does fight a good fight for angling politically - as he did, often - and its members enjoy fishing, without the competitive streak Dick disliked. So the whole thing has gone full circle and one can almost sense the change that is taking place, in many branches of the sport, towards spending more time smelling the flowers along the way.

A letter written by Dick to Eric Hodson at the time of the formation of the NASG reveals yet another side to Dick's character:

Dear Eric,
Thanks for your letter of 1st June, 1972, and for sending me the application

form for the Pike Society. Quite frankly, I am not prepared to fill up a questionnaire of this sort, nor to move an inch to make application for membership. I don't give a bugger whether I become a member or not. If you chaps think I can make a useful contribution and want me in, I am quite willing to join and to pay whatever subscription you consider necessary; but I am certainly not seeking membership in any positive kind of way and I am not going to fill up a form that implies that I am doing so.

Best wishes,
Dick

Apart from being quite funny this letter corroborates something that Dick's contemporaries in *primary* school pointed out: that he was a very social boy, supportive of activities, but seriously disliked the formality of joining something. He clearly despised form-filling. (I know another angler, not an inch from this pen, who reacts similarly.)

Imagine Dick's reaction, then, to another form that Eric sent him. Note, especially, question numbers 5-8. (To be fair to Eric, his covering letter did have a rider to the effect that Dick did not have to fill in the form if he didn't want to.)

NATIONAL PIKE CLUB
Application for membership

1. Name
2. Address   Postal Code   Telephone No.
3. Age
4. Profession or Occupation
5. Number of years spent angling
6. What period of this has been devoted to pike angling?
7. Do you specialise in any other species, and if so, what?
8. How many hours do you spend fishing per year?
9. Please give a brief résumé of the larger fish you have caught.
10. We anticipate that as a keen angler you would support the Clean Rivers Society or the A.C.A.
11. Please feel at liberty to give any further information which you feel will enable the National Pike Club to give fuller consideration to your application, on the reverse of this form.

Signature   Date

Please complete and return this form at the earliest opportunity to Eric Hodson.

A famous picture of Dick, on the Great Ouse at Beachampton, trotting the water for chub and roach. Despite the weather he looks comfortable, in his equally famous greatcoat.

At Wilstone Reservoir with one of those 'slimey things'.

But although Dick didn't believe in form-filling, he did support the fledgling NASG, sending subs in, and becoming its first President. The following is one of his addresses to an NASG conference:

PRESIDENTIAL ADDRESS: BY DICK WALKER

This Association has grown amazingly largely due to the efforts of Peter Butler, Eric Hodson and one or two others on this Committee, and we have all of us to strike just the right note between being keen researchers, keen pressers for the sort of fishing we like on the one hand, and retaining a proper sense of humour and a proper sense of proportion on the other. In other words, it's going to be a bad day for specimen hunters when they can't laugh at one another and laugh at themselves. We have not got to conduct ourselves too seriously but we have to conduct ourselves seriously enough. We are living at a time with a lot of younger people who could be doing a lot worse than going fishing, and we have considerable responsibility to the future in showing that fishing is not just someone sitting on the bank getting bored catching nothing, but a really exciting adventure, one that exercises mind and body.

A whole lot of challenges are to be met, both from the point of view of catching fish and guiding the sport. We shall have more to say about this later on.

During the last year I have been on the Executive of the National Anglers' Council, and although theoretically I represent individual anglers, in actuality I represent specimen hunters. I want to say now that I was under the impression, to be perfectly frank and to mention names, that people like Halliday and Davison, and chaps of that sort, were miserable old dodderers, and we should never get anything done. How mistaken I was - they have proved wise and statesmanlike individuals, and we have to work with them and perhaps make concessions, to save angling from the apathy we have had over the last few years.

I would just like to welcome you here. Thank you very much.

Note Dick's insistence that the sport of specimen hunting should not become too serious. It did, of course, and it paid the price in the demise of individual groups and the falling out which anglers indulged in. I do suspect that if Eric Hodson had not written to Dick in such formal terms then Dick would have been in touch anyway.

In modern angling it is not the bivvying-up and session fishing in itself that is so very different from the days of the Carp Catchers' Club; it is the way it is being done that would bother R.W. I cannot believe for one moment that

Dick would have disapproved of improvements in rods, reels, buzzers, or camp beds and bivvies. What he *would* frown upon are the more antisocial habits of some of today's specimen hunters.

Dick did have reservations about specimen hunting but he also supported the burgeoning new specialist carp angling groups. With the fading away of the Carp Catchers' Club (Chapter 9) the void had to be filled simply because the now-inspired anglers were fishing for carp as never before. Even though Dick had more or less stopped fishing for carp and had moved on to other areas, he still gave his support to the new Carp Society and British Carp Study Group - both of which have been extremely successful (more of which later).

So was Walker to blame for all the ills brought on by specimen hunting? Bernard Venables thought he was. But can you blame the man who invented the tool just because some of the subsequent artisans cannot use it? Could Bernard possibly be justified in throwing blame Walker's way? I don't think so; it's my view that there was much more to Bernard's gripe than meets the eye, as we'll see in Chapter 18.

If you look again at the NASG Presidential Address by Dick it is very clear that he understood fully the dangers of becoming too fanatical, and he warned against it. In all his angling writing published and unpublished, he repeatedly made the same points. When you spoke to him, or listened to him at a meeting, he was as a rule cheerful, humorous, and chippy, and occasionally he was serious. So I think Bernard Venables really did get it wrong, and really was unfair to blame Dick for any change of emphasis after the days of the Carp Catchers' Club.

Now take a look at the third paragraph of Dick's Presidential Address. Here he mentions the National Anglers' Council. This was a matter of enormous importance for anglers at the time. Never before had there been a single voice representing angling, and it is clear from Dick's remarks that he considered that the body was making progress, led by stalwarts Halliday and Davison. Those two were themselves experienced anglers, largely in the sphere of match fishing. Major Brian Halliday was then President of the National Federation of Anglers and himself a force in the world of angling. I met him initially at an angling conference in London where he quite took me under his wing after we bumped into each other in the bar (where else?). He was an impressive and knowledgeable man.

However, even from the very beginnings there were problems with the National Anglers' Council (NAC). I, along with a considerable number of specimen members, attended the inaugural meeting of interested organisations; indeed, most of the people at this meeting were specimen hunters, which perhaps reflects just how seriously they took their sport. Other bodies, such as the NFA, were represented by just one or two people, but the National Association of Specimen Groups (NASG) was there in force, with Dick Walker as its President and dozens of others as well. It's important to recognise this aspect of participation. Specimen hunters were not merely seeking representation, but viewed the progress of angling in a much broader and more fundamental way than other interest groups in the sport.

A deal of scepticism was evident as the meeting got under way, not only concerning proper representation for each angling body, but also with regard to the planned function of the NAC and the manner in which it would or would not, appeal to the grass roots of the sport. Dick spoke powerfully in support of setting up the NAC, arguing that a failure to do so would leave angling lacking representation in the country, in government, and would probably set the sport back decades in its quests for clean water, fairer tackle taxes, financial support for the clubs, and so on. His main critic in the discussion was Peter Mead, a very successful tench angler and a thoroughly professional person. He was not opposed to the NAC being formed, nor to the point raised by Dick, but, speaking just as eloquently as Dick, though with brevity, he pointed to the weaknesses in the proposed constitution which would leave specimen hunters (ie, the NASG) in a seriously weak position. After a little back and forth discussion involving others, Dick again took the floor and made a speech as powerful as any I ever heard from him. In effect he talked out Peter Mead's worries, and carried the great majority of those present with him. It was an emotional speech and it led to the NAC being formed there and then, with the constitution and structure presented on the day being accepted in its entirety.

However, Peter Mead's worries came back to haunt the specimen hunting movement, because within a short while they were ousted from the NAC and thereafter, for many years, had no political voice. The NAC failed to address the concerns of ordinary anglers; and letters that I sent them myself, on a variety of issues important to anglers, were dealt with (if at all) in an ignorant and derisory manner. Dick may have enjoyed his short term on the NAC, but after he left to do other things there was no voice at all for the NASG. It is ironic that, had it not been for specimen hunters and Dick, the NAC would not have been formed in the first place. The NAC itself eventually paid the price for its ineptitude and it foundered, not to be replaced. Only now could one argue that a single body is again representing angling (FACT: Fisheries and Conservation Trust) and in this body the (now) specialist anglers (with myself as President) are playing a major and at times pivotal role.

It is easy with the benefit of hindsight, to blame Dick Walker for the poor position specimen hunters found themselves in, but this is probably unfair.

Perhaps he *should* have been worldlier in dealing with anglers who had played politics for most of their adult lives, and perhaps he and the specimen hunters present at that NAC meeting should have listened more to the intellect of Peter Mead. It's easy to say in retrospect . . .

Specimen hunters or specialist anglers, call them what you will, approach angling in a way that is fundamentally different from 'pleasure' anglers, and from match anglers who are constrained in time and place (and, often, in tackle and bait allowed). In their search for the biggest and the best, they are constantly looking for new, and often revolutionary, techniques and approaches and, in so doing, they advance angling on all fronts. None of this means that they are too serious a lot; my own experience of them is quite to the contrary. At their best Dick Walker would thoroughly approve of them: and neither he nor they can be blamed if the tools invented are misused by the less inspired.

Dick at Tring reservoir.

Chapter 15

On resistance and streamlining: battles lost

T HERE are very few areas of angling where Dick Walker seems to have got
things wrong, but in this chapter I want to look at two areas where this
may have been the case: one where I *think* he made errors of judgement which
may actually have hindered developments; and the other where he made errors
of calculation surprising in an engineer. The first concerns lead weights
and resistance during bites on leger. The second relates to float design and
interpretation.

Walker always argued that if there were no resistance to the take of a fish
then it would not be suspicious and would bite confidently. (There has to be
at least some truth in this, despite what I shall write in a moment or two.) His
feelings on this led him to fish free-line tactics for carp, that is the line had a
hook on the end, plus bait, but no encumbrance of a lead. He designed rods,
the Mk IV Carp rod, and Mk IV Avon, so that free-line tackle could be cast
easily without losing distance or the bait. Anyone who has freelined lobworms
with a Mk IV Avon will testify to the quality of the design in this regard. I also
think that Dick was influenced in his design by his early experience of high
quality split-cane fly rods which, of course, do exactly what he wanted, but
with a fly line (the weight in the line in this case rather than the bait). Thus
the Mk IVs are through-action or soft-action rods.

One of the consequences of his thinking, that resistance to the take should
be avoided, was that all specimen hunters became imbued with that spirit:
pike anglers fished deadbaits with no lead or float; chub anglers fished a crayfish deadbait without lead or float; and many anglers fished lobworms in a
similar way for a variety of species such as tench, chub, and bream. If you read
carefully the Carp Catchers' Club rotary letter you will see that this thinking
not only predominated but that Dick was quite forceful in pushing it: large
baits, freelined, on an appropriate rod, avoidance of leads, avoidance of small

baits, and a good bite-indicator at the rod butt end of the outfit (such as a buzzer, the Heron, or silver paper). His forcefulness, as revealed in those letters, did, I think, if not suppress experimentation, certainly discourage it.

I first became worried about these concepts in the early 1960s and I raised my worries when I met him at a meeting of the NASG in Chelsea and subsequently several times when we had more time to talk. At the root of my disquiet, at least initially, was a a series of experiences whilst tench fishing at Carlton Towers lakes in the West Riding of Yorkshire. Using free-line tactics, or very light floats, I was reasonably successful, usually taking a tench or two on each trip: freelining after dark was also relatively successful. During the whole of one summer, however, I fished alongside two Polish anglers who were fishing for eels, for the pot. Their tackle was quite powerful: solid glass 'pike' rods, monofil of 20-25lb, and fixed leads of 4oz or 5oz. The leads were ones you'll probably have seen - fish-shaped, with a hole at the tail end and used in the 1960s and 1970s by sea anglers. These two Poles, with whom I became very friendly, caught many tench on their heavy gear and out-fished me by about 3:1. They also caught good eels, though not as many as their nets full of tench! It seemed to me that these tench did not mind the resistance at all or, if they did, it did not adversely affect the fishing. On the contrary, it improved catches: I was fishing the same swims as those Poles, often sitting between them as we swapped stories. Their tackle may, of course, have comprised early and crude bolt-rigs. When I raised this with Dick he was inclined at first to dismiss it as a one off, but when I gave him the full story he accepted that there must be something in what I was saying. Yet he still insisted that 'frictionless' rigs were better in the long run.

A few years later, in the 1960s, I was fishing a now famous carp water near Selby, which was then a noted tench water producing occasional six- and seven-pound fish. One day I was out in my boat using the tip of a 14-foot fibatube match rod to uproot water soldier plants from the bed of the lake. I wanted them for my own pond! However, I ran into a certain difficulty in the form of tench! Each time I got a plant half way to the surface (in about nine feet of clear water) the tench would attack the plant and pull it off the rod, and I do mean *pull*. On some occasions the rod was bent almost to breaking point, and they won most of the battles. In fact, I only managed to get three plants to the surface until I returned later with my (tench) drag. These tench were feeding and they expected to pull for their supper or were fully prepared to pull for their supper. They really were not a bit bothered about heavy pulling in the other direction.

Once again Dick was quite ready to dismiss this experience; but I became convinced that fish, generally, really did not worry about resistance and to some extent expected it as a result of their normal feeding strategies - strategies that included uprooting weed, catching prey in thick weed growth, and so on. At that time we began to use heavier fixed leads in our pike fishing, whereas previously we had followed Walkerian principles of using the minimum needed to hold the tackle in place. We noticed no drop off in results: in fact, because our tackle control was better, the results improved considerably. Our fixed leads were up to 3oz: in the past we had used no leads or a single swan-shot or mega-swan-shot. I think Dick was wrong about leads and resistance and I was not at all surprised when carp anglers made the bolt-rig discoveries. It seemed to me to vindicate my side of a private debate with Dick.

Some anglers have pointed out to me that if you disagreed strongly with Dick he ostracised you from that point on. I did not find this. He remained as courteous and friendly as he had ever been, often going out of his way to do things for me. My own feeling is that he liked a good well-argued debate and that the information gained, in whichever direction it took, was a bonus to everyone. Dick was not completely against the use of leads on the tackle, even in carp fishing, and in several letters to people he suggested that they add lead if struggling for the desired distance. But these were running leads, like an Arlesey Bomb, not fixed leads. In much fishing fixed leads are better.

I confess to a small, sneaking doubt about my own side of this argument. Dick thought it debatable. What is not debatable, however, is the argument he really did lose, with Dr Terry Coulson the physicist. In a classic, but at all times friendly debate in the now extinct magazine *Fishing*, the two of them clashed over floats, float materials, and shotting of floats. It was physicist versus engineer, and the physicist won. As it happens I knew both anglers, and in Terry's case fished with him on several stop-over trips to a tench lake near Selby. Both Dick and Terry were good company to be with and were similar in several respects. They were good scientists who liked to understand the nature of the problem before they tried to solve it. Neither of them had a bad word to say about anybody, unlike most of us anglers who regularly let off steam about somebody or other who happens to upset us. So a debate between Dick and Terry was always going to be valuable, and it was.

I suppose it began in June 1964 when Terry published a series of definitive articles, in the high-brow magazine *Fishing* on such matters as float antennae, inertia, streamlining, resistance and related matters. Then in August 1965 Anthony Goldstraw wrote an article about getting the best out of the lift method - but he didn't get the best out of the physics involved and may well, one suspects, have missed Terry's 1964 series. Be that as it may Dick took him politely to task, suggesting that Anthony had the wrong lift rig in that he'd put extra weight down near the hook and the float-carrying weight up at the float

A force to be reckoned with.

itself - so that the shot near the hook was additional to that needed by the float and would have to be carried by the fish when it lifted the bait. Dick argued that all the weight should be down at the business end, and that weight should be no more than was needed to sink the float antenna to its tip. He then went on to say, 'The weight of lead, provided it is not more than the float can carry, has nothing whatever to do with what the float lifts.'

Enter Terry Coulson in the 17th September (1965) issue of *Fishing* which I quote in its entirety for what I hope are informative reasons:

> I read Anthony Goldstraw's article on the lift method (*Fishing* August 20) and Richard Walker's reply (September 3) with great interest. I am in sympathy with many of the objectives Mr Goldstraw is trying to achieve, but his means of trying to achieve them are not well founded. My articles on float mechanics in *Fishing* last year, and especially the one published on June 12, would serve to set Mr Goldstraw on a more fruitful path, if he would care to look them up.
>
> In particular, the buoyancy of the antenna material (except insofar as it influences the total density of the whole float) has no effect on sensitivity;

contrary to Mr Goldstraw's advocacy, a cane-splint antenna needs just as much weight, no more, no less, to sink or lift it as an antenna of the same dimensions made of any other material. No experiments are needed on the use of aluminium rods as antennae; the effects are entirely predictable: they confer no advantages and involve a number of serious disadvantages.

Aluminium tube, which can be obtained in useful gauges from model shops, is of more interest to the float-maker; but it tends to get flattened and is generally not so good as the plastic bristles I offered to readers some time ago. Again, there is no merit in building lead into the float; indeed, it is less effective there than on the line. There are any number of other points in those articles which I feel sure would be of help to Mr Goldstraw.

So far as truly still water is concerned, I am broadly in accord with Richard Walker's comments. However, in conditions of even slight drift, the perfectly balanced, effectively weightless rig Dick advocates has the disadvantage of being all too easily moved out of one's swim. In such circumstances, a slight degree of overload has a very useful anchoring effect.

I am afraid, however, that Dick is not wholly correct in his statement that 'the weight of the lead . . . has nothing whatever to do with what the fish lifts.' It appears to be true, if one considers the rig before and after the lift, each as a static system. It may, in fact, be near-enough correct for practical purposes with really slow bites - say, the slow pick-up often given by bream.

As Fred J. Taylor has often explained, though, he and his brothers developed the lift-method primarily as a means of striking very fast bites, especially those given by tench in their 'suck-blow' mood. For a fast bite, we have to consider the dynamics of the gear, not its statics; in short the inertia of the shot-load near to the hook must be taken into account.

The self-same shot that a bream might move slowly and feel little or nothing of, would produce a substantial resistance to being moved rapidly by the 'suck' of a tench.

This inertia effect occurs whether or not the rig is exactly balanced. Ways and means of dealing with this, so as to get a rig which 'fishes' well yet presents the least practicable resistance to the fish, need more space to describe than I have here, and I hope to write about them in more detail on a future occasion.

Apropos Anthony Goldstraw's desire for a vertical lift, Richard Walker asks 'who cares if it does keel over?' The answer, I would think, is that an angler fishing at fairly long-range, and/or in poor light, might care. A vertical lift brooks no mistaking; but a keeling over, especially if it chances to be in the line of sight, is much less apparent to the eye. This is not of great importance, maybe - but since there is no difficulty in designing floats and tackling them up so as to get a good, vertical lift, one may as well do so: it cannot hinder, and may help.

Terence Coulson
London W.6

Dick came back at Terry on 15th October (1965) and, again, I quote it in full, followed by Terry's reply which more or less ended the debate.

From Fishing, *15th October, 1965.*
Well, well, fancy an erudite contributor like Dr Terence Coulson confusing weight with Inertia (*Fishing*, September 17). I was not wrong in saying that the weight of the lead in a lift tackle has nothing to do with what the fish lifts. It is true, however, that a fish may feel the inertia of the lead. Whether it does so will depend upon how fast it tries to move the lead.

One is tempted to worry about the possibility of missing fish that are sucking in the bait from an inch or so away, but whether there is any need for worry is doubtful. The Taylor brothers caught hundreds of big, shy-biting tench on simple lift tackles, using swan-shot and pieces of peacock quill as floats. If they could do this with such large shot and without benefit of antennae, the point about inertia would seem to be rather more academic than practical in relation to a sensitive antenna float loaded with a single BB shot.

With regard to the effect of drift on a perfectly balanced lift-tackle, if a shot is added to counteract the effect of drift, then surely, if the right size of shot is chosen, it will be almost on the point of being lifted by the drift, and little will remain for a biting fish to feel?

On the matter of the float keeling over, Terence is right in saying there is no difficulty in making a float that will rise several inches before it keels. I cannot agree, however, that a rising antenna is easier to see in difficult conditions than a tilting one.

On the contrary, if you can see your antenna at all, you can detect even a slight deviation from the vertical much more readily than you can a fraction of an inch of rise. No tilt can be directly in the angler's line of sight, unless he has only one eye.

Purely from the point of view of visibility, I would much rather watch for a tilt than a rise of the float at dusk or at long range, and fortunately, the demand for extreme sensitivity in practical fishing is so very, very rare that I can nearly always do so. In all my angling experience I have encountered only one little lot of fish - some big roach in the river Beane - that demanded an extra-sensitive long-antenna float, and I caught those at a range of about 10 ft. from the rod-point.

Nobody admires Terry Coulson's factual articles more than I. He has corrected some cherished fallacies, and I am not ashamed to admit that some of them were mine. It is important to know the facts applicable to float design, but I am sure Terry will agree that there is some risk that relatively inexperienced anglers may run away with the idea that successful fishing demands extreme attention to float design and tackle sensitivity, whereas in truth, simple natural materials like porcupine and bird quills will suffice to make entirely satisfactory floats for 99.9% of our fishing.

Richard Walker
Hitchin

From Fishing, *5th November, 1965.*
I see that Richard Walker is pulling my leg again (Your Opinion, October 15). He knows perfectly well that I was not 'confusing weight with inertia'! It is true that the elementary ideas of weight, mass, and inertia, often are confused, but as a simple explanation of them in angling terms appears in a letter of mine (October 16, 1964) we need not waste space on definitions here. In any case, no angler will go far wrong if he takes it that the greater the weight of a piece of lead, the greater its inertia!

Two points are at issue, it seems to me. Question one concerns the physical facts of the behaviour of lift tackle. Question two concerns how important or unimportant these facts may be in practical fishing. It is essential to deal with them separately, for it is futile to argue about question two until one has agreed the answers to the first question.

Firstly, Dick writes that he 'was not wrong in saying that the weight of the lead in a lift tackle has nothing to do with what the fish lifts.' Well, just for the record, I never said he was 'wrong'; I said he was 'not wholly correct' - there's a world of difference! The point I made was simply this: 'The inertia of the shot-load near to the hook must be taken into account . . . This inertia effect occurs whether or not the rig is exactly balanced.'

Dick now goes on to say, 'It is true, however, that a fish may feel the inertia of the lead.' Well, quite; that's exactly what I said. The point is that even if the weight of the lead is exactly counterbalanced by the buoyancy of the float, the fish still has to put effort into the lift to overcome such inertia-effects as may occur, and the greater the weight of lead the greater the effects of inertia, other things being equal. So, in every-day language, the weight of lead does have something to do with what the fish lifts!

Dick then goes on to the second question, and suggests that the effects of inertia are of academic rather than practical importance when comparing a

BB shot with a swan-shot. Now, this may run away with the idea that the weight of lead has nothing to do with it, what's to stop him using an ounce or a pound of lead, let alone a swan-shot? Of course, this would be a nonsense, and I am quite sure that Dick did not intend to suggest any such absurdity. Nor need we argue about how often or how seldom inertia has a significant effect on results - as Dick has often told us: if it can't do any harm, and may do some good - do it! Surely we can agree that unnecessarily great inertia can't do good and may do harm? In my book, that's reason enough for trying to keep the inertia down.

Quite apart from any effect it may have during the lift, it is obvious that a large chunk of lead near the hook may have other undesirable effects. It may result in soft baits being sucked off the hook; or in the bait behaving unnaturally to the point where a fish loses interest in it, or even takes fright.

On the question of whether it is easier to see a 'tilt' or a 'vertical lift', I think we had best agree to differ. I know which I prefer - but it is so subjective a matter that it is pointless to argue. Provided, always, that the chap who does want a vertical lift knows how to get it.

Finally, it is a real pleasure to acknowledge the kind and courteous words in Dick's final paragraph; I am sincerely grateful for his encouragement I heartily endorse his point that successful fishing does not require the extremes of float design or tackle sensitivity; in fact, I have said repeatedly that almost all my own fishing is done with simple and perfectly ordinary gear. It is an odd thing that I am recommending ultra-sensitive tackle. Yet I imagine I might say, for example, 'the speed of a film is important' without being accused of recommending the use of ultra-fast film!

Still, it is useful to know how to achieve ultra-sensitivity on those rare occasions when it is needed - with those river Beane roach, for example; or in the case of an angler with poor eyesight. And, above all, it is vital to get the facts straight before trying to decide whether or not they are important in practice: on this point, I am sure Dick will agree.

Terence Coulson
London, W6

There is no doubt in my mind that Terry's arguments here are better than Dick's. Of course, they are more or less agreed that when one moves on to practical fishing the amount of inertia to be overcome by the biting fish probably does not matter unduly as long as sensible tackle is in use - but it *must* have an effect (which could be easily measured if necessary). They differ on antennae and vertical as opposed to tilting rises and here I am with Dick rather than Terry, although, as Terry says, it's a very subjective matter. I do need to emphasise something that is not too apparent in the debate and that is that Terry Coulson is a very experienced and competent angler who did a great deal of float fishing in those days.

But you will have noticed just how much stress on weight and inertia is implicit in the writing of both writers. Both imply that one should use the minimum amount of weight that you can get away with and this does not accord fully with the modern angler, or with some of my arguments in the first half of the chapter. You may think it odd that Dick was off-beam a little in this debate, but, as I hinted near the beginning of the book, Dick may not have been the brilliant engineer he was often reported to be. What he *did* have was a brilliant mind, good scientific training and logic, *some* engineering training, and an outstanding practical commonsense.

Apart from this particularly public debate in *Fishing,* it is difficult to find other evidence of arguments where Dick was bettered. In the privacy of his correspondence, though, there are some debates with experienced game anglers that, you might say, stretched his ingenuity to the limit. In most cases he won the arguments on purely pragmatic grounds but he wasn't always right in principle. Let's not pursue this further, though: I think the point has been made well enough.

Dick Walker, 1984.

Chapter 16

Dick Walker as a trout angler

MANY COARSE anglers subscribe to the view that Dick Walker was one of, if not *the* greatest coarse angler of all time; however, the reactions to his *trout* angling achievements are more muted. While researching this book I interviewed dozens of young and youngish trouters on several of our trout reservoirs. Most were very unsure of Dick's contributions to the sport, even though many were, at the same time, using flies designed by Dick! The response is not the same, though, when the more experienced trout anglers are consulted.

Consider an article, for example, in the *Fly Fishers' Club Journal*, written by Brian Clarke, in which he says:

> In later life Walker began to devote significant time to the challenges posed by the growth of stillwater trout fishing in lakes like Grafham and Rutland and to write about them in the game fishing magazines. Some of the old hands writing at the time and who knew nothing of his background, or felt it was not relevant, or who simply resented his directness and formidable self-belief, were incensed as though by an upstart. It caused not a few established trout writers, destabilised by his knowledge and logic, to attempt to dismiss him - attempts which were not only ludicrous and futile given the manifest sense of what he was saying, but which were to diminish these writers' own reputations in the process.
>
> Trout anglers have much for which to thank Walker. Amid all else he seized on carbon fibre when it first appeared and designed the first fly rod in the world to be made of that material - and he created a veritable hatch of new artificial flies and lures. It helps to illustrate the thinking Walker brought to stillwater trout fishing - the contrast between his approach and the conventional approach - by touching on just one of these dressings.

Dick selecting . . .

Tying flies at Gerry Berth-Jones' house.

7th December, 1982

Dear Richard,

Thank you for your letter of 24th November with its very kind thought to tie a small collection of flies for the Club. The President wants me to tell you that we shall be delighted to accept such a small collection.

We are glad to learn that your health is improving slowly. We send best wishes for continued progress.

Yours sincerely,
Norman Fuller

Dick did send the fly collection, although this set went missing and he had to send another set to the Club via Pat Russell. The following letter from R.W. to Commander Fuller gives a description of flies and some comments upon them.

Commander N.T. Fuller, R.N. (Ret'd)
The Flyfishers' Club

37 Ivel Gardens,
Biggleswade, Beds.
10th January, 1983

Dear Commander,

Here, as I promised, is a selection of flies that I have devised over the last forty years or so. There have been many others that enjoyed brief success, perhaps for a season or more, but which then lapsed into mediocrity or even uselessness.

These that I am sending are those that have remained successful, and they are as follows:

Left to right, back row:

1. Short Green Partridge

This and its friend the Short Orange Partridge are examples of how the bronzed hook itself may be used to emphasise similarity to a natural insect.

There is a larva, which I am unable to identify entomologically, that inhabits the alga which grows on the bottom of clear, alkaline still waters. When this alga, in hot weather, rises to the surface through gases that generate from decay and expand, the larvae are trapped. They extricate themselves, or attempt to do so, and then sink back to the bottom. The most common kind has a sepia head and rear and a bright green centre section. In my pattern, the bend of the hook suggests the sepia rear section.

The fly is, therefore, one for special circumstances, but when these occur, the results may be spectacular. My best catch with the Short Green Partridge consisted of four trout weighing $10^1/_4$, $11^1/_2$, $12^1/_4$ and $12^1/_2$lb, a bag limit for the water, all taken in two hours under the eye of Mr Peter Lapsley. On the following day in identical conditions, the fly took two more fish of $12^1/_4$ and $12^1/_2$lb; I then had to leave to keep a lunch appointment. The pattern has the great advantage for big fish in that it uses a substantial hook, No. 6.

2. Leaded Shrimp
This is now a well-known pattern and I need say no more about it.

3. Bumblebee
My friends describe this as a chub fly and it is indeed a highly successful pattern for catching chub. It also catches trout, often when they appear to be preoccupied with a food-form too small to imitate.

4, 5, 6 and 7
These are sedge pupae and winged sedges; named Green Longhorns, Amber Longhorns, Green-bodied Red Sedge and simply, Red Sedge. The first two are wet flies; the others may be fished wet or dry. They succeed on a very wide variety of running and still waters.

8. Hawthorn Fly
All that need be said is that this pattern does very well when the natural is present in quantity.

9. Crane Fly or Daddy-long-legs
When this insect is at rest, its legs spread all round it. When flying or when in the water, they all trail behind and the artificial is tied accordingly.

10. 'Chicken' or Ghost Swift Moth
For many years, I regarded this as a late evening fly; it has accounted for many large trout on both rivers and still waters at that time. However, in recent years, it has proved very successful, on occasions, in broad daylight. Normally fished dry, it has also succeeded when sunk.

11. Pale Watery
It catches trout and grayling when they are eating the natural insect; the appearance of a very little primrose silk at head and tail-roots appears to add to its attraction.

12. Russell's Iron Blue

This is the invention of Mr D. A. (Pat) Russell of Romsey; I include it because he and I both believe that a touch of what we have come to call a 'key colour' adds to attraction. This principle is seen in the Red Sedge (No. 7) and the aforegoing Pale Watery.

Second Row

1 and 2. Midge Pupae

These are but two from a wide range of midge pupa imitations for still-water trout fishing, in which the basis of the patterns is the same, the only variation being in size and colour. All have bronze peacock herl thoraces, white cock hackle fibres in bunches at head and tail clipped to length and white cock hackle stalk for ribbing. They vary only in the colour or colours used in the abdomen, which consists of dyed swan secondary feather fibres.

3. Sweeney Todd

One of a large family of black flies with silver-ribbed bodies, this one stands up very well to the stresses of long casting, and the presence of a touch of fluorescent magenta wool behind the wing is believed to direct the attack of a taking trout further forward, increasing the likelihood of successful hooking, rather than a fruitless pluck. This pattern has accounted for a huge number of still-water trout.

4. Mrs Palmer

The pattern was named after a lady of my acquaintance who was as blonde and as attractive as the fly, which does well in still-water trout fishing, specially when the water is coloured and the fly is fished comparatively slowly.

5. Dambuster

A variation of the well-known Worm fly, this was originally devised for casting from a boat on to the masonry of reservoir dams in a wind, in which conditions trout, specially brown trout, are likely to be foraging for anything that the waves wash from the interstices in the stonework. The use of stiff cock hackles instead of soft hen hackles as in the Worm fly reduces the likelihood of the hook catching up. This fly is also useful in other conditions, and unlike the Worm fly, its use is permissible on waters where only one hook is permitted.

6. Mayfly Nymph

I could almost write a book about this one, having experimented with imitations of the natural, of one tying or another, for fifty years! This is the latest version; I think it is important to suggest the ciliae, the appendages along each side of the abdomen. In my earlier patterns, this was done with cream ostrich herl, but the replacement of that by teased-out and clipped Angora wool makes the nymph both durable and, I think, more attractive.

The curious thing about this nymph is that not only does it catch trout throughout the season; not only in mayfly time; it also catches them on waters where no mayflies are found, or ever have been.

It can be tied leaded or unleaded; the former for general use, the latter for when trout are taking the rising nymph but not the hatched insect.

I must apologise for the brash modern plastic box enclosing the flies; if you think them of sufficient interest to members, you may be able to find alternative accommodation for them.

Yours sincerely,
Richard Walker

Another great angler who recognised Dick's contributions to trout angling was Peter Maskell. In the twentieth anniversary edition of *Trout Fisherman* (June 1997), twelve years after Dick's death, he writes, 'Dick Walker was also a great trout fisherman, starting in his childhood when his grandfather taught him the rudiments of fly fishing on long since disappeared Hertfordshire rivers and streams.'

Dick was responsible for many famous trout fly patterns - the Polystickle, Sweeney Todd, Walker's Mayfly Nymph, the Chomper and the Amber Nymph to name a few. He also wrote many articles for *Trout Fisherman*, which, according to Peter, were 'packed with sound advice, practical common-sense and humour - all based on a lifetime's experience of practical trouting.' In the 1970s, when Dick was writing regularly for the trout magazines, many old, long established characters took umbrage, and, rather rashly (as any coarse angler could have told them) took Dick on. They were made to look rather silly, not by Dick's responses, for he was always careful not to belittle the opposition, but by their own pig-headedness. The same thing had happened with the *Fishing Gazette*, twenty years earlier, when both coarse and game anglers had been after his scalp, equally rashly, and unsuccessfully. What none of the correspondents seemed to realise was that Dick had begun his fly fishing at the age of seven: he spoke from a position of experience.

Peter Maskell's book helped to place Dick Walker firmly in trout fishing history and he also edited several books of Dick's contributions to trout fishing, including *Dick Walker's Trout Fishing* (1982) and *Trout Fishing on Rivers and Still Waters* (1997).

Dick on the river Test at Mead Mill.

Dick with two 7lb rainbows at Dermot Wilson's Nether Wallop fishery.

Dick with a catch at Damerham.

In 1995 Peter Lapsley, writing in *Fly-Fishing and Fly-Tying*, attempted an appraisal of Dick's contribution to trout fly design and dressing. Peter described Dick's contribution to fly fishing and fly tying as 'no less important' than his contributions to coarse fishing. As he pointed out, Walker considered it both impossible and undesirable to imitate flies exactly, believing it far more beneficial to identify and exaggerate the features by which trout identify natural flies. That is the way most of us think today. It might, in fact, be possible now to create an exact imitation of a natural fly, but whether it would last five minutes, and whether it would have the correct hydro-dynamic response in water, is very doubtful.

Peter Lapsley went on to point out that Dick discovered and extolled the value of still-water dry-fly fishing long before it became popular with reservoir trout fishers, 'despite the widespread prejudice against it generated by Tom Ivens' book *Still-Water Fly Fishing*'. So, we can see, Walker made an enormous contribution to trout fishing practice and theory, and to fly tying practice and theory. Indeed, the long-term impact may have been even greater in some respects than in coarse fishing because successful flies last a lot longer than successful baits! It is surprising then that so many modern trout anglers are unaware of his inventions.

Dick began fly fishing at the age of seven, and he certainly continued fly fishing during his later school days and his undergraduate years in Cambridge. I recall him telling me of his favourite fly fishing sections of the river Cam where he pursued dace, roach and chub on the fly. He must have cut an unusual figure because in those days most of the anglers on the river Cam would have been 'maggot drowners' to use a crude title. Many of the better-read coarse fishermen would have been aware of Dick's fly fishing origins because they would have read *Drop Me A Line* (1953), a record of the correspondence between Dick and Maurice Ingham. Maurice was not, at that stage, a trout angler, but Dick set about encouraging him and instructing him. This aspect of the letters is one of the most enjoyable in the book, a series of threads which appeared to result in a fully developed fly fisher by the end of the book. It all began when they had corresponded for a mere two months, and Dick asked Maurice if he had ever done any fly tying. Maurice replied that he had tried neither fly tying nor fly fishing. Thereafter, we see many sketches of the natural insects from Dick, the flies, how to cast, and so on until he has covered for Maurice all that he really needed to know to cast a fly, including casting round corners and obstructions with a right bend or a left bend. Many pages have the most beautifully artistic drawings of flies and tackle, and it is in this book (p.133) that Dick advocates the use of the forefinger aligned along the rod handle rather than the thumb as used by most anglers.

Having recently examined one of Dick's early trout rods and its shaped handle, I can imagine that a big man - and he was - with large hands could wield such a weapon in such a way, but I don't think that I could, unless the rod was a tiny, light brook rod. As it happens he was writing about small stream fishing at the time but he seems to have maintained this handgrip even on bigger waters. *Drop Me A Line* was never a good seller and I have wondered from time to time whether this was because it was marketed to the coarse angler. About 50% of the book actually relates to trout fishing so maybe it falls between two stools: too much trout for coarse anglers; too much on carp for trout fishermen. But Walker was not constrained by subject in the way that so many were, and are, and that is, perhaps, the root of his greatness.

Interestingly, Dick probably wrote more letters on the subject of trout fishing than he did on coarse fishing. (Perhaps because trout anglers were more educated, and therefore used to letter-writing, than most coarse anglers.) Perusing Pat's carefully maintained file of correspondence, one notices the odd letter or two from individual coarse anglers but dozens from many trout anglers. The correspondence between Dick and Bob Church is a delight to read, and this exchange of ideas came at the time of the great revolution in reservoir trouting, whereas the Ingham-Walker letters reflected the earlier, more traditional fly fishing. Walker embraced and experienced both periods and was at the heart of the revolution beginning in the 1960s, as the Church-Walker letters make clear.

The importance of the Church-Walker letters is that they began in the 1960s and continued until the mid-1970s, exactly that period when the greatest changes in the history of trout fishing took place. It's also worth noting that Dick reveals he'd already fished Blagdon Reservoir for trout, thirty years before this period - nothing like getting in early! Many of their discussions revolve around the development of flies, and Bob was as inventive at times as Dick: the two of them tested and improved each other's designs and commented on the flies of the day. At one point Dick points out that Dick Shrives' missionary fly was actually invented by Captain Dunn in 1914: Walker was extremely well read about ancient flies!

The manner in which Dick transferred his coarse fishing thinking to reservoir trout angling is well seen in one comment to Bob when he points out that 1960's trout fishing was similar to those early, heady days of carp fishing when 'everyone was accepting what the so-called experts said and not doing much logical thinking.' He certainly brought logic, commonsense and practicality to trout fishing, through his involvement in the improvement of casting, initially with the use of compound taper fibreglass. He notes that Ray Brecknock was casting over fifty yards with a number 9 shooting head, for example.

Fred Buller and Dick Walker choosing flies.

Dick as a young man, in his cluttered tackle room, tying flies.

Dick also fished a great deal himself, something some of his antagonists occasionally forget. In 1965, for example, he fished Grafham Water fifty-seven times taking two hundred and forty-two trout with twenty-two over four pounds. Dick was undoubtedly a very skilful trout fisher, often taking fish when others failed. Brian Clarke recalls Walker sitting well back from the bank of a small still water, on a low stool, pulling out trout after trout, whilst Brian himself struggled. Yet he congratulated Brian on his efforts that day and went on to help him a great deal: another example of Dick's generosity of spirit.

Dick's dry humour is also revealed in his letters to Bob. In 1966 he argued that he had two motives in writing for *Anglers' World:* 'one was to get paid . . . and the other was to leave an opening for a follow up.' Yet we know he would happily write for no payment at all. In the same year he makes the choice remark: 'If there is one thing that gets up my wick it is a bloke (who) is always chasing up the last water that produced a big fish.' In the year 2007 his wick would have been got up rather often I think!

In 1967 the letters show them concerned with stickle flies, and the poly-stickle and Peter Thomas' use of white raffine instead of polythene, which they considered a step forward. The Sweeney Todd was also discussed at about the same time; and Dick became involved with an argument which, in a nutshell, said he couldn't cast a shooting head forty yards. He could, for certain but he chose not to embarrass certain individuals by demonstrating in front of them. Rather he demonstrated to others. In 1967 too, he was attacked for his views on the use of dry flies on reservoirs, despite his well known success with floating sedges. He had used floating sedges on rivers as a boy, of course, so it was natural for him to try them on any trout water.

In 1968 the debates in the press continued. Of course, Dick always invited 'trouble' by writing in such a fashion that persuaded some readers that he had fired all his cannons in his first salvo. But he never did that, preferring to target the enemy once they had, so to speak, 'exposed' themselves. Topics of that year included the crowding of the banks on Grafham Water in the evening and the antics it resulted in (I remember that myself); the new light rods versus the heavy, cane Northampton rods; and attachment of the fly line to backing and the development of the nail knot. It was unusual for Dick to query other people's catches, but in 1968 he scorned one man's claim of three hundred trout in one year, not because it was impossible at all, but because in the fifty-seven visits Dick had made to the same water in that year he hadn't once laid eyes on the man! He argued that the gentleman must have fished at least fifty times to amass such a total. As an example he quotes the legendary Cyril Inwood, who did have similar catches in that year, but who Walker had bumped into on at least thirty occasions. Acrimonious discussions became increasingly common at that time because the sport was expanding so very rapidly and there were people about who wanted to make names for themselves come what may. It does occur to me that the Grafham Water logbook should at least show how many times an individual fished, though it hardly seems an important matter to look into now.

In 1968 too, in his letters to Church, Walker mentions carbon-fibre, the material with which he was to make a major contribution to rod-building. He pointed out that for similar strengths carbon-fibre rods will be 20% lighter, have a 30% smaller diameter, have less air resistance; and will easily generate more line speed. He arranged for Bob to receive a 9½-foot Superlite Hardy; and Bob returned the favour by providing the foam plastic for tying in the bodies of floating or buoyant flies. As always, there is humour in the letters between the two, Walker once talking about an encounter with a game bird that appeared to have ended up in his bag: 'and a pheasant met with an accident from which it was unable to recover, being too ill.'

In 1968 Church and Walker still hadn't solved the problem of very buoyant, large flies, finding that if balsa strips were used the fly really did become *too* big. In 1970 they had it solved with polyethylene foam. (Walker was enthusiastic about this and sent me some as well, although he must have been aware that I was a very raw fly fisher.) For fly fishermen at the time it was a most useful material, not only for building buoyant flies but also serving as a base material in fly wallets and boxes: hook points could be stuck in it and taken out frequently without damage to the material. It is still useful for these purposes.

The final notes between the two in 1968 refer to the breakdown experienced by Fred Wagstaffe and the latter's serious criticism of Dick Walker's fly fishing. It is rare to come across serious criticism of Dick, as this book surely makes clear, and it was a pity that Dick had to be on the receiving end of, in this case, unwarranted comments. I only heard Walker speak positively of Fred Wagstaffe. Fred made his name in pike fishing but like Dick became an ardent exponent of the rapidly changing reservoir trout scene (before giving up the sport altogether). I remember that even in his piking days he had little time for Dick and deliberately shunned one of the definitive pike meetings because Dick was associated with it (see Chapter 13). I don't think either Dick or Bob took Fred Wagstaffe's remarks seriously.

Grafham Water declined a little in 1970 and became overrun with eight-inch jack pike according to Dick. The policy at the time was removal of all pike and I am sure that Dick pointed out to the authorities that this would undoubtedly result in the water being overrun with small pike. Which it was. Eventually, they learned the lesson, to some extent at least, and these days earn money from pike angling as well as trout fishing.

The early 1970s saw Bob and Dick continuing to develop flies, including the Leaded Shrimp, and Bob's Baby Doll (which Dick requested when he heard of Bob's design). The dry flies continued to do well to Dick's rod, especially the Red Sedge, Daddy-long-legs and Dronefly, which he rated in that order, and also the Dog Nobbler. It was a very lively and productive time and their findings spread far and wide.

One of Dick's problems was that he was now doing rather more game fishing than coarse fishing and was covering this in his column in *Angling Times*. The newspaper asked him to curtail his writing on trout and to concentrate on coarse fishing matters. The problem was probably solved by a new trout fishing column that Bob started in 1972, and which, I'll bet, he didn't expect to last for thirty years! So Dick Walker was writing a (mostly) coarse fishing column for over thirty years, which then overlapped with Bob Church's column of similar duration. Between them they helped millions of readers for over half a century, an amazing achievement and a stupendous contribution to angling literature. Perhaps the only columnists to rise to these levels are Des Taylor, who took over Walker's mantle at *AT* (but who writes more widely than Dick) and Graham Marsden who has written each month for *Coarse Fisherman*, again for thirty years or so. There have been some comparable writers on game fishing in other countries, of course and one who springs to mind is the Tasmanian game fishing writer, Joe Thureau, who wrote a weekly piece for at least forty years; this was reportage, though, rather than innovational, as he told me himself.

Bob Church and Dick Walker worked together as equals, each making numerous, serious contributions to the sport. Walker didn't 'pinch' Bob's ideas, as some have suggested, (nor did Bob 'pinch' Dick's) but they simply sparked off ideas in each other and reported accordingly in their writing. Walker had similar relationships with a number of other leading trout anglers. Brian Clarke has already been mentioned, and of course, Fred Buller, but another notable one was Geoffrey Bucknall. He and Dick struck up a long term friendship, exchanging ideas regularly, and in Dick's last year of life Geoffrey was possibly his closest confidant (see Chapter 20). But he and Dick also did something else: they had what one might call polite but very forthright debates in the angling press, on such subjects as the static trout fly. While he had fished Grafham, Dick had discovered that a fly lying on the bottom, absolutely static, caught fish quite often. In a letter to Bob Church he even went so far so to suggest to Bob, tongue in cheek, that you might just as well cast out and put the rod in a rod-rest! Geoffrey Bucknall challenged him on this issue, arguing that in a water as deep and turbulent as Grafham, no fly would sit still on the bottom. Other people pitched into the debate, often

Concentrating on the retrieve.

quite hotly, and a real controversy resulted. The only two calm individuals were Dick and Geoff and there was a good reason for this: between them they had set up the whole controversy. Geoff explained what happened. After the publication of one article or letter on the subject, say by Dick, Geoff would telephone him and they'd discuss the tactics of Geoff's reply the following week and try out a scenario for the week following! The readers, including myself, thought it was spontaneous, but all the time they remained good friends, as the letters between them very clearly indicate. Dick's relationship with Geoff was rather different, then, to the one he had with Bob Church, and many other game fishermen, but it was probably equally productive. It is commonly held that Dick was involved in the inventing of the shooting head, and some have even suggested that Dick pinched the idea from someone else. In fact, Geoffrey Bucknall introduced this innovation to the UK from the USA (where he had extensive game fishing contacts) and he quickly passed it on to Dick and others for development on UK waters. This they did, and they all had to battle with traditionalists who, inevitably, dubbed it unsporting.

Returning briefly to the static fly controversy, it's important to realise that Dick really did believe in the static fly, and he seriously recommends it in a letter to Bob Church. Being Dick, he even invented a fly for the technique! This had long, stiff hackles, which allowed it to sit on the bottom without getting smothered or hidden by bottom debris or growth. If trout leapt over bridges Dick would have invented an airborne fly, a static one! The flies Dick caught 'on the static' included also muddlers, Polystickles, midge pupae and big spiders. His special static fly had body of peacock, peacock and brown ostrich mixed, or lumina plastic. The hackle (fore and aft) was reddish ginger for the peacock body and black for the lumina plastic.

One fascinating aspect of Dick's correspondence with the trout anglers is the extent to which the letters were illustrated. Quite often the letters he sent, and also those he received, were decorated with little slips of the appropriate material being recommended and literally dozens of superb drawings. On half a dozen of the letters to Bob Church, for example, there were no less than eleven excellent drawings of flies, plus a clear descriptive text. Within the letter files there are literally hundreds of working drawings and ideas. (There must be a good book here for some enterprising trout man.)

We've seen, then, that Dick Walker was concerned with the catching of trout by the best possible methods. But there was more to the man than that. He also battled for trout anglers just as he did for coarse anglers (on such questions as angling 'cruelty' and swans and lead shot). The following letter to the MP Eldon Griffiths, who was at the time Minister for the Environment, shows just how seriously and carefully Dick would chase up problems on behalf of anglers. The letter also goes to show that, as far as government is concerned, things have not really changed much for anglers in the subsequent thirty-five years.

Eldon Griffiths Esq., MP
Department of the Environment.
Whitehall
London SW1

24th March, 1971

Dear Mr Griffiths,
By a series of forwardings, your letter of January 13th addressed to Reginald Paget QC, MP, has come to me. This letter, you may remember, consisted of some comments made by you on an article of mine which appeared in *Angling Times*, November 26th, 1970.

No doubt your many commitments prevented you from reading the article fully, or you would have noticed that the comment that I made in it to the effect that anglers 'haven't had a cent' referred particularly to Grafham Water, not to the whole of angling in Britain. It is perfectly true that anglers at Grafham have not had a cent, whereas the yachtsmen have had upwards of £100,000 of public funds. The result is that it costs anglers £40 a year or £1 a day to fish at Grafham, whereas adult yachtsmen pay only £10 a year, with lower fees for their wives and for young people under twenty-one years of age.

It is true that a Clubhouse was built for the anglers, initially at the expense of the Great Ouse Water Authority but the cost of this, and of the boats and other equipment provided for anglers, has been recovered out of the fees that anglers have paid so that, in fact, the anglers have themselves paid for all the facilities provided for them as well as the wages and salaries of the fisheries staff and for the periodic stocking of the reservoir. Their fishing has therefore been entirely self-supporting, while at the same time they have been taxed, by having to purchase Great Ouse River Authority rod licences and having to pay purchase tax on their equipment. You are of course aware that yachting equipment is not subject to any tax whatever, nor does a yachtsman have to buy a River Authority licence.

I notice you say, 'It is a pity when one sportsman seems to resent the good fortune of another in another sphere.' You are not of course familiar with my writings generally, or you would have seen that I have repeated, time and time again, that we anglers do not grudge other sports the grant aid they receive; all we ask is that we be similarly treated. In fact, such grant aid as has been paid to anglers throughout the country is less than that given to the Grafham yachtsmen alone and what aid that has been given, has for some reason gone largely to Wales, where the pollution and other problems which anglers have to face are considerably less than they are throughout England, especially in the industrial areas.

I repeat, no angler wishes to see a reduction in the subsidies paid to other sports but it seems to me a most inequitable state of affairs, when our own sport is quite unable to obtain anything like the financial aid from public funds that other sports are, and when our sport is singled out for taxation in so many forms.

I also note that you say in your letter, as you have said in speeches, that many miles of river have been regained for fishing. I should be greatly obliged if you could find time to tell me where these miles of regained river are. I travel about this country probably more than any other person engaged in angling and I have yet to find a single yard of river that can be said to have been recovered for fishing.

If you can tell me where these recovered stretches of river are, I should very much like to pass the information on to the angling public, who like me are at present unaware of any such waters.

You also say that there has been a slow but steady increase in the number of reservoirs opened up for recreation. Here again, I should very much like to know which reservoirs are involved. The only reservoirs that I can discover, that are open for recreation are those that have been made available for that purpose from the time they were originally constructed. I know of no reservoir on which either angling or sailing were formerly prohibited, which has now made these recreations possible. If there are any such waters, not only I but anglers generally would be glad to know about them.

We are of course only too familiar with the long list of reservoirs on which both sailing and angling are still prohibited, and in respect of which the Authorities who control them persist in their obstinate refusal to make these recreational facilities available, usually without being willing to give any reason whatever for their attitude.

Of course, we anglers are all very pleased by your actions since you came to office, in trying to persuade these recalcitrant water undertakers to bring their ideas about recreational facilities into line with modern thinking but as I said in my article, any success you may have seems to me likely to be only marginal and if the majority of water supply reservoirs are to be opened for recreational purposes, it will only be accomplished by legislation, not by exhortation.

An interesting slant on the whole business of aid from public funds is found in the fact that it costs as much to hire a boat for a single day's fishing on the reservoir at Chew Valley, in the Bristol Waterworks complex, as it does to be a member of the Grafham Yacht Club for a whole year. At Grafham itself, the boat hire is cheaper; you can have two whole days' fishing for the same price that it costs for a year's membership of the Yacht Club!

Finally, you will forgive me if I show some amusement at your use of the phrase 'Built with the aid of generous funds', in respect of a fishing pavilion that you have opened somewhere. I would hardly call the sum total of Government aid to angling in Britain generous, having regard to the fact that it amounts to no more per head than the purchase tax on half a dozen floats, and that the entire Government aid to angling in Britain from the moment when it became possible to give Government aid for sport, is less than the yachtsmen at Grafham received in the year the reservoir first opened.

'Parsimonious' would be a better word to use than 'generous'.

Yours sincerely,
Richard Walker

Dick cooking freshly caught brown trout, on a trip to Scotland.

Chapter 17

Walker on match fishing

DICK WALKER did not like match fishing. His writing and letters make that clear. He took part in matches from time to time, for sociable or charitable reasons or to support a club, but he disliked the competitive component of them, especially under such artificial conditions. Writing in his *Angling Times* column 'Walker's Pitch', he pointed out that matches often began *after* the best of the early morning fishing and ended *before* the best of the evening fishing. Nor did he like the idea of having his swim chosen for him. After all, two of the main tenets of *Still-Water Angling* were to fish in the right place at the right time; and matches negated both at a stroke. Nevertheless he was quite successful in the matches that he did fish, mostly locally in the region of Hitchin and in Bedfordshire, but also in a now-famous classic match-angler versus specimen-angler contest, usually referred to as the Tom Sails Match (of which more later).

If he did fish a match, he applied himself seriously to it. On one water he reckoned that what was needed was a big heap of maggots out in the middle of the big river, on the bottom. He'd then drift a float rig over the bed of maggots. Obviously it was good thinking. What he did next wasn't. He made a container out of pastry that would take about a pint of maggots. In fact the container was similar in shape to a pint bottle. He then sealed it with a pastry lid after filling it up with the maggots. The whole was then heaved out into the centre of the river. Brilliant . . . except that it *floated!* It was a mistake he found hilarious, but it does show the lengths to which he would go to succeed at fishing. In fact, if you think about it, had Dick not been so averse to weight on the tackle (see Chapter 15) he might have invented a swim feeder or a method feeder!

Although he was opposed to aspects of match fishing Dick did make many friends amongst match anglers, most notably the famous Billy Lane. For some reason they hit it off very well. Walker, of course, would have defended to the last the rights of anglers to be match anglers if they wished, but he became uneasy if they started to tell him how to fish outside the realms of match fishing.

One of the battles he had with the match angling fraternity concerned the use of left-hand wind reels for right-handed anglers. He argued that if you were right-handed then that hand should do the most important jobs, and the heaviest jobs, namely holding and casting with the rod. The weaker left arm/hand merely had to turn the handle of the reel. Now, this opinion was voiced, and then defended, at a time when ambidextrous reels were few, and most reels had the handles on the right. So match anglers - indeed *most* anglers - were quite literally handicapped from the start. There was a great deal of huffing and puffing from the match fishing legions but their case was weak and Walker eventually won. Reels became more readily available in either left- or right-hand wind. For example, the famous Mitchell reels came in both. Some cheaper ambidextrous reels were also produced, such as the Intrepid range, and bit by bit, the angling community came round to them. Nowadays it's a forgotten debate because most reels are ambidextrous and most right-handed anglers, including match anglers, prefer the handles on the left: what is the point of changing hands in order to play in a fish, especially if in that initial split second of the battle you give away control to the fish?

And yet . . . there are two remaining quite illogical legacies. One is that most multiplier reels are made for left-handed anglers, whilst most anglers are right-handed! Of course, you can buy ambidextrous multipliers and the demand for left-hand wind access grows by the year. But we are not there yet. It is common still, for example to observe sea anglers and big game anglers struggling to hold the rod up with their weakest arm. (Perhaps more practice is needed in the pub, using first one arm as the drinking arm, and then the other!) It is worth making the point that if you are casting, say, lures, with a multiplying reel and you are right-handed, then the cast is made with the right hand as the main lever, and as the rod comes down to the horizontal the reel handles drop neatly into the left hand. It's as simple and neat as that. Dick didn't write much about multipliers because he used mostly fixed-spool reels, centre-pins and fly reels (the last being merely a modified centre-pin). Centre-pins could be fished ambidextrously provided you could remove the line guards which were invariably set for left-handed anglers! Most experienced centre-pin anglers remove the line guard anyway because rather than actually guiding the line all the time, they do have a nasty habit of fouling it.

Now for one of the paradoxes that is, beyond question, part of the Walker psyche. Having converted almost the whole of the angling world to his way of thinking on where the reel handles should be, what did he do whilst fly fishing? Take a look at any picture of Dick wielding a fly rod and you'll see that he does it contrary to his case! His argument was that the fly reel rarely comes into play during fishing and is little more than a repository for line. This is not a good argument and no salmon angler could sustain it for five minutes, or any angler attached to a big trout. When I began fly fishing in the late 1950s I, quite automatically, put the reel handles to the left, removed the line guard, and cast with my right, drinking arm. It is just so much more comfortable and efficient.

Another argument Dick had with match fishermen concerned closed-face reels. Match anglers really liked these because they helped prevent line flap of the very fine lines they often had to use. (In recent years there has been a swing away from them, probably owing to the fact that modern fixed-spool reels are so much smoother and more efficient.) Walker, quite unsurprisingly, examined the innards of the closed-face reel and discovered that the line went around several 90^0 bends before it finally arrived on the reel spool. Obviously, he said, this would create excessive friction for anyone playing a big fish, but that really wasn't a concern to the match angler chasing smaller silver fish. Today, of course, the match fisherman may be catching sizeable carp, and a closed-face reel may be unsuitable if they have a rod rather than a pole.

Another reel innovation from which the match anglers benefited as much as everyone else, resulted from Walker's pressure on manufacturers to produce rollers in the pick-up heads. This seriously reduces friction and makes the reel a greater pleasure to use. Intrepid were the first firm to incorporate Dick's thinking in their Intrepid Elite reel. It wasn't an expensive and finely engineered reel, but I was involved in testing it for Ken Morritt the MD, and I did find it rather nice to use. I gave it away to an Intrepid enthusiast, quite recently.

Dick was also involved in a float shotting debate with the match anglers. He argued that one big shot, or a close bunch, down near the bait was all that was needed in most cases. This would propel the bait along at the preferred depth and, what is more, get it down more quickly than a string of shot spaced at varied (and hotly debated) positions along the line. What I think he didn't fully realise was that whilst his method was probably good for trotting for big chub or barbel, it wasn't as well suited for the match men, who were chasing smaller fish, and who therefore needed much more flexibility. The match men needed to vary the sink rate, the hold-back rate, the overrun rate and so on, which couldn't be done easily on Dick's scheme.

In the 1960s and 1970s Dick was also opposed to the use of (weaker) hook lengths favoured by the match angler. Dick simply tied his eyed hook or spade-end hook directly to the reel line. He made the point that if the line was

En route to the water: the famous Tom Sails versus Dick Walker match.

Left to right: Peter Tombleson, Phillip Sutton, Maurice Ingham, Richard Walker, Harold Ludlow, W. Kelsey, Tom Sails, Ken Sutton, Percy Smith.

Dick and Tom competing on the river Witham.

in good nick, then in the event of a break, the break would take place on the hook knot and the fish would be left only with a hook in it, not a length of line as well. The match angler, by contrast, did not want to fish a gossamer line through the whole reel length, not least because of wear and tear and the risk of damage to a long length of fine line. This debate between them was eventually shelved, but it's interesting to note that in his later years Dick actually did fish with a finer hook length. I have no record of his conversion, but it may be buried somewhere in one of his 1,700 or so *Angling Times* articles. Alternatively perhaps, Dick, being Dick, if he thought he'd got it wrong, may have simply changed his method without telling anyone.

Most of the time Dick got on well with match anglers, probably because he regarded them as brothers of the angle, and fair game for a good debate, but things may have changed just a bit when Ivan Marks came on the scene. Ivan took match fishing to a new level, and there was a period when he was as famous as Dick himself. I have it on good authority that Dick did not respond too well to the rise of Ivan Marks. Could he *really* have been concerned that his 'top dog' position would be overturned? It is just possible. I knew Ivan Marks reasonably well because he used to come down annually to Cambridge to help Percy Anderson and I run the local council's children's angling course.

He did this with the same generosity of spirit that Dick helped others and he also, like Dick, had real charisma. He was a superb angler, of that there is no doubt, but of course, in a much more restricted sphere than Dick who did just about everything except sea fishing. Ivan was not only charismatic, he was crafty! I well remember accepting his challenge at an angling conference in Reading, to cast a half-ounce Arlesey Bomb into a plastic bucket (as he could do regularly). Note that he was using *Dick's* invention, the Arlesey Bomb, and as soon as he saw me coming down the aisle he moved the bucket into the corridor outside the hall! I hit the bucket at least.

I never spoke to Ivan about Dick, which was short-sighted of me, but other leading match anglers of the day held him in great regard: people like Billy Lane, Kevin Ashurst, Bill Bartles, and Percy Anderson - all England team men. Percy was very pro-Walker and we once organised together a grand evening with Dick as the guest of honour and speaker at the University Arms in Cambridge. Dick had an audience of three hundred and fifty or so (an all-ticket occasion) and he held them spellbound, match anglers, and all.

The big, much talked about, match-versus-specimen contest between Dick and Tom Sails was, in reality, a very friendly affair. Dick had insisted that apart from a certain media hype (low key by modern standards) there should be no animosity; as, indeed, there was not. It was fished in three stages, one venue favourable to each man - Tom Sails and Dick - and one neutral venue. All in all I think Tom probably had the advantage in the three matches because Dick tended to fish for biggies, and these were more likely to be spooked by the gathered officials (though Dick actually won by two matches to one). I also think that one consequence of this good-natured affair was to draw match and pleasure anglers closer together rather than drive them apart. Most certainly they got to understand each other's position rather better. Perhaps this was Dick's intention, or hope, from the outset. Today, we have a situation where, by and large, both pleasure and match anglers recognise the skills of the other sphere of the sport. Dick would have been pleased, I think; and he did contribute considerably to the skills of both.

One thing Dick got wrong about match fishing, though, was his firm assertion, in the letters of the Carp Catchers' Club, that at least carp fishing would never be involved in it. How times change! Not only do we now have hundreds of matches each week catching small carp on small lakes, but we even have World Championship matches which involve catching large carp. I do not think Dick anticipated that the country would ever be so full of carp and carp fishing that competitions would become inevitable. Did anyone at that time?

Chapter 18

Bernard Venables v. Richard Walker

I N THE second half of the twentieth century Bernard Venables and Richard
Walker were the most famous names in angling, the former known for his
artistry and literature, the latter for revolutionising the sport. But Bernard and
Dick were not friends. In fact, it seemed very much that Bernard was wholly
against Dick, although there is no indication from Dick that he felt the same
about Bernard. Several people who knew Dick well have confirmed that
Walker and friends often had a laugh at Venables' expense, but only in a good
humoured way, gently mocking his writing style or his, at times, sentimental
view of fish and nature. So why was Venables so anti-Walker? What were his
views on Walker and why did he hold them? Were they correct? And which of
them - Venables or Walker - contributed more to angling and its development?

In his autobiography *A Stream of Life* (p.174) Venables describes R.W. as
'Combatively logical rather than passionate, brilliant rather than inspired.'
And the following too: 'I found in him an oddity I could not for a time
identify'; 'He was not intelligent, but was almost boundlessly innovative. He
was, as someone said of him a brilliant fifth former. He was and remained
immature. I also detected coldness of spirit which lay behind the various
aspects he displayed'; 'I found him a publisher and helped the book on its
way to publication. The book (*Still-Water Angling*) was very successful: it is
unfortunate that its long-term effect has not been for the good of angling.'

It is pretty damning comment and we can be clear about one thing:
Venables did not like Richard Walker. Here we see the other great man of his
day, Venables, kicking hell out of Richard Walker and, moreover, kicking him
after he was dead. Venables goes on to record that Tiny Bennett, the *Angling
Times* photographer of those times had told him that Walker was determined
to push him, Venables, from his position of eminence in the angling world and

No sign here of the animosity that B.V. was later to show towards Dick!

replace him. But Tiny Bennett was on good terms with Walker: in 1972, from his base in Ontario, Canada, he was still writing to Dick on the subject of scents and fish. Tiny Bennett is now dead so we cannot corroborate B.V.'s account: indeed, because Venables completed his autobiography so late in his life (and it was published posthumously) many of those he criticises in its pages for adversely affecting his career were already dead. It is a rather one-sided story in some instances. There was a brief letter in *Angling Times* in the 1990s claiming that Walker had had Bernard sacked from *AT* yet the *AT* editorial staff, when questioned during the research for this book, could find no evidence of this at all.

Bernard claimed that Dick was not intelligent, but on what did he base this? After all, Dick had won a place at Gonville and Caius College, University of Cambridge, and pursued successfully an undergraduate career in Mechanical Sciences (ie, Engineering) until the war intervened. He had to pass serious examinations to do that, and surely must have had reasonable intelligence at the least. And those who knew him well talk of his prodigious general knowledge and sharp intellect. (That was my experience of him too.)

The charge of immaturity is more difficult to counter, not least because most extrovert and confident people have a degree of immaturity about them in their willingness to entertain without reserve or embarrassment. Walker certainly had these qualities. Yet he was mature enough to tackle skilfully the threats to angling, and in particular those from politicians and other officials. And he did it in a manner that gained their respect and, quite often, their compliance. This question of maturity is purely one of opinion and may simply be a thoughtless addition to the invective Venables heaped upon Walker, probably for the reasons I will shortly outline.

Coldness of spirit? Now this is an interesting charge! Venables was an artist, in oils and watercolours, and also had strong drafting skills. He, presumably, considered himself of a warmth of spirit which he would equate with his appreciation of the very ethos of angling. This he tried to capture in his artwork as well as in his writing. Walker's writing style is not as convoluted as that of Venables, but it is clarity itself, a fact many have commented upon. This does not stop him capturing the very essence of angling and to illustrate this we only have to read his account of the capture of the 44lb record carp: I have never visited Redmire Pool, but I have in my mind a most vivid picture of the swim and of the events of that night, thanks to Walker's sparse but emotive prose. And Chris Yates, one of the greatest angling writers, wrote in 1988 in *Dick Walker: a memoir,* 'There was no glaze over his prose. He used words economically and succinctly, yet he could be beautifully evocative and quietly poetic as he described his pleasure, problems, moods and triumphs of his fishing day.' Arthur Ransome achieved the same, quite without the convoluted and at times very stilted style of classic Venables. Fred Buller told me recently that he and Dick Walker had quite independently come to the conclusion that Venables' flowery writing style was based upon the style of the poet Edmund Blunden, but that it wasn't as good. I agree with them.

But was Venables trying to tell us that Walker was not artistic? I think he was. So let us have a look at that aspect of Walker. Many anglers of my generation will probably remember the small incident in the Walker column in *Angling Times,* when it appeared one week illustrated by a sketch of a great crested grebe. This naturally led to a query from a reader as to the identity of the artist: it turned out to be R.W. himself. Given Venables' views on matters of art, and of R.W. in particular, I began to look into the artwork of the latter. I found plenty of evidence of considerable artistic ability. In the first place he was a good draftsman as one might expect from an engineer, but he also liberally illustrated many of his letters with sketches of all sorts of things - insects, tackle (naturally) and scenery too. And look at the classic *Drop Me A*

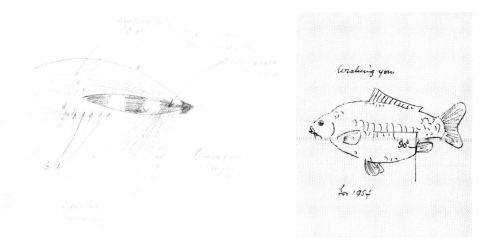

Walker was a keen artist, and his letters and books are full of sketches and drawings.

Line: there you will see evidence of considerable artistic skill. If Venables was equating warmth with artistic skill then he was wrong there too: Walker had warmth, most certainly. All his friends testify to that, as do people who barely knew him.

Consider now B.V.'s description of Walker's classic *Still-Water Angling* as merely 'very successful', and not for 'the good of angling'. In actual fact the first edition was not, in financial and sales terms, very successful: one letter from R.W. to, if I remember correctly, Gerry Berth-Jones, mentioned that it had sold only 1,500 copies. I must say that the figures surprised me and I am certain that Venables was unaware of them. But the book *was* successful in that four editions later it is still with us and regarded as a classic. Can the same be said of any Venables book (apart from *Mr Crabtree*, of course)? We know why Venables claims the book was not for the good of angling: he did not like what he saw as modern angling. But look at the books that *Still-Water Angling* inspired: the books of Bob Buteux, the Clifford-Arbery classic *Redmire Pool*, the letters between Chris Yates and Walker, or between Peter Stone and Walker. And look at the letters between Maurice Ingham and Walker (*Drop Me A Line*). In this, and all those others mentioned, you will find the very fabric of angling. You may scoff, as I'm certain B.V. did, at the way the small tents of R.W. and colleagues at Redmire became the bivvies of the modern angler, but it is an arrogant person indeed who claims that the modern carp angler in his bivvy cannot and does not enjoy the aesthetics of angling.

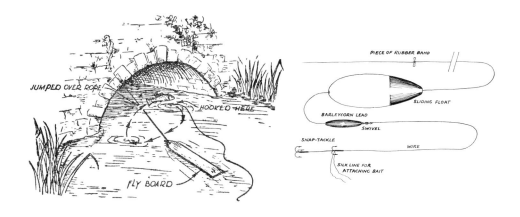

All great discoveries have a downside in the way in which they are received and interpreted by those that follow. I have no doubt at all that some modern anglers do *not* appreciate nature or man's hunting role within it, and would be as happy playing darts (which I also like!), but that was not Walker's legacy. What Walker did was to show ordinary anglers how to be successful hunters in a natural environment, rather than merely sitting there 'communing with nature'. Venables taught only the communing bit and in consequence had a small following, which included, it must be said, myself and many of those mentioned above. But we saw both sides of the coin. Venables' 'position of eminence' was to a degree one that existed in his own mind rather than in the real world. In those days most anglers had never heard of him (despite *Mr Crabtree Goes Fishing* and its huge sales) and those who had, often didn't read him because of his flowery writing style. This last is a pity because his books are written in a less stuffy and fussy style than his articles, where concentration of a theme into one or two thousand words was essential.

Finally, lets look at Walker's supposed lack of passion. Obviously, the charge is to some extent refuted by the quality of his artwork. But what I have been told repeatedly by those who knew him well and fished with him was that he was not only fanatical about angling - and all fanaticism contains an element of passion - but that he deeply loved the sport too, and the natural framework within which it operated. When I first spoke to Alan Brown the rod maker, who as a young man knew Walker well, it was this he remembered most -

Walker's passion, without restraint or reserve. Now here's a puzzle for you. Who wrote the following words, Venables or Walker?

> The wisps of cloud were like purple bruises edged with magenta. The western sky changed from the vermilion of a wild poppy to the purple crimson of a peony. The reflection of the sky on the water made changing patterns like moving cobblestones in a street of blood.

It comes from an article in *The Field* in 1969, and you can guess that it wasn't Venables. This is not romanticism. It is Walker's observation reflecting his passion for angling in the natural environment.

I spoke often with Richard Walker and on only two occasions with Bernard Venables. I have read both men extensively over many years and have witnessed the impacts they have had. I think that Venables' anti-Walker remarks in *A Stream of Life* reflect in small part an element of jealousy of Walker's fame, but perhaps in greater part a resentment of, or disagreement with, some of the things that were happening in angling and which he thought were Walker-led or Walker-inspired. Both achieved greatly in their own spheres but in angling Walker's legacy is and will be immensely the greater.

Walker toasting Venables and other angling luminaries.

Chapter 19

Richard Walker and Izaak Walton

THAT THESE two anglers are often referred to in the same breath and mentioned in passing, as a pair, by leading angling writers, makes it clear that they are of similar and great stature in the annals of angling. One never hears anyone else paired with Izaak Walton, only Walker. So let us attempt to weigh up the relative contributions the two have made to our sport.

Walker has, at first consideration, an unfair advantage in such a comparison because he is relatively recent, his writing modern, and his impact on the details of the sport plain to see.

Nevertheless, we cannot dismiss Walton in the way that Martin James has done in describing *The Compleat Angler* as poor literature and not adding to angling knowledge. It would be better, I think, to take as a starting point Brian Clarke's more measured comments (*The Times*, 26th July, 1995), when he writes, 'Nobody would argue, of course, that Izaak Walton is not more generally famous than Richard Walker and that Walton's pastoral hymn, *The Compleat Angler*, has outsold the dozen or so books that Walker wrote a hundred times over and more, but Walton's was a work of literature, not intellectual force.' *The Compleat Angler* has run to more editions than any book except the Bible: millions have been sold. I have conducted my own straw-polls over the years and I have discovered that relatively few anglers possess a copy of Walton's work, and even fewer have read it, and yet it is a great work of literature, quite easy to read even in the first edition (which I think is the best) and, allowing for the word usage, phraseology and spelling of the time, the prose is sparse, clear, to the point, and very emotive. In fact, he had exactly those attributes, which others and I accord to Walker elsewhere in this book (Chapter 18). In fact I find it rather puzzling that Tom Fort, himself a master of clear writing, should describe Walton's prose in the following way (*Telegraph Weekend,* 26th January, 2006): 'The dialogue form is clumsy and the language often obscure.' It seems that G. E. M. Skues considered Walton a 'miserable old plagiarist'. Miserable? Surely not! And Jeremy Paxman, too, had it in for Walton, dismissing him as 'unreadable'. None of this do I agree with.

Walton's great work is not an intellectual force, for sure, but it cannot be argued that it did not contribute to the angling of the day. There were few books to do with angling and I should imagine that every written and published word was devoured by literature-starved anglers, and acted upon. There is a great deal of angling sense and useful instruction in *The Compleat Angler*, so it would not only have been enjoyed as literature, but it would have been useful to the practising angler. Walker himself is said not to have rated it highly as an instructional book, but he recognised its value as literature. I'm a little puzzled that he thought this but he may have meant that it was not particularly useful in the twentieth century - and I would certainly agree with that.

So, in terms of writing styles and communication skills I think it is fair to say, allowing for the passage of time, that Walker and Walton were not dissimilar. However, we cannot know whether Walker's classics *Still-Water Angling* and *Drop Me A Line* will still be referred to in a hundred years' time and, if so, whether they will seem as quaint as *The Compleat Angler* does to us now. And what of Walker's 'intellectual force' which pervades all his writing and to which Brian Clarke rightly drew our attention. This does distinguish the two quite markedly and to Walker's advantage in this debate. Walker's writing is likely to stand the test of time because it is inevitable that compilations of his work will appear, as is already happening to some extent. What if his thirty years of writing, for *Angling Times*, week in and week out, was collated? The mind boggles a little, but with modern advances in publishing why shouldn't it be feasible? Think of it, almost two thousand articles. Are *Angling Times* missing a trick here, I wonder?

The equation so far, then, is tilted in favour of Walker because of the strength of his writing and the undoubted fact that almost everything he wrote helped anglers in their practical fishing. There are a few factors that can be cancelled out on both sides of the equation. For example, pike and pike fishing. I refer you to Chapter 13 for more details of Walker and pike, but if you read Walton's pike chapter, and Walker's in *Still-Water Angling,* there are close parallels. Neither had pike fishing as their strongest point; both used, with acknowledgement, the ideas of others; and Walker's earlier ideas on pike ecology might have been taken straight out of Walton. So in the equation measuring one against the other we can cancel out the pike factor as evens.

What we need to do now is think about the impact upon angling of the two. I think it is fair to assume that Walton's writing would at the time have had some significant impact, for the reasons stated above, and we do see his ideas carried on up to the present, not only in terms of the pike ideas just mentioned, but in other matters too, such as line clips (widely used today and first mentioned in *The Compleat Angler;* Walker also used them, a slight modification of those mentioned by Walton). There is nobody alive to speak directly of the value of Walton's ideas, obviously, but those ideas did have a great impact on the sport.

In the case of Walker it is easier to see the impact he had, and there are plenty of anglers living who can, and do, testify to it, but few anglers realise the sheer breadth of Walker's influence. If you are a carp angler you may be unaware of his contributions to trout fishing; and vice-versa. In all probability most coarse anglers of experience will be aware of his achievements in chub fishing, but may be totally unaware of his extensive involvement with the tackle trade (an altruistic involvement on the whole, I might add).

Let's just look briefly at carp fishing. No so very long ago I walked around a large carp lake very close to Cambridge. It was peopled by a considerable number of carp anglers, all under the age of thirty, in small groups of associated bivvies, on long fishing sessions. They had two to four rods each, on pods or rod-rests, each topped by a buzzer. I did an informal poll, asking them if they were aware of Dick Walker and, if they were, whether or not they knew anything about his carp fishing exploits. Very, very few (three if I recall correctly, out of more than thirty) had heard of Dick and of those three none had any idea of his contribution to the fishing they were now enjoying. Of course, had I done a poll at an angling gathering with anglers over forty in predominance the answers would have been totally different: indeed, in such gatherings, the role of Dick Walker is *frequently* discussed.

Let us look again at their tackle. The buzzers those youngsters used were developed by Dick and Jack Opie. The rod-rest head design was Dick Walker. (I have in my possession one of his originals given me by Alan Vare: with the rod rested in position, the line runs freely below it.) The reel handles are on the left. The rods have long slim handles of various kinds (another Walker feature of design). They do not fish at night by means of Tilley Lamps, as sea fishermen do, because R.W. argued against excessive use of lights in the dark hours. I could go on and on, but let's end on boilies.

Now, boilies were not invented by R.W. - Fred Wilton was responsible for that and for the vigorous philosophy that accompanies their proper use - but R.W. did develop baits that were designed to avoid the attention of small fish (as are boilies) and baits that the carp liked to eat (except, perhaps, potatoes). I have no doubt that Fred was inspired by Walker's ideas and simply extended them logically, adding the brilliant Wilton ingredient as he went. I helped

Martin Gay test Fred's early (successful) boilies so do have some idea of their origins and the thinking behind them, and I have talked to Fred about them. Today, you can buy boilies in many parts of the world.

In short, almost everything those youngsters were doing, and almost all the tackle they had, stemmed from original Walker initiatives and inspirations. This kind of effect on our fishing can be found in almost all areas of the sport, especially freshwater, game and coarse fishing. I don't think Izaak Walton had this breadth of impact even though some of his 'discoveries' did come down through the ages.

I haven't even mentioned the philosophical components of Walker's world. He argued that successful angling was not a matter of chance, but of thinking like a fish, of understanding how a fish lives and feeds. It was necessary, he said, to use the correct tackle for the anticipated fish and weight of fish; to use the right bait, in the right place, at the right time; and, of prime importance, to avoid scaring the fish. Some of this is implicit in Walton's writing, but with Walker it is explicit, fundamental, and often carefully argued for each and every species.

Izaak Walton is commonly described as the father of angling or, occasionally, as the greatest angler ever. I think Dick Walker achieved more, and effected greater changes in the sport that were more fundamental and longer reaching. Here are just some of the things that have been said of him:

' . . . a man who many believe to be the most important figure in the history of the sport.' Brian Clarke (*The Times,* 26th July, 1995).

' . . . has done more to increase the skill and knowledge of the average angler than anyone in the history of the sport.' Colin Willock (*Country Fair Magazine,* April 1958).

'Dick Walker was one of the greatest anglers of all time. His achievements are without parallel.' Peter Maskell (*Trout Fisherman,* June 1997).

'Walker . . . by his own efforts, drew angling from the dark ages: who brought science and logic to a sport that up to his appearance had largely been lost in myth and adrift on potion.' Anon. (*Flyfishers' Club Journal*) (From the style of writing I suspect this was written by Brian Clarke.)

'Time has canonised Izaak Walton: if history has a sense of justice time will surely elevate Dick Walker above all others as the greatest man to emerge from the angling ranks . . .' Tim Paisley (*Dick Walker: a memoir,* 1988).

' . . . in language everyone could understand, he laid out a coherent approach to the water, to replace the sense of cast and hope that had gone before. Year by year, angling attitudes changed. So did angling practice. So did tackle. So did pretty well everything else.' Brian Clarke (*The Times,* 12th May, 2001).

'The greatest freshwater angler of all time who . . . was not just the greatest charismatic angler of the 20th Century, but of any Century . . .' Martin James (*Memorial Meeting,* Oxford, 2004).

'Dick Walker turned angling upside down and inside out.' Peter Stone (*Angling Times,* 7th August, 1985).

' . . . is responsible for more original thoughts about angling than anyone else.' Peter Thomas (*Angling Times,* 7th August 1985).

'His was the greatest mind angling has ever seen . . . He was the most influential angler of all time.' Christopher Yates (*Angling Times,* 7th August, 1985).

Fred Buller once remarked that Dick Walker was by far the best read of any writer he had come across and, moreover, one with a seriously photographic memory who could often give chapter and verse of ancient books quite readily. I think these written words by some of the most experienced anglers of the last half century accurately portray what has been argued in this chapter: Richard Walker's achievements and inspirations really do eclipse those of Izaak Walton and time will surely confirm this.

Chapter 20

The death of Dick Walker

DICK DIED on 2nd August, 1985, aged sixty-seven. It was an event which, it is no exaggeration to say, shook the angling world. *Angling Times,* for which he had written a column for thirty years, until shortly before his death, simply entitled their article telling of his death 'End' adjacent to Dick's 'Voice of Angling' byeline. All the anglers I spoke to at the time felt exactly the same, even those who did not know him personally: they felt that something very, very important had been removed from the world of angling, something they would all miss. How right they were.

Of course anglers had been aware that he was ill, because he had said so in his column; and towards the end one article was written for him by Pat Walker to let readers know how he was progressing. The many letters he received were answered for him by others including Graham Marsden the veteran specialist angler for whom Dick had a great respect. Of the letters he received so many were solicitous for his health and praised his unfailing good humour. Although his friends and family knew that he had cancer I'm not sure how widespread the knowledge was. But he must have announced his cancer in his column because I can recall that a letter was published saying, in effect, that Dick only had himself to blame because of his habit of smoking. Dick's reply was quite typical of him; he pointed out that never in his life had he smoked a cigarette where he had cancer. Dick was polite in his reply; but the letter criticising him does serve to illustrate how insensitive people can be towards famous people, as though they do not have feelings. One of his other jocular remarks concerning his cancer was, 'I'll beat this thing if it kills me'. He died of a form of prostate cancer.

For several short periods during his illness, Dick perked up quite a lot or certainly gave this impression to others in his letters to them, and it gave rise to some optimism that he might survive the cancer, as others have done.

But it was not to be. In his last year there were signs of frustration, mostly communicated in letters to Geoffrey Bucknall, his old 'antagonist' of the angling press, to whom he became increasingly close. The letters dealt in forthright manner with matters to do with angling and people and were scathing at times. In the end Geoffrey decided, correctly I'm sure, that they were written by a seriously ill Dick Walker, not the man we all knew, and so he destroyed them. This anger, If one could call it that, was part and parcel of the courage he showed in his final year, to which Pat and the family can testify.

Dick died at home, cared for by his wife Pat, and assisted from time to time by other members of the family, especially Tim and his wife Lynn. I asked Pat to tell me a little about that time and these are her words:

> In the last few months of his life when they visited to spend time with Richard, I was assisted from time to time by my step-children, but they had responsibilities with their young children. Robert was young too, and Janet and Simon kindly took him away on holiday with them to the seaside. Lynn and Tim, being freer of children, often had Rob to stay or helped me by fetching him from prep-school. In the last weeks of Richard's life Lynn and Tim visited most evenings and in June they kindly stayed for a week to enable me to go away to have a rest - I went, not knowing that Richard's end was so near. It was on Monday, 1st July, that Dr Mary Greig answered Richard's direct question 'How long have I got?' - the reply came that it was just weeks.
>
> When it was apparent that it was very close to the end, I asked all the family to come and say goodbye to Richard, who was in bed in his study, and there was always someone staying quietly in the room with him, until he died. My sister Mary Routley, who gave us both great support, came with my step-son Richard to wake me to tell me that Richard had just died, and I note that in my diary for Friday, 2nd August, 1985, I have written, 'R. died 3.17'.

There was a Service of Thanksgiving for Dick, held on 20th October, 1985, at St Andrew's, Biggleswade. The church was packed and included many anglers, famous and otherwise. Dick's eldest son Richard gave the first reading, followed by Ken Sutton, then Director of the ACA (I had walked to the church with him and, despite his intention to celebrate the life of Dick, he was very sober in mood). The superb address was given by Dick's old friend Fred Buller and later published in *Dick Walker: a memoir* (The Carp Society, publication department, 1988).

It was an emotive day for all present, but if one thing sticks in my mind of the day it is of over two hundred voices, many of them ordinary anglers, thundering out 'Onward Christian Soldiers'.

SERVICE OF THANKSGIVING

RICHARD STUART WALKER

1918 — 1985

Sunday, 20th October 1985

ST. ANDREW'S BIGGLESWADE

THE BIDDING

We are met together in the presence of God to give thanks to Him for the life of Richard Stuart Walker and pray that all sorrow may be replaced by the joy of remembrance.

. . . .

Never say in grief he is no more,
Only say in thankfulness he was.

S. Baring-Gould, 1834-1924.

Onward, Christian soldiers,
Marching as to war,
With the Cross of Jesus
Going on before.
Christ the royal Master
Leads against the foe;
Forward into battle,
See, his banners go!
Onward, Christian soldiers,
Marching as to war,
With the Cross of Jesus
Going on before.

2 At the sign of triumph
Satan's legions flee;
On then, Christian soldiers,
On to victory.
Hell's foundations quiver
At the shout of praise;
Brothers, lift your voices,
Loud your anthems raise.

3 Like a mighty army
Moves the Church of God;
Brothers, we are treading
Where the Saints have trod;
We are not divided,
All one body we,
One in hope and doctrine
One in charity.

Unison.

4 Crowns and thrones may perish,
Kingdoms rise and wane,
But the Church of Jesus
Constant will remain;
Gates of hell can never
'Gainst that church prevail;
We have Christ's own promise,
And that cannot fail.

5 Onward, then, ye people,
Join our happy throng,
Blend with ours your voices
In the triumph song;
Glory, laud, and honour
Unto Christ the King;
This through countless ages
Men and Angels sing.

THE FIRST READING

"My duty to my neighbour..."

Mr. Richard C. Walker

THE LOST CHORD

Words by Adelaide A. Proctor
Music by Arthur Sullivan

THE SECOND READING

The Wisdom of Solomon Chapter 3
Mr. Kenneth Sutton

ADDRESS
Mr. Frederick H. Buller

THE HOLY CITY

Words by F.E. Weatherly
Music by Stephen Adams
Solo by Mrs. Christine Underwood

THE PRAYERS

William Blake, 1757-1827.

And did those feet in ancient time
  Walk upon England's mountains green?
And was the holy Lamb of God
  On England's pleasant pastures seen?
And did the countenance divine
  Shine forth upon our clouded hills?
And was Jerusalem builded here
  Among those dark satanic mills?

Bring me my bow of burning gold!
  Bring me my arrows of desire!
Bring me my spear! O clouds, unfold!
  Bring me my chariot of fire!
I will not cease from mental fight,
  Nor shall my sword sleep in my hand,
Till we have built Jerusalem
  In England's green and pleasant land.

THE BLESSING

"DANNY BOY"

Words by F.E. Weatherly 1848-1929

Traditional Irish Tune Londonderry Air

I doubt if there was a dry eye in the church at the end of that hymn. Dick had never been particularly religious but one can imagine him being pleased at this rendition of a hymn he was known to have enjoyed in life.

Whatever problems there had been for a while between Maurice Ingham and Dick were forgotten when Dick was ill and the two came together again as good old friends, Maurice visiting Dick and Pat several times. I shall let Maurice have the final word on Dick's last year with the following recollection from him of their last fishing expedition (the remainder of Maurice's piece can be found in the Personal Recollections at the end of this book):

Although we lived far apart I was fortunate in being able to visit Dick a few times during the later stages of his tragic illness. By then his strength and stamina were sadly diminished but his great spirit and love of angling were unimpaired and on one memorable visit he insisted that we should have a 'crack' at the trout in his local water - a former gravel pit on a farm at Roxton. I had not gone prepared for fishing but there was never any shortage of fishing tackle in the Walker household, and in no time I was equipped with a superb fly fishing outfit. I am sure that his motives in suggesting this outing were totally unselfish and were prompted by a desire to provide a change of scene and occupation for his devoted and solicitous wife, Pat, and, for me, a chance to enjoy the sport that he was able to offer.

Pat drove us the short distance to the lake and parked the car on an elevated vantage point about 20 yards from the bank. Having seen us satisfactorily tackled up and having given me a few words of advice on where and how to fish, Dick returned to the car from which he watched the subsequent activities. It was not long before Pat, who is a highly skilful fly fisher (as befits the wife of Richard Walker - and being a Marston) caught a lovely brown trout of about 3 pounds. Meanwhile I was having problems in casting into the slight wind. Seeing my difficulties, Dick left the car and, taking over my rod, he gave me a brilliant exhibition of casting technique, not only explaining where I was going wrong but demonstrating how it should be done. During the course of his demonstration Dick caught another nice trout which I had the pleasure of netting for him. This short burst of activity had exhausted him, however, and he was obliged to return to the car.

Regrettably I was not able to give Dick the satisfaction of knowing that I had caught a trout as a result of his tuition - at least not on that occasion, but I have many times proved its worth in other places and on other occasions - an appropriate and enduring souvenir of a dear, dear friend.

Chapter 21

A personal perspective
by Patricia Marston Walker

ORSON WELLES wrote: 'Writers go into total eclipse immediately after their deaths'. However, I had thought that one day soon, or in the far future, there would be a need for a biography about Richard, so, while he was ill I asked him to talk on tape for me. He covered his early life, school, university, war and the later years, intermingled, of course, with his fishing. Now, in 2006, I am contributing to this biography, and I am glad that I have much material to hand, to add to my memories.

My husband was born in Hitchin, Hertfordshire, on 29th May, 1918 - Oak Apple Day, restoration of the monarchy and hence the Stuart in his name - into an end-of-terrace Victorian house, which was much bigger than it looked as it had two attic bedrooms, as well as a commodious cellar. It was in the days when nearly everything could be delivered to the house, and he even remembered 'a horse drawn sort of wheeled vehicle, selling meat for cats'. Cats became one of his loves.

Most of the living took place in the kitchen, with the parlour, and its aspidistra, being kept for guests and regular visits from the vicar. The scullery was at the back of the house and a fire was lit under the copper, for bath nights on Fridays, and for washing-day on Mondays. Richard told me that vast amounts of water were needed for the hip-bath, which was put in front of the range in the kitchen.

Richard's father, who was in the First World War, was invalided out of the army and given a job at the War Office in London, and so he was brought up mostly by his mother, with help from his four grandparents. His mother's family came from the Stanbridge area of Bedfordshire and, sadly, her only brother was killed soon after the outbreak of the war. Richard's maternal

Annie Foulger.

Grandmother Walker (née Annie Foulger) and Edwin Halford, Dick's stepfather.

The Coopers at Wood Lane Farm.

Grandfather Cooper, of farming stock, was a good farmer and a wonder with animals, he also knew every bird and beast and creature and insect about his farm. However, there has been a great change in the bird life of the area in which Richard grew up, and he commented, in the Eighties, that it must be thirty years since he had heard a nightjar, and corncrakes were practically extinct.

It was this grandfather who taught Richard an enormous amount about wildlife in Britain in general, which, he told me, he didn't appreciate at the time but he realised later that it was of great help to him in his subsequent fishing. He thought that the most important thing his grandfather taught him was that a wild animal is a wild animal and it does not hang about if it sees you coming. This, of course, he soon learned applied to fish as well, because one of the boundaries of the little farm was the river Oughton, which was then a fine trout stream; it was one of many excellent chalkstreams in Hertfordshire at that time and held a large number of trout - many of which were quite big by the then standards, fish of up to five pounds.

Grandfather Cooper was not an angler but he had ways of getting a trout out of that river if he wanted one. Apparently they were most unorthodox and involved things like pitch-forks, snares and night-lines. Another time his ducks were being attacked by a large pike: he extracted it with the aid of the clothes prop, a piece of sash cord, a butcher's hook and a piece of pork! The pike weighed 25lb.

After working in the Post Office, Richard's mother, in 1921, joined Lloyds & Company of Letchworth, makers of fine grass-cutting machines. By gradual stages she rose from a £2 a week clerk to be Managing Director, and Chairman - which involved very long hours. Richard told me that his mother was always very kind and thoughtful to him, and that one of the most important things she did was to teach him to read long before he was five, by simply recognising words. If he took a book to her and said, "Mummy, what is this word?" she would say rather impatiently, "Well, what does it look like?" and he looked at it and he knew what the word was. I suspect there was a bit more to it than that! There was never any shortage of books in the house, of all kinds, and the natural history ones were his favourite.

When he was quite small, Richard was taken by his family to see the Flying Scotsman train when it pulled into Hitchin Station, and as they knew the engine driver, he was lifted up to the cabin. Something he remembered well. However, at Christmas when he was given a new train set, his family could not understand his apparent lack of interest - but, it was the wrong colour, not green, but maroon.

Richard said that he was useless with a shot-gun. But because of his mother's teaching (not his grandfather's), and she having started him with a Diana air rifle when he was ten years old, he became a pretty good shot with any kind of rifle. She had taught him to shoot straight with a rifle over open sights, and later with telescopic sights, and if properly aligned he reckoned he could kill a man stone dead at three hundred yards provided he didn't move.

Richard Walker, Richard's other grandfather, was apprenticed to the Oxford University Press but after a few years ran away from home to join the army. He served on the North-West Frontier and later he was involved in the unsuccessful expedition to rescue General Gordon from Khartoum. As a sergeant he became the Personal Servant to Lord St Levan and through this job he met his future wife, Annie Foulger, who was a farmer's daughter. She had been 'taken up' as a lady's maid by Lady Blanche Lindsay who took a great interest in her and taught her a great deal about music, the arts and poetry - so that she became an extremely well spoken and well-read lady. They apparently fell in love at first sight and as they were both in their thirties they were shortly married. Both were given substantial wedding presents, sufficient so that they could put down a deposit on a house at Hertford.

As a boy Richard used to spend a good deal of his time at 'Highfields', then the highest house in Hertford, and apart from being very kind to him, more important still, this grandfather, born beside the Thames at Oxford, was a very keen and very capable angler and would take his grandson fishing with him. When very little he was tethered to a convenient tree or bush by a piece of rope so that he could not possibly fall in!

Richard's grandmother Annie always claimed to be descended from Charles II. The mistress who bore him the most children was Barbara Villiers, later created Countess of Castlemaine and although the King never acknowledged royal descent for his bastard children he did create titles for them. One son was given an estate and became the Duke of Grafton and in due course a later Duke of Grafton, according to Richard's grandmother's story, contracted a liaison with the daughter of one of his tenant farmers and a son was born and at maturity he was given the farm as owner. His name was Foulger. Simple maths will tell us that by now there must be many tens of thousands of people who could also claim descent from Charles II, but Richard liked to think that there might be some truth in this because he considered that the King, apart from being perhaps the best loved, the kindest and the most tolerant king, was also a very keen angler.

As Richard grew up there was not a lot of money but his mother saw to it that they had what was essential and there was never any shortage of food from the farm. One source of food that Richard used to exploit in due season was the eggs of moorhens and coots from the reedy swamp between the pasture and the river itself - called 'the bog' - which was full of Norfolk reeds, *Phragmites*, and also tussocks of grass which the youngsters could use and, by jumping, get across right to the river's edge for the eggs. There were no refrigerators in those days, let alone deep freezers, no washing machines, no television and work was from dawn to dusk preserving food - nothing on the farm would be wasted.

Both the grandmothers cooked the most delicious meals. One used to make his favourite puddings: steamed marmalade pudding, or alternatively choco-late blancmange and orange jelly with lashings of cream poured over the top. I myself remember another later favourite which was banana fritters - but always lashings of cream and some pudding!

Richard said that when he was twenty-one his farm grandmother did some-thing that has recently become 'fashionable'. She got hold of the most enormous turkey, inside the turkey she put a small goose, inside the goose was a teal, and inside the teal was some stuffing and one or two snipe. And all this was dished up with all the usual side dishes for the group of male friends and the family. With full stomachs and plenty of beer there was just no room for the steamed treacle pudding, another favourite, and Richard recalled that Granny was terribly disappointed and said, "What's wrong with you young fellows, haven't you any appetite?" But he added that it was the most marvel-lous meal.

This farm granny was a pretty tough old bird yet very compassionate when tramps called at the house (quite a frequent event in those days) asking for boiling water to make tea. The enormous kettle was always on the boil and she would give them a spoonful of tea and sugar for their billy-can, and pour on the water. With a polite "Thank you, Ma'm" they would be off.

Richard's education started at Miss Darby's School, a little school near to where he lived. He said Miss Darby was a dear old lady, and she had the assis-tance of a young lady. As Richard could read by the time he joined at five, he was more advanced than the other children. They learned their multiplication tables by reciting them in unison and they used to sing hymns and songs. Richard told me of the confusion that he had with the 23rd Psalm: to him it sounded as if what they were singing was 'surely good Mrs Murphy will follow me all the days of my life and I shall dwell in the house of the Lord forever' (supposed to be 'goodness and mercy' of course) and he didn't know who Mrs Murphy was and did not like the idea of dwelling in the house of the Lord forever - because he wanted to go fishing!

At the age of ten Richard started school as a boarder in the autumn term at the Friends' School, Saffron Walden, a Quaker School (the Society of Friends as it was known). It was by this time that his mother - who he would describe

Elsie Walker, Dick's mother.

The wallet of Dick's father,
Richard Harry Walker.

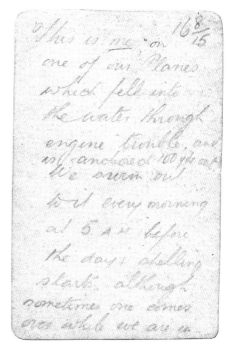

Dick's father aboard a downed plane during the
First World War.

as a brilliant woman - had raised enough money to build a new house at 11 Bearton Avenue, Hitchin, to her own design, completed in 1928. At first at his new school Richard recalled being 'hideously unhappy, bullied mercilessly', but fortunately he and three other boys, Bunny Cannon, Brian Gillett and Jimmy Hunt, all from farming backgrounds joined forces. Together they were a force to be dealt with and so were soon left alone. Apart from some oppressive masters he said that his boarding school days were happy.

Pocket money was the same for all, regardless of whether your parents were rich or poor, and was strictly rationed. You started in Forms 1 and 2 with sixpence a week, but Richard remembered that it was quite surprising how much you could buy for that in those days.

The school was co-educational with a headmaster, Mr C. Brightwen Rowntree, who administered the school, and a headmistress who was Miss Florence Priestman of the Priestman Earth Moving Equipment firm. Miss Priestman was 'a real darling' and nothing pleased her more than to show the boys little models of various earth-moving machinery that she got from the family business. These Richard found fascinating and perhaps this is what engendered his interest in engineering, which became his main career.

Richard particularly hated two of the masters and on the final day of his last term at Saffron Walden he had great pleasure in assisting one or two other boys in throwing one poor teacher fully clothed into the swimming pool! They hoped he would drown - but fortunately he didn't.

Mr Stanley Beer was the history master and he really made his subject come alive and the boys loved and respected him. Richard's love of poetry and literature was due to another special master called Walter Baldwin. His biology and natural history master was a Mr Hindle - a kind and gentle man, as are most naturalists, and Richard really enjoyed his company. He became rather a favourite of Mr Hindle - without being given special concessions - because, thanks to his grandfather's tuition, Richard already knew a lot about this subject, and was even better than the master at identifying the birds and animals when out on nature walks.

As with his later fishing Richard was not competitive with school sports. He was more concerned with having a good and interesting game. He played cricket and football and thought that if he had been keener on the competitive angle, he might have scraped into a football fourth-division league side. He said that his cricket was very much inferior but he could bowl quite well. He remembered one match when he was last man in - he said that he was always last man in - and the opposing bowler was very fast and he was frightened to death. So he just shut his eyes and swung the bat. By the grace of God, or sheer good luck, bat and ball connected and the ball flew until it smashed the skylight window of the swimming pool, saving the day. As a result of this the pool had to be drained to clear all the glass, and the next swim resulted in icy cold water, which Richard never forgot!

Although I never actually witnessed Richard swimming competitively I understand that he won a good number of the events held in the excellent twenty-five-yard long school pool. Compared to the swimming speeds of today Richard felt there was no comparison, but by the time he left school he could swim a hundred yards in sixty-two seconds, swim two miles 'without any sweat', as he put it, and dive off a fifteen metre board, without being frightened.

'Matriculation' came in 1934 and Richard got credits in most subjects, failed in none, and to everyone's amazement got a distinction in history. This was not entirely because he'd absorbed an awful lot of history as taught by his admired master Mr Beer, but because, thanks to his grandfather who had told him so much about his army campaigns, he was able to answer questions on the North-West Frontier and the Rescue of General Gordon.

The story of how Richard came to go to university is quite an unusual one. There were two aunts, married and fairly affluent but, as he said, 'mean as muck'. At a family gathering, they were sympathising with Richard's mother about her predicament of having no husband to support her and asked, "What is going to happen to poor little Dickie?" To which his mother replied, "He will have as good an education as his father, if not better." So when one of the aunts said sarcastically that she supposed she was going to send him to Eton, his mother answered, "I'll do better than that, I will send him to a University."

To achieve this, as there was little money to spare, his mother worked and worked, apart from her job, making anything she could sell, as there were no grants in those days. Mrs Walker was determined that her son would go to university - she favoured Cambridge as at the time they mostly won the Boat Race! In due course Richard did go to Cambridge, in 1936, to Gonville and Caius College to read Engineering.

University was still in the future, though. Having got his Matric he was unable to stay at the Friends' School, as there was no option to do this at that time, and he could not go to university until he was eighteen. So for this gap period Richard's mother sent him to the St Christopher School at Letchworth, where he found things curiously different. At Saffron Walden the rules were quite clearly laid down; at the new school it was the opposite, very 'free and easy', and it was up to the pupils themselves, individually, to do what they thought was right. He found it hard to settle down.

At St Christopher most of the teachers were called by their Christian names, but Richard, on being 'choked off', discovered that this did not apply to new boys, which he thought was most unfair. It was a school with a very gentle atmosphere but there was an occasion when one of the boys wanted to be in a classroom with his girlfriend so decided to throw Richard out. Now Richard never took kindly to anyone assaulting him and would always give as much back, but this sent the other boy screaming to the Headmaster. Well this resulted in the Headmaster telling Richard to do four hours digging in the kitchen garden, which he did, but being accustomed to the strict rules of Saffron Walden he dug and dug down and produced a hole so deep that he could not see over the top of it. The Headmaster, Mr Harris, said, "Walker, I don't know whether you are incorrigible or not, but you appear to take everything I say literally. You must learn to take the spirit of what I say and not just the letter of the law."

However, before Richard had taken this on board he went to his first swimming lesson. There were prizes for the first pupil who could learn to swim - but nobody had thought to ask him if he could already swim. So, after being towed backwards and forwards on a wire across the pool, they were told to see if they could swim across on their own, which of course Richard did with no trouble and was awarded a penknife! In due course, after a swimming match against his old school, his teacher became aware of his prowess and took the penknife away telling him that he had been acting a lie.

The things that Richard remembered most about St Christoper were how extremely nice the teachers were, and two matches that he played in. One was football and the other cricket and in both these matches apparently, unexpectedly, he excelled. When he had been at Saffron Walden he had been unable to restrain what seemed to him then an enormous boy who was a good ball player and who could run rings round Richard. A year later, in this match at St Christopher's, he was playing an attacking centre-half and stopped this chap dead. He could not get past Richard. They won the match 3-nil, scored by Richard, and he recalled, "That was the first, of several special occasions, that the trumpets sounded for me." The cricket match was one played against Newport Grammar School and the Captain had put Richard in to bowl due to a lack of his regular bowlers. Richard was six feet tall and about twelve stone at the time and he could put the ball down pretty quickly and make it turn both ways and curve in the air. He felt that his success at bowling possibly arose due to the fact that he had been fly casting since the age of seven with an old greenheart fly rod. He believed that over ten years (he was seventeen) this had developed very strong muscles in his arm enabling him to really make the ball spin: "You could almost hear it buzz in the air," he said! He took four wickets for seven runs and then the big hitter came in, and he hit two fours and a six off the other bowler. Richard then bowled him three quick ones on the off-side, which he could hardly reach, and then with his usual run up, bowled a real floater at half-pace which pitched outside the leg stump and broke back and hit the top of the middle stump. (At Saffron Walden, as already mentioned, Richard was, on one occasion, successful with a bat, but on the whole there he considered that he was a totally incompetent batsman. However, he had since learned how to do a square cut from what was known as a 'flicker', a little book consisting of a number of pages of some famous cricketer performing a particular stroke and if you whizzed the pages you got the impression of actual action.)

The finale to the Newport match story was that when Richard went in to bat, last man as always, fourteen runs were needed to win. The Captain had been very successful bowling rather short balls on the off side, which was producing edges and getting the batsmen caught in the slips. Richard's first strike was such a thick edge that it went right over the head of slips. In those days they had a man positioned at what was called Long Stop, and he ran like a stag and stopped the ball from reaching the boundary. Richard, with two runs scored, had to face the bowling again, much to his horror! But to his amazement the next ball was exactly the same and this time he got it right in the middle of the bat and it reached the boundary. The next balls were similar and Richard was able to play the only stroke he was capable of playing, and struck the balls smack in the middle of his Gun and Moore Cannon bat, and so they won the match.

When Richard was at Cambridge he had one more sporting success, excluding fishing, when he played for Caius XI against another college. By this time he'd been promoted to centre-forward and there were two chances in that match, both from outside the penalty area and he hit both with his right foot. "The goal keeper never even saw them go past him into the net, wham!" he said. In those days you didn't get hugged, but Bradley, the Captain, quite out of character, slapped Richard on the shoulder and said, "Bloody good shot, Walker." This sent him away so proud and that was another time when the trumpets sounded.

Whether Richard would ever have been any good at rowing at Cambridge we shall never know as the first time out on the river he broke an oar. At the time if you wanted to row you were allowed to break one oar and get away with it, but you had to pay for the second one. Richard decided that he could not afford to continue, but he still used the river a great deal, taking a canoe rather than a rowing boat. He'd paddle up to Grantchester, drag the canoe over the rollers, and continue on and on, up the Cam, very often fishing. He had always loved water.

In those days, as I've said earlier, there were no student grants and although his mother could afford his university fees Richard had to earn money for clothes or food. During the vacations he took jobs in all sorts of factories, an experience which, he said, stood him in enormous good stead when he later reached managerial status in business. As a manager there was nobody in the factories, in any of the places where he worked, who could tell him what could or couldn't be done on a particular machine tool - he had been on those machine tools himself. If a man tried to tell him he could only do twenty parts in an hour, Richard would say, "Move over and I'll very soon show you how many you can do," - he could do it. Richard believed this was one of the reasons why, in his industrial career, he enjoyed, he liked to think, both respect and affection from his own employees - they never tried to fool him. He told me, "They would not be so silly, they knew there is nothing that they could do that I couldn't, or if I could not do it as well they knew they would be suitably rewarded. If a man could do more parts per hour than I could on any machine, well then he was worth more than he was being paid and I would see that he got it."

While at Cambridge, Richard got to know some other rurally oriented undergraduates (as he had at Saffron Walden) and they augmented their food supply in all sorts of ways including fishing for pike and perch and bringing them back to cook. In fact Richard soon learned to cook all manner of things that didn't cost too much!

Richard was so busy trying to earn money in one way or another that he did not have the time to get too involved in sport. However, after spending his early terms washing down taxies for a shilling a go, or washing up dishes after banquets at the Blue Boar or the University Arms, he decided that there must be an easier way of earning money. He knew a little about radio and fishing, so he decided to have a go at writing some articles and trying to sell them. This was when he was paid for his first fishing article, which I think was published in the *Fishing Gazette*. In fact by the time he had been at Cambridge a year his writing income was making a useful contribution to the money he needed for food and clothes (topping up what he earned in the vacations). Richard told me that although he was so busy dealing with his various jobs as well as studying, it would have been indiscreet to list his temporary romantic attachments in this phase! Later, during the war, he appreciated the 'bon mot' from his driver Vic Page: 'Never chase women, they're like buses and trains, if you miss one, stick around, there will be another coming along presently.'

There were usually no problems working at the factories, but towards the end of his university years Richard was working at the Chator Leigh Manufacturing Company when word got amongst the workforce that he was an undergraduate. This caused a certain amount of resentment because of the

Another one into the net.

Dick with chub.

Gonville and Caius College, Cambridge.

Playing the ukelele in Hitchin, 1959. He also played the guitar.

unemployment at that time; why should a 'toff', as they thought, be taking the bread and butter out of the working-man's mouth, just for him to have a bit of 'fun'. The upshot of it was that he was challenged to a fight by a chap who was considered the factory 'strong man', and if he lost Richard would have to leave. But by this time Richard was 13$^1/_2$ stone and had been well fed all his life, he had done various sports and some boxing, and therefore had a considerable advantage over this man whose physical condition was not comparable. Having won, he was not happy and felt that the fight was most unfair.

When the war started, Richard was working with Murphy Radio at Welwyn as a tester on the production line of radio receivers. However, when the company won a contract to make transmitters for fitting in tanks, and the management discovered that he knew about transmitters (in his teens Richard had been a very keen amateur radio 'ham'), he was transferred, albeit for a short while. It was not long before he was requested to attend an interview at the Admiralty. Richard was amazed at how much they already knew about him, even that he liked fishing, and he told me, "One of the questions, which I shan't forget, was: 'Having been to a Quaker school, Mr Walker (and they were very polite) are you a conscientious objector?' and I well remember my reply, for having heard of the atrocities that the Nazis were committing against the Jews, I said, 'In any other war I might have been, but in this one I feel if ever a war was justified this one is.' They said, 'Very good, Mr Walker, will you proceed to Aberdeen?' " In some notes that Richard left for me he wrote, and underlined twice, that he dearly wanted his war years to be minimised. He hated being involved in producing devices to kill people, even Nazi enemies of our country, however necessary to preserve our freedom and way of life.

Richard's stay in a bitterly cold Aberdeen was brief because after a very long interview, in which they told him about radar, he was sent off again to St Athan in South Wales, to work on airborne radar equipment.

It was soon after this, on 21st March, 1940, at the age of twenty-one, that Richard was married for the first time, to Ruth Burdett-Holcroft.

It was after about three months in St Athan that Richard was moved again to Farnborough and placed in a section which was involved in night fighter radar. He was appalled to find at Farnborough the sluggish way in which everything was done, and the fantastic amount of red tape to be dealt with before anything could make any progress. Having installed radar in night fighters it was essential to explain it to the aircrew, but the senior crew were not prepared to accept 'orders' from a sergeant and of course this kind of attitude, which was common, resulted in a very much poorer performance on the part of the pilot. Richard believed that if the pilots had been chosen from the kind selected for a bomber or a coastal command crew, they would have had greater success, as they would not have ignored the instructions given by their navigator or wireless operator.

In those days there were no transistors, radar sets failed for a number of different reasons, and the pilots were suspicious of the 'black box'. The pilots wanted, and eventually got, a pilot indicator. However, it was found to be difficult to hold the 'blip' of an enemy aircraft in the brightened area, and Richard contributed to solving this problem by putting a little U-shaped dip in the trace. If you got the 'blip' in the middle of this little U, you knew you were spot on, and you could quickly see it moving off in either direction.

Richard became involved with what he felt was a hair-brained scheme called the Turbine Light Havoc programme, the aim of which was to facilitate the shooting down of enemy fighter planes by first using a searchlight to illuminate them. He sent in numerous memoranda pointing out a variety of drawbacks to this scheme, but felt that because he was twenty-three years old the officers were not prepared to listen. Richard's extreme opposition to this turbine searchlight stemmed from his early game-hunting experiences, from which he learned that a game-keeper does not catch a poacher by searching for him in the dark shining an electric torch. However, my friend Gill King's husband Roy has told me that the system was used with success in the Bay of Biscay. As the U-boats surfaced, they found themselves under a shining light, and were depth charged.

When Richard was older he gave his views on whether older men should listen to younger men in their twenties! One of the things that he was proud of was that he always managed to keep an open mind. He was prepared to listen to anybody. The sole criterion was: is this man likely to be right, not how old is he? He would tell of a very good example at his own lawnmower company when the chief engine mechanic died at the age of fifty-eight from a heart attack, and his second in command was a young man not yet in his twenties. The co-directors were dubious about promoting this man to be in charge of the section. "He is too young," they said. But Richard said, "I don't care how old he is, I only want to know how good he is. If he is good enough for the job, give it to him." So they gave the job to him, and he did the job very successfully. (In fact, this man, very many years later, and after Richard and his mother had died, became and is still the Managing Director of the company, bearing out Richard's foresight.)

There was an interesting sequel to Richard's wartime experiences. Many years later, after he had met the Taylor brothers Fred and Ken and cousin Joe, who were all very keen anglers, there was a fishing match arranged between the Westcott Rocket Projectile Research Department and the RAE at Farnborough. Fred was then the chef at Westcott and as they were short of anglers the Farnborough team agreed that they could recruit from outside, and needless to say Fred soon recruited Richard! The match was to be on a little tributary of the Thames, called Whitewater, and when the Farnborough team arrived they were two men short. Richard was soon recognised, and the Farnborough Captain insisted that being a 'Farnborough' man Richard should even things up and make eleven-a-side and fish with them. As Captain of Westcott, Fred had to agree.

Although Fred caught a lot of fish during the match he would have done better if his keepnet had had a smaller mesh, as many of his fish were small gudgeon and they managed to escape. Richard caught many more fish than the others, so it resulted in the match being won by the Farnborough team. Nobody minded because it was a happy day and a good booze-up followed at the pub afterwards. Richard said that it was one of the happiest fishing days of his life, which amused him because he was not by inclination very keen about match fishing (see Chapter 17).

Needless to say Richard's fishing experiences in the war were somewhat limited, but it was possible for occasional trips to be made to the Basingstoke Canal, and Mytchett Lake near Camberley where, using his favourite method of floating crust, he did catch a 14lb carp, and that was in 1943. They tried eating tench caught from this lake, but he said that they were horrible! He vividly remembered one occasion when, while crossing Hartford Flats, with his rod strapped to the cross-bar and with tackle in his saddlebag, he was shot at by a Messerschmitt 109. Somehow, without stopping pedalling, he jumped off and went head first into a ditch. Sparks were striking off the road as he landed and slid along the ditch - but most unfortunately a dog, and it must have been a large one, had been there to do its business first. So he received a stripe from right cheek down to right shoe, and it stank! When he reached the canal he washed all his clothes as best he could and as it was a hot August day they did dry out enough to put them back on later to go back to his digs. But much more washing, and lots of disinfectant, was necessary to get them usable, which was essential in the days of clothes rationing. Richard didn't wish any real harm to the Messerschmitt pilot, but he would have liked to return the favour, and having done that, shake hands with him!

There was once a major incident at Mytchett Lake when, with a friend Frank Hart, Richard was able to save four stupid people who had overturned a punt and couldn't swim. Richard had very strong feelings about fishing in a boat. He would never, ever, fish from a boat in which his boat partner was going to stand up. If a man in a boat with him stood up, he would promptly say, "SI' DOWN!" and if he or she wouldn't sit down, then he would say, "Right, we will go back to shore and I am getting out of this boat." We know from his school swimming achievements, that the issue was not about swimming.

Richard and his colleagues supplemented their rations with various items of wildlife but only once were they caught for poaching. They were driving through Norfolk to Bircham Newton once with Richard's driver, Vic Page, and two pheasants were shot. They had not gone far down the road when out of the ditch, covered with camouflage vines, sprang one PC George Mortar, appropriately named, who stopped them and said, "You will be charged with killing game." Then, having examined the pheasants, he said, "Gor bugger boy you don't miss much do you?"

Vic Page had a firearms certificate and they had with them a 45 revolver and a 22 Remington rifle with a telescopic sight, which Richard had used. When the policeman said he was going to search the van, the revolver was pointed at him, and he was told that he couldn't as it contained secret equipment. The PC had the good sense not to press the point, but he did report them and they were charged with killing game without a licence.

At the magistrates' court they pleaded guilty. The constable gave evidence in the most formal 'out of the notebook' terms. When asked by the Chairman, "Have you anything to say?" Richard said, "No, Sir, except the evidence that the constable gave was not quite exact. He didn't say, 'I have reason to say that you have just shot a pheasant' but, 'Gor bugger boy you don't miss much do you?' " - to which there was 'much laughter in court'. After conferring, the magistrate fined them £1, the usual price for pheasant poaching, but he added that they were to remain at the back of the court until the court rose.

At the end of the session the magistrate, a retired colonel, strode up to them and said, "Now you young devils if you want to shoot my pheasants in future do me the courtesy of asking my permission first, and you may come and shoot two or three whenever you want." They never abused his hospitality, and it did help out the meagre meat ration. This episode gave Richard much amusement. He learned later that they had fallen into a trap not destined for them: some Canadians had been shooting, with everything they had, at anything that moved, and it was them that the Norfolk police were after. It was the only time Richard got caught poaching although he admitted that he had done much poaching through school days, university and right through the war.

On another occasion, Richard recalled narrowly missing a dressing-down for wearing the wrong uniform. Because he worked as a civilian through the war, he had to join the Home Guard, where he rose to the exalted rank, as he put it, of lance-corporal, 27th Battalion, Hampshire. However, when testing the radar in planes overseas, he was given a courtesy rank of wing commander, and on one occasion to get to the Home Guard Parade *on time*, he had no time to change uniform, which could have resulted in a who should salute who scenario!

When the war ended Richard soon applied for permission to leave Farnborough as he had decided to join the family business of Lloyds and Company. He had decided that working in government service was not going to give him the opportunity to use his creative abilities, and he *wanted* to create - he wasn't so much concerned with *what* he created, but he just knew that by nature he was inventive. The move meant starting as a designer and parts order clerk, at a considerably lower salary than he had been enjoying at Farnborough. By 1951 he was Technical Director and by 1955 General Manager as well. Richard's mother remained Chairman and Managing Director until she died in 1990.

Lloyds was first established in 1878 and moved from London to Letchworth, Hertfordshire, in 1916. Until the 1930s it was simply an agency for the importation of American lawnmowers and other horticultural equipment. However, with the financial crisis of 1930-31, which caused increased import duty, the prices of the machines became prohibitive and it was decided by the directors to close the firm down. There was one dissenting voice, that of Richard's mother, who argued that if they could not get the machines from America, then why could they not make them in Letchworth. And that was what they did. The meeting took place on a Friday and by Monday Richard's mother had acquired a very competent Works Manager, her cousin Edwin Halford (whom she later married), who soon put into production British-made equivalents of the American machines with very few modifications. Apart from the factory being given over to munitions during the war, this production line carried on until Richard joined the company and brought in many new ideas.

Glen Bray, the present Chairman of Lloyds, told me the following in March 2006:

> As someone who worked for and with Richard Walker for over twenty years I can say that, without contradiction, he was respected as a fair and honest employer. Richard's attitude was that if you could do the job well, age and length of service did not matter, all he was concerned with was that Lloyds had a good product, and he encouraged those who met his requirements. Conversely if you did not meet his standards he had no hesitation in telling you, but in all his dealings with the staff he was fair. Richard was also noted for his kindness and willingness to help. Anybody who had a problem could talk to him and receive advice. He always made time for the workforce, from the cleaner to the Sales Director.

Dick with his mother Elsie.

Dick night fishing, possibly on the Beane.

Pat's father, R. L. Marston, fishing.

He was a skilled designer and his personality made him an excellent sales-man, something he put to good use at the many demonstrations and field days he attended. It was in the Sixties when his design skill came to the fore. Most Lloyds machines were still as they had been pre-war and Richard led the team that brought the mowers up to date, to meet the new requirements demanded by time and motion experts at many local councils. He also designed the framework for a fifteen-unit gang mower for use at Newmarket racecourse, at the time the largest mower in the world, and as such was included in the *Guinness Book of Records.*

The only downside to Richard's relationship with Lloyds was that as the demands of the fishing world became more and more and took up most of his day, his involvement in the day to day running of the company dimin-ished. This did lead to a small amount of friction between himself and other directors but, through it all, he remained respected by all who came into con-tact with him.

Richard, with his first wife Ruth, settled down in the house that he had lived in with his mother and grandparents in Hitchin, Hertfordshire. They had decided previously that it would be wrong to have children during the war and their first son Richard was born in 1946 (21st July), followed four years later by twins Simon and Tim (7th April, 1950). Richard told me about his chil-dren and said that Richard was the quieter son, and he felt that he had to get young Richard 'going' by turning things into an argument. In contrast the twins apparently got up to all sorts of mischief. Their garden backed on to a football pitch and on one occasion the twins decided to blow up the goalposts. Recently Simon told me that there were many such happenings, but that they were ably assisted by their 'chemist' brother!

At this period, Richard would go on long, and late night, fishing trips, and needed to make up sleep when he got home. The fact that the twins thought it great fun to let off fireworks under their father's window produced a very angry and irate father! It wasn't always easy for him to catch two children, but they certainly knew about it if he did. Discipline was made more difficult, Richard told me, because it was very difficult to tell them apart; it was always the 'other one' that had done this, that, or the other crime! But Simon tells me now, that that's a myth! However, there were compensations because there were times when they would make coffee for their father, "At sixpence a time."

There were always some cats about, and Simon tells me that there were quite a few Siamese ones when his parents were breeding them for sale - Richard had loved cats ever since having one for company as a child. It was at this period that he kept and bred Flemish giant rabbits, for which he told me that he won a 'tremendous' number of prizes and he had a small book published entitled *The Book of the Flemish Giant* under the name Stuart Walker. He had a reason for taking up breeding rabbits. Through the war years, and with the help of the late Dr J. N. Pickard of Cambridge, Richard had been studying the subject of inheritance genetics and how the characteristics of creatures are passed on through the generations, and of course rabbits are very useful for this purpose! The first Flemish Giant stock adults weighed an average of nine pounds, but after close inbreeding for nine generations Richard's rabbits were averaging about fourteen pounds; the biggest, a doe called Laura, reached just over sixteen pounds, and she was a triple-champion. If Laura was placed anywhere on the judges' table, she would promptly hop up to the top position! Richard thought that he was the only man who achieved this championship result, and I think that he was very proud of this.

At the same time Richard was virtually feeding the family with all his own vegetables, and he kept chickens at the top of the garden. But this did take up a lot of time and in due course he realised that he could earn more by returning to writing articles, this time entirely about fishing. He wrote for magazines, some now sadly defunct, including the *Fishing Gazette*, the *Angler's News* and the *Midland Angler*. Later, starting in 1953, he wrote for the *Angling Times*. After some years writing purely for angling magazines and having had some books on fishing published, Richard began writing for other publications like the *Field*, *Shooting Times* and for a time the *Evening Standard* and the *Daily Mail*.

By the end of the war Richard possessed just three fishing rods, two of which were later stolen from Edwin Halford's car in which they had driven to Arlesey Lake, while they were fishing across on the far bank. These were both split-cane rods, one of which was a Wallis Wizard which he had bought from Bill Raison at Farnborough in the earlier years of the war. He was devastated by the loss of these rods because in 1946 the fishing tackle industry - which during the war had been devoted to making various forms of war material - could offer you nothing in the way of replacements.

So, apart from design work with lawnmowers, he was drawn 'willy-nilly', as he put it, into making fishing tackle because rods and reels were just not available. Edwin Halford (later Richard's stepfather), was very skilful with his hands and used to repair violins and he had said, "Look, if Antonio Stradivari can make a violin, surely to goodness you can make yourself a fishing rod." Richard said he commented that it was terribly difficult to plane six strips of bamboo to exactly 60°, let alone knowing where to find the bamboo - but was told, "All right, go and do it!"

Richard wrote to the Managing Director of Allcocks, the late Major

Courtney Williams, stating that he wanted to make fishing rods, not in competition with them, but just to make one or two for his own use and of a sort that they didn't sell, and were not likely ever to sell, namely rods for carp fishing. (It seems ironic that many of Richard's handmade rods - mostly given away by him - now fetch a lot of money!) In the same letter Richard stressed that he would not be using fibreglass as this was not a material suitable for amateur construction, except when making up ready-made blanks.

Now this was a pretty cheeky request from a young man of twenty-six or twenty-seven, but he got a most charming letter back from Courtney Williams telling him that he was despatching to him a dozen excellent bamboo poles, which they had had in store for something like ten years, and that were beautifully seasoned. He wrote, 'Go to it, you can make fishing rods and I am also sending you a little booklet, which was published a good many years ago, but nevertheless is still relevant, which will tell you how to do it.'

To cut a long story short, Richard did it! He found it much easier than he thought it would be, and after a good deal of hand planing and that kind of work, he developed a little machine for milling out the sections of the split-cane rods. How many rods he eventually ended up making he couldn't tell, although he did write in a note one hundred. But there is another aspect of this story. He had always assumed that fishing rods should have a straight taper, that they should get thinner and thinner from the thick end to the thin. Then he began to think, 'Well, Walker, you are supposed to be an engineer and that isn't the way they design a cantilever bridge or lighthouse. They would use a complex compound taper for that, to get the minimum of material for the maximum stiffness.' He realised that he had forgotten a good deal about the theories of structures but had the idea of finding out whether his old tutor in Cambridge might be able to help. Mr H. W. Feare, who was a delightful man, was still at Caius College, Cambridge, and Richard received in reply a nice letter saying, 'Dear Walker, please do come over and see me and we will go into this together.' So they did and Mr Feare, who was also an angler, went through all the calculations that Richard would have to do to work out the proper compound taper. Richard never forgot that Mr Feare had told him that the design of a fishing rod was not just engineering, but also part art. You have got to know what it is you want, and you have got to be a good enough angler to find out - when you have done your calculations, and made your prototypes - whether you have got what you want.

When all the poles that Courtney Williams had kindly sent were used up, Richard got in touch with a new firm which had just started up at Hythe in Kent, called J. B. Walker & Company, run by a very nice man called John Walker (no relation), who could supply not only bamboo but also things like ferrules and rings and whipping silks, corks and so forth. Richard proceeded to make a number of rods and John Walker said, "Will you not write a little booklet that I can send out to my customers telling them how to make fishing rods?" Richard proceeded to write what he thought was a little booklet and sent it to John Walker. The response from John was, "You haven't written a little booklet, you have written a full sized book! We must get this published." And so they did. *Rod Building for Amateurs* was originally published by a firm called Belfield and Bushell in hardback but the firm eventually disappeared, and there was a slight hiatus until sometime in the late 1950s the book was reprinted, by the East Midland Art and Publishing Company, a subsidiary of East Midland Allied Press (the publishers of *Angling Times*).

At about this time there was a considerable upsurge in carp fishing, inspired not a little by the Carp Catchers' Club members who talked of big fish ranging from twenty to fifty pounds. However, the available tackle was not that suitable for such big fish and this gave Richard the impetus to design some. He set about making a suitable rod and in this he was greatly aided by three people: Denys Watkins-Pitchford ('BB'), Peter Thomas and Maurice Ingham - all of whom had had considerable experience of carp fishing. The first three rods were not satisfactory and after trying a double-built split-cane rod, which proved heavier but didn't add much else, they reverted to a single-built taper 10-foot two-piece split-cane rod, which became known as the Mk IV. As is now known, it became successful beyond their wildest expectations.

At first the tackle trade resented the fact that Richard's little book was telling anglers how to make their own rods, but it actually worked in their favour, stimulating a whole new interest in rods amongst the angling public. It became apparent that keen anglers wanted and needed quite a battery of rods, and the firms began to design and sell rods for a variety of purposes. Some of Richard's designs were put into production, the most notable of the firms he worked with being B. James and Son, later called Bruce and Walker. I think Richard felt pleased that the work he did, after losing his rods, benefited angling.

Mention has already been made of Richard being taken fishing by his paternal grandfather and being tethered by a rope, and one of his earliest memories at the age of about four was being left, in this way, to look after his grandfather's leger rod, which had been cast out in the hope of catching an eel. It was an extremely powerful rod with strong tackle, including a big hook baited with three big fat worms. Apparently Richard saw the reel begin to revolve and not knowing about reeling in he clamped down on the reel and ran backwards, and kept running. Out of the water, perforce, came a large trout. The Lea was fished well in those days and a lot of anglers came running and assessed the fish at four pounds. Richard said that he had to push his nose through their legs to look at the fish *he* had caught!

By the time he was sent off to boarding school at ten, his grandfather had taught Richard an enormous amount about fishing. His grandfather used a much wider range of baits than the modern angler, was well versed in every aspect of coarse fishing, and was very successful. He used the stealth of a Red Indian and, as with Richard's other grandfather, shared the view that a fish is a wild creature and if you scare it you are not going to catch it. When Richard was quite little he remembered him saying to him, "Just pretend that the fish has got a gun and if it sees you before you see him, it will shoot you dead."

In 1928, when the family moved to 11 Bearton Avenue, Richard found a nearby pond of a couple of acres in extent, which contained the usual range of still-water fish including carp. Bearton Pond belonged to a Dr Arthur Foster who was a very keen naturalist and an entomologist, and he allowed anyone to fish the pond provided that they had a note from their parents to say that they could swim. If he was satisfied with the note then he would give you a red card entitling you to fish the pond, and this is where Richard fished a great deal. Although Richard did not normally keep a score of the fish he caught, he did at that time and by the outbreak of war he had caught fifty-three carp of over ten pounds, most of them on floating crust. This was quite a feat because at that time if a carp of over eight pounds was caught it was considered a 'notable fish'.

When, in 1931, Hitchin Angling Club was formed Richard joined as a junior member. The club very shortly afterwards managed to get the lease of Arlesey Lake which was quite a large old marl pit with very, very deep water with almost no shallows. At first the anglers could only catch little roach up to about six inches and it was many years later, starting in 1950, when Richard learned to catch the very big perch - a story that has been well documented in his articles and books. But in the early days a Londoner joined the club and he would cast out seven or eight lines baited with small dead fish to catch eels, which he used to take back and sell. Richard, then about twelve years old, asked him how to kill an eel and his verbatim reply was, "Well, my son, first I stamps on 'em with me 'obnailed boots, and then I 'its them on the 'ead with me bleedin' great 'ammer," - and then he took out of his rucksack the sort of hammer that a blacksmith would use for flattening horseshoes! Richard never discovered if he was having his leg pulled! But he did enjoy eating eels and he killed his eels by holding them by the head and cracking their tails against a post, or something like that, which numbs them and that kills them as they have an important nerve centre about three inches up from the tail.

Richard still continued to spend part of his holidays with his father's parents at Hertford and in those days there were some quite marvellous trout streams, second only to the famous rivers Test and Itchen. One was the river Beane and it was a good full flowing river and in addition to roach and dace it contained quite a lot of trout, escapees from stocking further upstream. At first Richard used to catch the trout on worms using coarse fishing methods, but with the rod that his mother had given him, the 8-foot Hardy Casting Club de France split-cane rod (he 'loved his beautiful new rod'), he began to fly fish for them. Richard used this rod for twenty-five years. He had already learned to cast reasonably well using an old greenheart rod that he had found in the attic, and he had got a proper reel, a tapered silk fly line, leaders and flies - which he had learned to tie when he was seven.

It was whilst staying with his paternal grandfather when he was nearly seven that he decided to start fly fishing, and having been an assiduous student of *Hardy's Anglers' Guide* he had seen some flies and so asked his grandfather for sixpence. "What do you want sixpence for?" came the reply, and Richard said that he wanted to buy three flies from Turners Tackle shop. Grandfather told him that 'he didn't want to spend good money on flies, he should make them himself'. When Richard said he didn't know how to, his grandfather said, "Neither do I, but I bet there is a book in the library that will tell us, let's go and find out."

They went off to the library, found a book by McClelland called *Silk, Fur and Feather* and on return they raided Richard's granny's work basket for silks, 'kicked the bejabers out of a pillow' and got all sorts of feathers, then sat down and 'in the crudest possible way' tied some flies. Without hackle pliers, vice or other fly-tyers' usual essential items they made some flies that were good enough to catch fish - dace and an occasional trout - from the river Beane. However, rather more than sixpence was spent in buying eyed hooks on which to tie these flies. This was the start of a lifetime of making flies, and, as we know, Richard introduced many new patterns and published articles and books on the subject.

Being away for more than three-quarters of the year at boarding school meant that Richard could usually only fish in the school holidays. Oddly enough at Saffron Walden with all the children and teachers that were there, he was the only one that was even remotely interested in fishing. There was a formal school walk on Sunday afternoons so he couldn't take a fishing rod on those, but at other times when allowed to go out Richard used to take his little Casting Club de France rod and no one objected to it - although there was a general attitude that anyone who went fishing must be mad because they never caught anything anyway!

There were one or two little ponds within cycling distance of the school where Richard could fish and he caught a number there but of no great size. Another pond where he used to poach was on the Audley End estate, and he caught quite a lot of rudd from there up to about a pound. At yet another very small pond, which was part of a 'marl workings', he used to catch crucian carp of about the same size. There was also the river Cam that ran through Audley End estate and there were some trout in there, a few of which he managed to extract. But while at school there was nothing he could really do if he did catch a fish except put it back, and throughout his life Richard always put back fish that he caught unless it was for food for either his family or his friends.

As already mentioned, Richard's farmer grandfather had taught him all about wildlife, and how to catch things. If you wanted to catch a rabbit, you would note where he goes hopping along, and put a snare one hand high above the ground, between two worn patches. If you wanted a hare, then it would be two hands high. His grandfather also taught him how to set a gate net: that is a net that you put where hares run under a farm gate. Then you go up the field to disturb them, and as hares follow their usual run, they get tangled in the net. Quite a few hares were caught like that and some were even caught on the borders of the Friends' School playing fields, unbeknownst to the teaching staff! For pheasants you would make a conical hat out of brown paper, smear it with treacle, bury it in the ground and then put a trail of sultanas along the ground leading to the 'hat'. Then when the pheasant got the 'hat' stuck on his head, he was easy to catch. (Richard said that he caught rabbits etc. to sell, to augment pocket money.)

While Richard was at the Friends' School, Saffron Walden he wrote his first ever fishing article at the age of about fourteen and it was published in the school magazine *The Avenue*: it was about how he caught a six-pound carp and he said that he stole a good deal of the phraseology from Zane Grey's book *Tales of Fishes,* which was largely devoted to catching fish in the hundreds of pounds. Minor plagiarism was never a thing Richard worried about too much; he wouldn't steal anybody's idea and sell it as his own, or copy verbatim great chunks of text, but he wouldn't hesitate to re-use a good turn of phrase if he saw one for an article or book! Richard A. Wright, in charge of the archives at Friends' School, kindly sent me a copy of the article in 1990, and it is reproduced in Chapter 3.

Now a little more ought to be said about the first fishing article that Richard ever got paid for, which was, according to Richard, in September 1936, after he had decided that there was a possibility of earning rather more money rather more quickly, than washing dishes and taxis in his first term at Cambridge. He wrote an article and submitted it to the *Fishing Gazette*. The Editor was then Mr R. L. Marston, who accepted it and to Richard's surprise

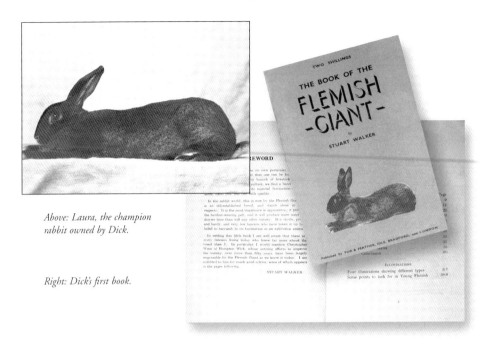

*Above: Laura, the champion
rabbit owned by Dick.*

Right: Dick's first book.

Dick, Peter Thomas and one of the children fishing the river Ivel.

he received a cheque for fifteen shillings (75p; but see Chapter 3). So, inspired by this, he wrote another article. This time it wasn't accepted and consequently Richard didn't get paid for it! What he got was a two-page letter from Mr Marston telling him, in effect, not to write outside his experience. Marston wrote at some length saying that he thought Richard had got a writing style that should be encouraged and he hoped that Richard wouldn't be discouraged by the rejection of this article, which was returned. He also said that Richard had clearly written about what he thought would happen rather than what he knew from experience did happen, and he was not going to publish that kind of article. However, he encouraged Richard to send some more articles, which should be based on his own practical fishing experiences.

Richard took the hint and sold many more articles to the *Fishing Gazette* and the *Anglers' News* under the pseudonym 'Water Rail'. He also wrote for the *Radio Press,* and between 1941 and 1948 about rabbit breeding for *Fur and Feather.* Richard said that he never forgot Marston's advice and he passed it on to many aspiring young angling writers - he said it was the best advice he ever had as far as journalism was concerned. He would also say, "Don't do what Napoleon warned his generals against, that is to say draw pictures of what you think might happen in your mind, and then write or organise things as if those pictures were real, because so many times they are not."

At university Richard had more opportunities to fish than when at boarding school. In the first place, although he had to work in the vacations, he had free evenings, especially in the summer, and most of the weekends. He was still dependent on his bicycle for transport, but it is an interesting reflection upon modern attitudes that in those days people thought nothing of cycling long distances.

During one long vacation he cycled, with another fellow undergraduate from Pembroke College called Donald West, in two stages, from Hitchin to Scarborough in two days. They stayed overnight at a youth hostel at Rossington near Doncaster and then carried on to Scarborough. They then made a tour of England in a week, going up to Scotch Corner, turning left over the Pennines, down through the Lake District, down the Welsh border to Ludlow and then turning east and following, more or less, the Thames valley back to Hitchin. And they did all that in a week! But, of course, the volume of traffic was minimal then and a cycle trip of fifty miles was not considered out of the ordinary. For a brief period Richard joined the Hitchin Nomads and almost became interested in competitive cycling; he told me that he completed a twenty-five-mile time trial out and home in one hour six minutes, which is not bad even by modern standards.

Cycling comparatively long distances opened up many more waters for

Richard and his friends to fish. They tied their rods and landing-nets to the cross-bar and they put most of their tackle and bait in a saddle bag - not in a rucksack - or if they wanted to carry more than that they used a couple of panniers. They could take food for the day and then go perhaps forty or fifty miles, fish all day and then cycle, probably about two hours, back home. At weekends if they were working on Saturday mornings then they would cycle off after lunch, take a tent so that they could fish into the evening, stay the night, and fish the early morning until the bites became few and far between. Then they would pack up and have a leisurely cycle home on Sunday afternoon.

This way Richard did get in quite a lot of fishing, and even in term time he found time to go and fish the Cam. He and a friend used to hire a canoe from one of the boatyards there and paddle upstream until they got beyond the urban areas and they used to catch some quite good fish - chub up to three pounds, pike perhaps up to seven or eight pounds. Many perch of two pounds were caught from Grantchester Mill Pool in those days, and as previously mentioned, the more edible species provided a welcome addition to their diet.

One of the things Richard used to enjoy very much was fly fishing for dace in the Cam. He remembered one occasion when he was cycling along the towpath from Cambridge out to Baitsbite Lock to meet a young lady (whom he subsequently married) on a very, very hot day - it was in the middle of a heatwave - and he spotted a shoal of dace on the surface. They were some of the biggest dace that he had ever seen and he got three in three casts, the three leaders of the shoal. Not having a keepnet, but having a landing-net, he was able to keep them in the net held in the water. This was on the outskirts of Cambridge, and on a little side road nearby there was a sweet shop; Richard was able to take these fish along to the sweet shop and as he put it 'ask the dear lady in the shop to weigh them' for him, which she did on her commercial scales without any complaint at all. He thought she must have had some angling connections! They weighed 1lb 1oz, 1lb 2oz and 1lb 5oz and Richard reckoned that it was the most remarkable catch of big dace that he ever made. The account of this catch is given in his book *No Need To Lie*.

Quite often Richard and his friends used to cycle further out into the Fens and fish the various fen drains, for all sorts of things. They used to spin for pike and leger for bream; they would put set-lines down, which was strictly illegal, to catch eels which provided, if they were big enough, good food.

Richard told me about another aspect of his time at Cambridge. When it became known that he was a fairly capable angler he was soon being invited by undergraduates who had their own cars, to stay and fish with them. He felt sure that it was his fishing ability that they were after, but he didn't mind as on some weekends he was taken to really super waters like the Test and the Itchen, and also Blagdon. Having 'Walker' along they got help with their casting, and if they ran short of flies Richard could tie them some more! But, to be fair to these rich young friends, it gave Richard quite a lot of fishing including experience of dry-fly fishing in the chalkstreams, where nymphs were considered strictly *infra dig*. The modern idea that the multi-hook lure is a new invention and only came in with the opening of Grafham Water is total nonsense because they were using these quite enormous flies at Blagdon right back in the 1930s and before.

During the war Richard managed to get home on leave for brief periods and at that time the Hertfordshire trout streams were still in good order, so he was able to keep his fairly short-range, very accurate fly casting in trim. Richard used to fish the rivers in the Hitchin area, sometimes with permission and sometimes by poaching, and this was possible because during the war the keepers were pretty thin on the ground. Then there were the Lea tributaries: the Beane, the Mimram, the Gade, the Ver and the Rib all of which were then excellent trout streams. It was not unusual to catch a trout of four pounds from them. The biggest that he ever caught from any of those rivers was from the Beane, on a bend in the river quite close to Hertford North Station, an area known as Seale Deeps. It was a brown trout of 5³/₄lb, and it was caught in the most gentlemanly way on a floating mayfly. Seale Deeps also contained at that time some excellent roach and dace, and on two occasions in the 1960s Richard caught a dace of over a pound and a roach of over two pounds in the same evening.

Perhaps this is the time to mention Richard's relationship with Peter Thomas, because although he had many other friends whom he loved dearly, Pete was the first of them. Pete's elder brother Stan was four or five years older than Richard and when he was a little boy Stan constituted himself as 'protector' and as the years went by Richard moved into that role in respect of 'little' Pete, who was a few years younger. This was in the early 1930s and except for the war years they fished together all Richard's life and Richard considered Pete as probably the best all-round angler he had ever known. Peter was a true and steadfast friend to Richard, he visited every weekend through Richard's illness, and I always thought of Pete as a brother.

Richard told me that he thought it was very curious when, in 1946, he was walking down the Arcade in Hitchin and it just so happened that coming the other way was his old friend Pete Thomas, whom he hadn't seen for the five years of war. They got together and from that time on did a lot of fishing together. Richard couldn't afford a car but Pete then had a J2 MG sports car. He also had a Royal Enfield 250 and later a Triumph Speed Twin motorbike and they used to go out fishing with either Richard sitting on the pillion of his motorbike or sitting in the passenger seat of his car. They went to various places within a range of about sixty or seventy miles, so they fished here, there and everywhere, sometimes with permission and sometimes without, and they caught quite a lot of what by any standards were good fish - not record fish but good fish.

Later on, when Pete's son Paul was born, Pete needed to have a more suitable vehicle and he bought a very beat-up pre-war Ford 10 de luxe. Then they used to go fishing together in that. It had a top speed, if you didn't mind it boiling, of forty-five miles an hour and it would cruise quite happily at thirty-eight miles an hour!

It was not very long after the war, when fishing with Pete Thomas and another friend Ken Richmond, that they discovered - under a culvert at West Mill at Ickleford, where Richard's grandfather used to farm - an exceptionally large trout. There were no holds barred when you found a trout of that size and Richard chucked a worm up under the culvert, hooked the trout and then they discovered that although they had brought the landing-net, they had for-gotten the handle! Pete jumped down from the culvert into the river up to his waist and attempted to net the fish but it eluded him and broke, shooting up under the culvert. Ken Richmond was leaning over the culvert watching all this. Having collected their wits, one of them suggested that if they wanted to catch this trout they had better give it a rest.

Now this was on a Saturday and they swore a solemn pact that none of them would try to catch the fish until the following Saturday. They all shook hands on it, so you can imagine Richard's anger and annoyance with these two chaps when he went down on Friday evening to find both of them hanging over the culvert with worms cast up underneath. He said, "You rotten lot of so-an-so's, we all shook hands on this, we all agreed we wouldn't fish for this trout. But," he added, "you are wasting your time because I came up yesterday evening and I caught it, and it is in my fridge now, and it weighs 4lb 2oz!"

You can't trust anybody, can you?

Around this time a number of rather odd things happened. One of them was that Richard was given a book called *The Fisherman's Bedside Book* by 'BB', Denys Watkins-Pitchford, and in this book 'BB' expresses particular interest in carp and reveals his ambition to catch one over ten pounds. Of course, Richard and Pete knew a thing or two about carp, Pete having caught his first big carp at the age of fourteen and, by an odd coincidence, it had weighed exactly 14lb! So Richard wrote and invited Denys to stay for a week, with the promise that he would catch a carp of over ten pounds. This would have been about 1946, when Richard was twenty-eight, when by the standards at that time a fish of over ten pounds would be a very big carp indeed. At that time Richard's biggest carp was 16lb 5oz which was another coincidence because he had been brought up on H. T. Sheringham's book *Coarse Fishing*, and *his* biggest carp was also 16lb 5oz.

Denys went to stay and Richard found it rather amusing because Denys was one of those fellows who was brought up to believe that real men don't like cats, only dogs, and yet he ended up sitting in a deckchair on their lawn with one of the Siamese cats on his lap purring like mad. He was stroking the cat and it was sort of pushing its nose into his hand so Richard said, "Well for a man who doesn't like cats you are not doing a bad job of making friends with ours, are you?" He just had to laugh! And, of course, as we all know from his writings 'BB' quite clearly liked all animals.

They went and fished Richard's then favourite method of margin fishing with floating crust at Bearton Pond and Denys caught five carp, one of which was just over the magical figure, 10lb 2oz, and so he went away very happily. He had met Pete while he was staying with Richard, and sometime later he wrote and suggested that they form a club for those people who were particularly interested in carp. Richard wrote back and said that he thought it would be an excellent idea, why not call it 'The Carp Fishers' Club'. Denys replied, 'No, we are going to call it "The Carp Catchers' Club". We catch carp: we don't just fish for them!' So the Carp Catchers' Club was formed and they kept their eyes and ears open for people who were perhaps more able than the average to contribute something towards the techniques, the methods and the tackle for catching carp; the club eventually grew to a strictly limited membership of twelve.

At about this time, fishing the lake at Hexton Manor, Richard and Pete caught a number of carp of quite modest size up to seven or eight pounds. But they saw some very much bigger ones, which they subsequently caught when they realised that the best chance of catching them was between the fading light of evening and sunrise the next morning. This is what led them to try out electric bite-alarms.

Also at that time, Bernard Venables was on the staff, first of the *Daily Express* and later of the *Daily Mirror*. He had begun there with an illustrated strip, being a fine artist, dealing with Mr Crabtree and gardening, but later it changed to the fishing cartoon strip 'Mr Crabtree Goes Fishing', which became very popular. The *Daily Mirror* had an enormous circulation, and the effect of this cartoon strip, plus news of what had been caught up and down the country, helped increase the number of anglers in Britain by leaps and bounds. Richard considered that the tackle trade owed a tremendous debt of gratitude to Bernard Venables. He felt that 'Crabtree' must have multiplied their sales enormously, and the effect still lingers on. Angling is now of course by far the greatest participant sport in the country, which means that the amount of value added tax taken by the government is immense, but unfortunately it gives very little back in the way of subsidies compared to other sports (see Chapter 16).

Coming back to Bernard Venables, in about 1949 he instituted a club contest for big fish - not for match fishing, but for big fish - and any club that wished to enter was given a form in which they could enter up to about twelve fish each of a number of species, for which points would be awarded. Richard and Pete Thomas thought 'well, we catch some pretty big fish, let's have a go at this'. They were both members of the Hitchin Angling Club; Richard spent some time as its chairman and Pete as its treasurer, and they went to various places on the club coach. They were quite honestly amazed at how easily satisfied their fellow members were with fish that they caught: it was quite an event if someone caught a fish as big as a pound and a half!

Richard and Pete conferred together and Richard said, "Look if this is the average standard of club fishing, we ought to be able to do something with this *Daily Mirror* Club Contest." So they recruited one or two other people in the club who they thought might be capable of catching some bigger fish, people like Bob Rutland and Trevor Lockhart, and Richard did an analysis of the last five or six years of the old *Anglers' News* magazines which used to issue an annual Notable Fish List, and from this he was able to decide just how big a fish they would have to catch in each species to stand a chance of scoring points in this contest.

Richard also realised that there was no point in spending all their time catching roach; they had got to catch a number of different species so as to fill in each column in the entry form. He and Pete organised this and when they thought they had caught enough roach to score a fair number of points for that species, then they went rudd fishing. When they had caught enough rudd, they went perch fishing and so on. Now around this time they were beginning to come to grips with the big perch in Arlesey Lake and they had learned a few things about catching carp over ten pounds. To cut the story short, they submitted their entry and to everyone's surprise, including theirs, they won the *Daily Mirror* Club Contest by the enormous margin of 464 points to the runners-up who scored 97.

It is well worth repeating the lesson they learned from this, and the lesson that Richard tried to pass on ever after: 'If you want to catch big fish you have got to go out to catch big fish. You don't just fish for anything that comes along and hope that sometime you will catch a big one.'

As Richard and Pete were also members of the Shefford Angling Club they decided to enter on behalf of that club too, and went to an enormous amount of trouble. On that occasion they did not win because, most unfortunately, the Secretary omitted to send in the form! They learned afterwards from Bernard Venables that they would, otherwise, have won, and by an even larger margin. This was at the beginning of what later came to be called Specimen Hunting - that is to say going out to try and catch a fish of what most anglers would regard as specimen size; what the Victorians would call 'a glass case specimen , a fish big enough to have set up and put in a glass case as a trophy. Richard always thought it a shame that the art of fish stuffing went into decline, but there were now 35mm cameras which were easy to use, portable, and produced good photographs that could be framed to display the 'trophy' catch. Having said that, however, my neighbour Keith Smith has a model of a fine barbel of 15lb 1oz in a bow-fronted glass case, so perhaps they are now coming back into vogue. Incidentally, Keith told me that he was recently in a tackle shop when Dick Walker's name came up, and a teenager in the shop exclaimed, "He's the Pele of angling!" - I was pleased to know that youngsters are being told about his methods.

Photography was a great interest of Richard's, encouraged and helped by Edwin Halford who was a member of the Royal Photographic Society. Richard had taken the subject very seriously, at one time attending meetings of the London Camera Club. He made excellent studies of cats and dogs, as well as fish and water scenes, and the photograph he took of an otter he deemed the best picture that he ever took. Photography was to become increasingly important to him because Bernard Venables, together with some other members of the *Daily Mirror* staff, including Ken Sutton, Tiny Bennett, Stan Worker and some others, had contracted with East Midland Allied Press at Peterborough to bring out a new and quite different angling publication called *Angling Times*. This was to have a newspaper format instead of a magazine format and was to be printed when their presses were idle.

They chose as their Editor Colin Willock who was known to most people as the television producer who produced the 'Survival' series for Anglia Television, and who wrote a good deal in the sporting press. (Richard told me that he was an extremely nice man.) Colin went to Richard's house and asked, "Will you do us a regular column for this new paper that we are going to start called the *Angling Times*? We will pay you £10 per week." This was quite a lot of money in those days and considerably more than the £3 or £4 a week Richard had been getting from the then popular fishing magazines. So he said yes. It was July 1953 when the very first *Angling Times* came out, and Richard wrote for it each week for thirty years - except for one issue when, as Richard put it, 'My wife Pat said that she would like to let the readers know how I was progressing after the first battle with the cancer that I got in 1981.' Bernard Venables was appointed Editorial Director, Colin Willock Editor, Ken Sutton General Manager and Tiny Bennett (who was 6 foot 9 inches and 19 stone) was the Staff Photographer. The *Angling Times* were to use very many of Richard's photographs in the paper's double-page feature spreads.

Mention has already been made of the Carp Catchers' Club and one of its twelve members was Bob Richards, who, in October 1951 discovered a lake called Bernithan Pool, near Ross on Wye (re-named 'Redmire Pool' by Denys Watkins-Pitchford) and caught a 31lb 4oz carp - a new record which won him the *Daily Mirror* individual prize. Bernard Venables knew of Richard's ability in fish taxidermy and asked him to set this fish up, so it was duly sent to Richard. However, it had lain in Bob's coal-hole for a while and arrived in a somewhat odoriferous state! Richard commented, "I don't know how many cigarettes I smoked at the time while I was 'taxiderming' this fish, but eventually Pete and I got it stuffed and put in a glass case and then it was sent to Bob Richards. He took one look at it and said, 'There is no room in my house for this'. This was a pretty big fish in a pretty big case, so it was eventually presented to Hereford Museum. What happened to it after that I really don't know."

Richard made a rod for Bob that would be more suitable for these big carp and he and Pete gave Bob a reel as well. In return for this generosity, when the closure of Redmire to anglers was threatened, Bob persuaded the new tenant owner to give Peter and Richard a day's fishing. This was duly arranged and on 17th June, 1952, Pete caught a carp of 28lb 10oz, the second biggest carp at that time. The owner, Colonel J. F. Maclean, went down to the water where they were fishing and, according to Richard, asked them a great number of questions. He said, "Colonel Maclean was chairman of the local magistrates and he put us through a most rigorous cross-examination about our attitude towards the countryside, towards fishing, towards game, towards wild fowl and after we had answered all his questions and shown him the fish he went off."

That night, just as they were preparing to drive home and had reached the exit gate, they heard an extremely loud cry and saw the Colonel running across the field. When he reached the car the Colonel said, "Look here you fellows, you've been telling me about your friends who are members of this Carp Catchers' Club which I understand has twelve members. Now I am extremely satisfied with the answers I got to my questions, I am extremely pleased with the way you have behaved while you were here and I think it would be most unsportsmanlike of me to prevent you from continuing to try and catch these very big carp from this lake. You may tell your fellow members that if they wish to fish here, they can write and ask me for permission and they may come not more than two on any one day." They fished on for many years and as the Colonel found that the estate was treated with respect, in due course the number of people was increased to four on any one day. The story of Richard's 44lb fish, Clarissa, has been told many times and aspects are considered again in Chapters 8 and 10.

Richard had started writing *Still-Water Angling* in 1950 and like many other would-be authors he was adding to it, correcting it, crossing bits out, and putting bits in, until one day when he got home his first wife said, "Oh, a very nice gentleman has been here, James MacGibbon. He is one of the directors of MacGibbon and Kee the publishers and he said that he had come to collect the manuscript of your book *Still-Water Angling*. He told me that Bernard Venables had advised him to come along and get it, and I gave it to him." Subsequently, Richard received a phone call from James MacGibbon: "I hope you don't mind," he said, "but if I had left you to yourself this book never would have been published, because you go on learning all your life and you never would have been satisfied with the book. But Bernard Venables, who you may remember had a chance to read your original manuscript, has told me to come along and steal the thing and publish it. And publish it I am going to do if we agree about terms."

They did agree the terms and of course the book was duly published and ran to a fourth edition, which included a chapter on zander or pike-perch by Barrie Rickards. James MacGibbon became a personal friend, and Richard considered him a thoroughly honest publisher. *Still-Water Angling* had an impact far beyond anything Richard could have imagined, and the message of the book was clear - if you want big fish you should go out and try to catch big fish on purpose. It was a message that Richard felt strongly about, as we've seen (described fully in Chapter 11), but he was always adamant that his 'fifth essential' relating to bait was of the least importance - his experience showed that fish, including big fish, will take an astonishingly wide variety of baits.

When the question of a fourth edition was raised Richard asked me what I thought (I had been for several years Editor of the *Fishing Gazette*). I said, "There are a lot of people who will want *Still-Water Angling* kept as it was originally written," but Richard replied, "An awful lot of it is out of date now, I mean people no longer use split-cane rods, and lines have changed and so forth." I said, "Well, in that case I think it would be very much better if instead of re-writing the whole thing, you added notes to the ends of each chapter explaining how things have changed," - and that is what he did, and events have shown that this was the proper course, as the book sold better than ever. Richard told me that he had asked one or two other people like Pete

Thomas, Fred Taylor and Fred Buller what they thought about the idea, and they had all said, "Yes, Pat is quite right, that is the way you should do it."

It was when Richard was first writing his book that he wrote an article which was published in the *Fishing Gazette* about carp fishing in which he had said that there was no rod available commercially that was really suitable for carp, and that he had had to build his own. About a week later he got a letter addressed to him through the *Fishing Gazette* from a man called Maurice Ingham who lived at Louth in North Lincolnshire, and it was a charming letter; the basis was 'will you tell me about this rod that you have built for carp fishing because I too am interested in carp fishing, and there is a lake not far from where I live where there are some big carp, and I would like to set about catching them.'

From this letter stemmed a correspondence that went on for some eighteen months or two years; it covered almost everything you can think of that would interest a freshwater angler. One day when Bernard Venables was visiting Richard they talked about the possibility of this correspondence making a book. So Richard wrote and asked Maurice if he still had his letters and he replied saying that he had every single one of them. When Richard told Bernard this Bernard said, "You should put these into a book, it would be fascinating." Richard was a bit dubious about this, but at any rate, to cut the long story short, they were put into a book which was published by MacGibbon & Kee, by our old friend James MacGibbon, under the title which my mother-in-law invented of *Drop Me A Line*.

Richard did not know how many copies of the first edition were sold, but he thought it was not a vast number. However, there was a curious thing about this book because Richard found that those who had read it, and liked it, were among the nicest anglers he had ever met. He felt that this was because there was a special quality to his relationship with Maurice which came through in the atmosphere of the book. He thought it was appreciated by the kind of angler who is cooperative rather than competitive, and who likes to feel that anything he discovers that might help others enjoy their fishing more ought to be passed on and not kept a secret.

That was Richard's philosophy, and Maurice Ingham's, and Richard felt it was a philosophy also shared by all his other dearest friends. He said that it should never be forgotten that fishing is for pleasure, and, as Fred Taylor wisely said, "If you aren't enjoying it, pack up and go home!"

In 1964 a second edition of *Drop Me A Line* was published, for which Fred J. Taylor wrote the Introduction. In 1989, after Richard's death, a third edition was published, prepared for publication by Maurice Ingham, who wrote a new Preface, and myself. I had not read the book before and found it a fascinating, stimulating read. The two men were so alive to their subject and extremely keen. They started, as was done in those days, by using 'Mr Ingham' and 'Mr Walker', and it was a considerable time before it became 'Maurice' and 'Richard', and later again before Maurice used 'Dick'. Maurice and I were both very disappointed with this third edition: the paper was poor, and there were no pictures - despite the fact that I had sent sixteen photographs to the publisher, giving plenty to choose from. I had also specifically asked for full-page frontispiece pictures of the two authors.

Most of this chapter so far has been culled from the tapes that Richard prepared for me before his death. What follows next is my personal account of our life together.

* * *

Although my husband had been writing articles for my father R. L. Marston's angling paper the *Fishing Gazette* since he was at university, we would have been unlikely to have ever met but for my father being taken ill with cancer. It had not been my plan to work for the 'family business', but when my father asked me, the decision was, of course, made for me. After my father died in 1957 I decided to carry on the business, endeavouring to keep the magazine going, as, although there were still some other angling papers, the 'new' *Angling Times* could not be allowed to become a monopoly. The following spring there was to be a big fishing exhibition at the Alexandra Palace, in north London, and I decided to take part to show that we were very much still alive. The stand was manned by members of the *Fishing Gazette* staff during the day and I would go up in the evenings. One Thursday evening I arrived with a parcel of 'just off the press' issues of the paper and as I swept by to the little office, I saw a man sitting at the back of the stand, noticing particularly his butterscotch-coloured eyes. I was told by one of the girls that it was Mr Richard Walker who having been told that I was due to arrive, apparently intended staying there till I did arrive. So I went out and introduced myself.

Over the next few years Richard Walker did his best to support the *Fishing Gazette* by writing numerous articles and sending in masses of photographs. He also worked hard to encourage other successful anglers to send in articles for consideration. One of the years that the Boat Show incorporated a Fishermens' Row, I decided to take a stand, and Richard visited with Peter Thomas. His presence, and Peter's, was helpful in encouraging anglers to visit us and there was much animated talk about all sorts of fishing matters. Other fishermen visited and helped, including Gerry Berth-Jones and John Nixon.

In 1959 I took a pitch at the Game Fair held near Basingstoke, in

Dick, Fred Taylor and Pete Thomas. A very early bivvy?

The Fishing Gazette *stand at the CLA Game Fair, Castle Howard 1960. The Editor, Pat Marston (centre) is talking to Mrs Lionel Sweet.*

Hampshire, and Richard Walker came and set up a tea making kit, kindly supplying our visitors. It was at this Game Fair that he entered the fly casting competition being judged by Lt. Col. Esmond Drury, and he came first - but he let the lady who came second have the prize of a fishing rod as he had his eye on the small silver dish presented by the *Fishing Gazette*. Little did I know that this dish would end up sitting on a small table in my house!

At about this time Richard invited me to fish with him and his friends at a few different waters, introducing me to the art of coarse fishing. I remember one occasion on the river Kennet, on a very hot day, walking up the river in search of fish with Richard and Fred J.Taylor; Fred had the bait but when we needed it there was none left - Fred had consumed the quite large piece of blue cheese that was our bait. And it was a very hot day!

Another time I was to use a lobworm, but I had not bargained for the strength with which they wriggle. Not to be beaten, I took myself off behind one of the cars and with great determination managed to get that worm on the hook, much to the amusement of Richard and the others in the group. I preferred fishing with a piece of cheese or sweetcorn, and I didn't even like using maggots - I guess it was being used to fishing for trout with dry flies that did not twitch.

On one occasion when I was fishing for barbel on the river Avon under Lt. Colonel Stanley Crow's supervision, Richard returned to find out how I was doing and I showed him a barbel of about one pound. "I didn't know they grew so small," he said. Oh!

Mention of Stanley reminds me of fishing at Two Lakes, the water that Alex Behrendt made. Richard used to fish there and once remarked to Stanley that he had left his bag at one of the 'fishing stations'. Stanley replied with great dryness, "Well if you hadn't, there soon would have been another old bag fishing there." He was very naughtily referring to one of the heavily waterproofed lady members! On another occasion we were fishing together when Richard got out some of the mixture he made for degreasing the line (it's one I still use - Fairy Liquid and Fuller's Earth mixed to a smooth firm paste). It did look a bit like the large piles left around by Alex's alsatians, and when Stanley enquired what he was using, Richard pointed to one of the lumps on the ground. Stanley said, "Oh, if the needs must," but was stopped from bending down any further. After that the mixture has always been referred to as 'DDS' (Dirty Dog Shit!).

It was in 1991 that I asked Alex Behrendt for his memories of Richard, and he told me that one morning among the letters he received was one from Richard Walker. Like many anglers he had read his books, and also many of the articles which had appeared in the angling press. Alex was curious as to why such a famous angling personality should write to him, but discovered that Richard wanted to know if he could bring a handicapped boy to fish at Two Lakes. Later Alex found out that Richard gave a lot of time to helping these less fortunate children, but also liked to encourage all youngsters.

Alex was to see Richard quite often at Two Lakes, and was even involved in one television programme. They both shared, as Alex said, 'this overwhelming love of all kinds of angling', so they became friends. Alex continued, "I found that Dick was usually a placid man and very rarely showed a temper, which description also applies to myself. However, over the years we had a few heated arguments about different aspects of angling, but we always made it up and remained friends, until on one occasion we rather overdid it, and as we parted the atmosphere was very cool. We just did not want to see the other's point of view!"

At a later date Alex's book *The Management of Angling Waters* was published and reviews began to appear. Alex told me that he was certain Richard would be asked to review it, and when one was published it was, "With great uneasiness I started to read, and it was to my amazement he had reviewed the book on its merits, concluding with the words: 'It is a pity that Alex did not write this book many years earlier, as it would have saved many angling clubs a lot of money'. My apprehension had been unfounded as was shown by Dick's fair-minded review, which was typical of him and showed that anything connected with his beloved angling was dealt with honestly; this was no place for personal bickering or feelings of animosity. Dick wasn't only a great angler - he was a great man. Anglers the world over felt his loss, and I agree with many other anglers who say that he had few equals."

I also fished at Two Lakes, and was very saddened to learn recently from Brian Clarke that the Lakes are no more. The fishery was very beautiful when I was last there.

It was with Peter Thomas that we went together to fish the Darwell Reservoir near to Hastings, and it was there that Richard discovered a new fly. He took photographs of it and in due course it was named *Siphlonurus armatus*, of the Ephemeridae. It is about the size of a crane fly, and has a bright green body and Richard said later, "I have never seen it on any water other than Darwell, and I never saw a trout eat it or its nymph there, nor have I found it in stomach contents."

As is well known, Peter was a very dear friend of Richard's and he often shared a boat, fishing with us not only at Darwell Reservoir but at Hanningfield, Grafham and Roxton. Roxton is a fifteen-acre lake, man-made by the Bath farmers who own the land, and you could fish there as a season member. Richard once received a call from Simon Bath because the members were complaining that there were no fish in the water, so he wondered if Richard would be kind enough to come and fish to see what he thought. Richard tucked himself in to a small run between the bank and one of the islands, and did catch some trout, so Simon was able to pass the information on to the members. As the water was not too far to travel we did become members ourselves.

When sharing boats it is quite amazing how anglers manage to avoid clashes, and with us there were very few mishaps. As soon as one of us hooked a fish, the others would immediately reel in until the fish was netted. I remember the very first Grafham trout that I caught: it tore off so much line that I was well into the backing, and when a fish leapt out of the water a long way out and Richard assured me that it was mine, I couldn't believe it. But it was, and it was duly landed. Richard told me that it was at Grafham in 1968 that he was, almost certainly, the first angler to catch a trout on a carbon-fibre rod.

Despite all the help that anglers gave to the *Fishing Gazette* (and I had also started a news format paper called the *Sea Angler*, which did quite well) we were not getting quite enough readers to be a viable concern. Although I had talks with the *Angling Times* directors, I was approached by my cousin, and finally the company was sold to him. It was a sad day for me, especially as the company eventually failed. I then worked for a publishing company for a period before joining the Nestlé Company Limited.

In due course the reason that I left Nestlé was because Richard had asked me to marry him and of course this meant that we could fish together far more often. We lived in Flitwick, Bedfordshire, and after three years our son Robert was born, named after my father R. L. Marston and 'RBM', his great-grand-father. Robert made his first fishing trip when he was six months old - to Broadlands where Richard had a rod on the carrier of the river Test, running through the estate. We were very fortunate to have help from Margery Russell, the late Pat Russell's wife, who very many times looked after Robert, enabling Richard and I to go fishing. As Robert grew up, Margery's daughter, Jean Russell, used to keep him amused by drawing for him, mainly horses - her particular love.

Now I think that I should include some details about the carrier. It was in 1964 that Bernard Aldrich was given permission to fulfil one of his dreams, which was to build a trout stream to his own design. There was an old water-meadow carrier, much of it filled in and very overgrown, which Bernard thought could be dug out and widened to make about a two and a half mile stream. However his plans were frustrated with regard to the amount of land he could have with the result that the planned 'river' became a stream, narrow with high banks, and Bernard wondered who would ever want to fish it. Then, Bernard told me, "Soon after opening, came news that the famous Richard Walker was coming to fish my carrier, and I awaited his arrival with some trepidation, looking forward to his opinion of it."

I asked Bernard to tell me about this meeting and this is what he recalled: "Richard was a big man, a very gentle giant, wearing his hallmark wide-brimmed bush hat and he set off to fish with me trailing along behind. I learned so much just watching him as he stalked the fish. He moved quietly, unhurriedly, but keeping low to avoid his shadow preceding him, watching and marking his fish, casting with great skill dropping the fly delicately in front of his quarry, invariably hooking, playing and landing the fish.

"He was as expert with the nymph as he was with the dry fly, adapting his technique to the prevailing conditions, his casting was a joy to watch and he was always willing to give up some precious time to discuss methods of fishing, or to help anyone, giving freely of his great knowledge of the sport and river-craft. I once told him that he seemed to think like a fish and was convinced he had been a fish in a previous life; he laughed and thought it was a nice idea."

Bernard was glad that Richard had happily enjoyed his trout stream and that he had fished it for many years, and he felt fortunate and privileged to have been a friend. He thought that the fishing world had lost a fine ambassador and added that he is greatly missed.

Pat Russell used to organise various fishing days for us including Mead Mill and Bossington on the Test and would also meet us on still waters local to him. We would meet at Damerham, which was at that time the water newly developed by Colin Harms, not so far from Fordingbridge where we used to stay at the Albany Hotel. On one stay at the hotel Richard decided to fish the river by the hotel car park, hooked a fish which somehow got itself caught up with something, and Richard landed a 'silver' toast rack - he was so tickled with his catch that he had it restored to pristine condition and we have it in the house.

Jim Hardy, of the House of Hardy, was the person who brought Richard and John Jacobs together. They had many discussions on fishing and on the methods John used in his teaching of golf, which might be of help in the teaching of fly casting. John Jacobs had moved with his family to Emery Down in Hampshire from Middlesex to be nearer good fishing. We stayed with them and I think John was anxious to be off fishing early in the morning and was surprised that Richard was in no hurry. I think that they fished the Parlour Pool at Christchurch, but there was another little lake, Leominstead, not far from John's home where I joined them. I do remember feeling uneasy fishing there from rather wobbly platforms jutting out in to the water. Later when we visited with Robert, Rita, John's wife, very kindly baby-sat for us, enabling us to go fishing. (Sadly Rita died in 2006.)

John told me, "Dick was great to fish with - always directing you the right way without ever telling you exactly what to do. In spite of his own expertise he was very quick to pull his own leg if anything did not work quite according to plan. I am sure there would be some who would find Dick somewhat overbearing and possibly not a very good listener. For me personally the breadth of his knowledge coupled with his tremendous contribution to all aspects of angling, made it very easy for me to forgive him any shortcomings in that direction. I am so grateful for having had the opportunity to actually fish with him. He always seemed to have the schoolboys' love and enthusiasm for the sport, which expressed itself not only in his own success but also in a delight in helping others. Hopefully just a little of his logical approach rubbed off. On difficult days I often find myself saying, 'now what would Dick try next and why?' "

We did, in fact, stay in Emery Down on another occasion, when we rented a cottage for a week, and with the help of a friend, Joyce, who looked after Robert, we fished the carrier of the river Test at Broadlands, Avington Lakes and other waters. Richard would remember all the fish we caught, their weights, and not only what fly he caught his fish on, but mine as well. It is a shame that I did not keep a diary, but I always thought there was no need as Richard had such a phenomenal memory.

When the Russells were away in Ireland they kindly let us stay in their house, and, again, Joyce came with us and therefore when we fished at Avington we did not need to take Robert with us. Richard had long discussions about genetics with Sam Holland, who was bringing on some very large trout. On other occasions Babs Holland had very kindly let us take Robert in to their bungalow, and she would provide me with welcome mugs of coffee. On one visit - it was hot weather, I remember - I had walked up to the top lake looking in the water for signs of trout. I stood by one large bush and waited. In time I saw a good sized fish swim through the water and a little while later he swam through again. In due course I hooked this fish and eventually netted it, as, at Avington, you used to have to net your own fish (I don't know whether that's still the case). It wasn't an easy task as it turned out to weigh 9lb 8oz. I did fish on, though, and caught three other fish to make up my limit - 3- and 4-pounders.

Another of Richard's friends, the late Peter Stone, in his book *Fishing For Big Chub* mentioned that after Richard landed a double-figure trout at Avington, Alan Pearson who had been watching him playing the fish said, "Do you know, my cock - you're shaking." To which Richard replied, "When the day comes when a big fish does not cause me to shake I'll pack up." It was one of many large fish that Richard caught at Avington, including one of 18lb 4oz which held the record for a short time.

Mention of Alan Pearson takes me back to our visit to Church Hill Farm Trout Fishery at Mursley. Alan had a lot to do with the beginnings of the fishery and we were invited over to meet Tim and Don, the most welcoming of owners. Whilst Alan took Robert, now about two and a half, on his shoulders, to see the lions and tigers in the back fields, we enjoyed some fishing with the other visitors on the opening day. There was a very nice fishing lodge with food organised for us and I caught a ten-pound trout to complete the day (of course, Richard caught fish too, but mine was bigger than his that day!) On another visit to the fishery Tim's sister was there and when Richard came in with his bag of fish she quoted a most apt piece of Shakespeare; Richard answered appropriately, and they continued quoting Shakespeare to each other for quite a while as we all listened and enjoyed the performance.

On one of our visits to Hampshire we paid a visit to the late Dermot Wilson and Rene Wilson's home and shop at Netherwallop, as he had invited us to fish his very large pond. Richard caught two trout and I do remember the weights as they were both, although slightly different shapes, exactly 7lb 2oz each.

I had a talk recently with Peter Thomas about Richard and salmon fishing, as I had found a picture in a copy of *Country Fair*'s April 1958 issue showing Richard with a twenty-pound fish. Pete thought that, as I understood, Richard preferred to fish for 'the more wily' trout, and that was the reason that he did not often take up the various invitations that he received to go salmon fishing.

Richard's involvement with BBC television included a number of outings, with George Cansdale, McDonald Hastings, Fyffe Robertson and Jack Hargreaves. One assignment with Trevor Philpott was filming on the Great Ouse at Beachampton where in 1961 he and the Taylor Brothers Ken and Den and others had built a hut, big enough for sleeping and cooking and therefore suitable for staying several days at a time. Ian Howcroft told me about the hut: "Dick was not a man to take chances, and so, before any construction began, he had some good solid concrete stilts, about two feet high, poured on site, thus ensuring that water was never going to get anywhere near the front door." He also commented on the fact that not being able to use electricity he thought, "Dick quite enjoyed watching the workers using saws, hammers, chisels and so on, while he gave instructions and advice," - good naturedly ignored! Ian said, "Dick was not a man who enjoyed physical exertion for the sake of it," and I would concur with that. Unless there were fish at the end, walking was not considered. Except for one occasion when we were out walking, on a country lane, in winter weather, and Richard said, "If my friends could see me now, they wouldn't believe it!"

The BBC2's Trevor Philpott and his crew arrived at the water to film Richard and Peter fishing for chub, and as usually happened for Richard, when needed for such occasions, he caught a fish for them. (I supplied food for the lunch break.)

One of the reasons that we went to live at Flitwick was because the house was by the river Flit, although Richard did not fish it. No longer was it the river that it used to be in Richard's earlier days when it held large shoals of big roach and dace, good chub and perch, and occasional trout. It had become dirty, with few fish, at that time, due to sewage from Ampthill and Luton.

Our neighbour, the late David Myers, was intrigued when Richard tried out new rods on the lawn, and it was not long before he was asking if he could watch Richard tying flies. Richard always had his fly-tying equipment set up and would take any few spare moments to sit down and tie a fly. He liked to have plenty because if he was asked, "What fly are you catching your fish on?" he would like to give three to the angler saying, "Here's one to use, one to lose and one to copy!" Having got David thoroughly intrigued with this 'fishing' business, it was not long before David was also being taught how to cast, was kitted up, and then came with us on our visits to Grafham Water. I think that Richard and I were trying almost too hard for David to catch a trout, and when we returned home, David's wife Jackie would come out to meet us, and time and again it had to be one of our trout that she was given. Eventually, with great perseverance, David did not only hook a fish, but it was netted and very proudly taken home and after that there was no holding him. He also caught fish on the carrier of the river Test with Jackie acting as ghillie, until she started fishing herself, and we would meet up at other waters too including Damerham and Roxton.

Jackie remembers the 'Great Trout Feast' in the summer of 1976. She recalled, "We were experiencing the hottest and driest period that we had seen for decades when Richard, Pat, my husband David and I had the idea of hosting a garden party. We chose the beginning of July to coincide roughly with David's and a close friend's birthdays. Any reason for a celebration would do! Richard took on the task of preparing and cooking the huge trout that he had taken from his freezer, caught earlier in the season. The rest of us prepared salads, alternative meats and desserts. The day dawned hot and brilliantly clear, as was the norm at the time. I set about filling the garden with chairs and cushions for our many guests, including all Richard's family. Then, less than an hour before the Feast was due to start, the dark clouds rolled in and the first ominous drops hit the patio. 'No worries!' said Richard, 'it will soon pass.' He was right, of course, the thunderstorm went over quickly and, just in time, the seats were re-positioned as friends and family began to arrive. Richard was in his element as he served the now beautifully cooked trout, and joined in the fun of firing the 'champagne' corks into the neighbours' garden! (Fortunately they were on holiday at the time.) The festivities continued well after night-fall and everyone agreed that the 'Great Trout Feast' had been an event to remember."

It was while we lived at Flitwick that Richard received a request from the Secretary of the Bedford School's Angling Club, Guy Hammersley, to give a talk to the youngsters. This was another example of Richard's keenness to help anyone to fish and I went with him on two occasions. On the first visit, a very dark night, we went straight in to school and Richard introduced himself and then said, "Let's just have a chat and some questions - now what's the first question?" So Guy asked about Grafham Water, and Richard produced his fly box, and Guy remembers the great gasps of amazement as the youngsters saw the rallied rows of thousands of flies. Guy also remembered that Richard smoked!! They found him an old paint pot, and he smoked continuously dur-ing the evening, which, of course, left a very smoky smell - and resulted in the boys being accused of smoking!

On the second visit Richard gave them a casting demonstration on the lawn in front of the main school building. He was using a carp rod with an Arlesey Bomb attached to the end of his line and Guy tells me that he made an almighty cast which resulted in the lead snapping off and landing, with a great clunk, somewhere on the main school roof - to the delight of the boys. (When I queried why there were no teachers present, Guy said that it was considered sufficient that the head boy, who was a member of the club, was there.)

Guy remembers: "Then a fly rod with a shooting head was assembled and, again, we were all utterly amazed at the distance that Richard was casting. However, he then turned to me and said I was to have a go, which I did, not very successfully, to which Richard said that I wouldn't go very far while I was standing on the coils of line!"

Guy's parents had a friend, comedian Eric Morcambe, who was very anx-ious to meet Richard and they invited us to dinner for this purpose. We agreed and met Joan and Eric (real name Bartholomew) there, but I remember that it was Richard who kept us all amused with his jokes and his many stories in various accents. Following the dinner we arranged to meet and fish at Little Brickhill Lake, but unfortunately the carp were not to be caught on that occasion and Richard was disappointed for Eric.

Richard had known May and Gerry Berth-Jones for coarse fishing a long time before I met them but we soon made up a foursome, getting together for fishing various waters, mainly for trout. We would have a boat each, but fish within reach for exchange of flies, food and chat. Gerry was a keen fly-tyer and when we stayed with them down in Kent, he would open up his fly-tying box, set up his vice, and let Richard tie some flies and they would discuss possible new patterns.

Richard enjoyed having family and friends for a meal and would be involved himself with the preparation, with either the starter, main course or dessert. He liked to serve the trout that we had caught, either smoked, or cooked and skinned and laid out in its four natural strips, garnished with prawns and salad, to have with his extremely thin brown bread and butter. When we caught big trout, we would get them smoked and then there was quite a performance: Richard owned a tall chef's hat and there would be a clinical demonstration on how to 'carve' the fish! This performance was greatly enjoyed by Dorothy Hancock and she told me recently that her husband Alec remembers, and still carves 'properly', as Richard taught him, when they have smoked salmon. Richard was very keen on making a steak and kidney pie. He would cook the meat but leave me to roll out the pastry! He once devised a dessert he called 'Cherries a la Ricardo': a tin of black cherries soaked overnight in Cherry Brandy, then put into a raspberry jelly, which I had made with the liquid. He would cover this with whipped double cream, with a touch of sherry, and decorate it with grated chocolate and some of the remaining cherries!

Fred Buller was one of our frequent visitors for meals, and used to bring different people with him. Hugh Falkus came a couple of times and I remember he so appreciated one oxtail meal that he asked for bread to mop up all the gravy! On that occasion he had a good go at Richard about something to do with writing for 'proper' publications - a criticism that I felt was uncalled for after our hospitality! Sometimes Fred's late wife Pauline would join us with Pat and Pete Thomas, but Pauline would soon leave the table to go and amuse Robert when he was small - she adored children. Fred had a Polish friend, a scientist called Tad Andrzejczyk, who had a great knowledge of freshwater fishing and who wrote articles for our angling papers. He visited Fred once to show him a photograph of a Polish record pike fish, and said that he was very keen to meet Richard. Fred tells me that on the drive home, after having dinner with us, Tad was very emotional, having finally met the 'great man'; he was even in tears. Richard was very well known in Poland, and on the continent.

I can only remember one occasion of our fishing with Fred, and that was when we joined him to fish for the Lady of the Stream - the grayling - on the Rookery stretch of the river Test, at Broadlands. Fred said that it was the first time that he had fished with Richard for grayling, and I do recall that it was a most enjoyable winter's day's fishing. Conversation between those two never faltered, and it was always stimulating as so many subjects were covered apart from, of course, fishing.

It was on 12th December, 1984, that Richard enjoyed having Fred B., Fred J. and Pete Thomas at home for a roast duck dinner; I think that was the last time the three sat down together, although they all made many visits through his illness.

After Richard's mother had her book published - *The Sportsman's Cookbook - Fish and Game* - she was invited to take part in one of the late Russell Harty's television programmes. Richard prepared for her, to take with her, a large dish of trout with the 'four strips' very beautifully decorated, despite being ill with flu at the time. We watched the programme and were disappointed to discover that 'Bumper Bushytail' (casserole of squirrel!) was given to the audience to taste, and not the trout. I suppose that there was more TV 'drama' to be gained from telling the audience what they had just eaten! Richard's mother had heard from Fred Taylor that squirrel was considered a delicacy in the USA and that is why she had included a couple of recipes in her book. We never saw the dish again though - although we could do with lowering the grey squirrel menace over here . . .

About that time Richard used to have a cookery column in the *Country Gentlemen's Magazine*, which was published monthly. He'd begun by writing about fishing, and I cannot remember quite how it changed to cooking. As he said, he was no chef, but he gave his short-cut ideas for other men who had to cook, or who enjoyed cooking.

We moved to Biggleswade in April 1978, and again we were able to find a house by a river, this time the river Ivel, with some fish in it. As soon as we had agreed the purchase Richard asked for permission to plant some willow shoots in the bank, and this he did on either side of the river frontage, in the hope that, in due course, it would encourage chub to take up home under the trees. The shoots grew into quite large trees, which acted as side curtains to a stage and we both loved to watch the martins flying in and out as they were feeding in the evenings, as we sat in the garden with a drink in our hands. They used to nest on the front of the house and Richard always said that they brought good luck to a house; now, apart from the occasional few, they've gone and we have only one of the willows left, a stump with a few tall branches.

Richard was very keen to find out all about the fish in the river, and on our first 15th June he was ready to start at midnight. Richard enjoyed fishing in those early months and caught some good fish: 1lb 12oz roach, 6oz dace, 2lb 8oz chub, 2lb 8oz carp and a 2lb bream with a variety of smaller species: gudgeon, bullhead and on one occasion a rainbow trout. He used a 12-foot Hardy Matchmaker fibreglass rod and an Intrepid reel, mostly using sweetcorn as bait. The automatic sluice farther upstream resulted in the river flowing very fast at times, very slowly at others, so he would use leger tackle in the fast periods and a float when running slow. He reckoned that the anglers who fished from the opposite footpath tended to use float tackle that was too light, and bait with maggots, which he thought would catch mainly small dace and gudgeon. Once the fishing was fully investigated Richard then preferred to watch others fish, but he loved to sit in the lounge and watch and note all the different birds, and to watch the grasses in the field on the other side of the river, shimmering in the evening sun.

I found a list in Richard's handwriting of forty-two birds which I think he must have seen from the garden. I was often amazed when he named birds and animals shown on the television. He put it down to the hard work of both his grandfathers who had trained him from an early age what to look for and where to look, and had explained how plants, birds, animals, fish, insects and the rest of the wildlife in the water and at the waterside are all involved with one another. It was this ability to 'look' and not exceptional eyesight that enabled him to see fish in the water that only few others could see.

Understandably Richard had a large collection of angling books, but he described them as a 'working library' because he usually only kept the books that he enjoyed or wanted to refer to. This is the list he made of his favourites: *Loved River*, H. R. Jukes (1935); *Sporting Sketches*, Francis Francis and W. W. Cooper (1878); *At The Tale of the Weir*, Patrick A. Chalmers (1932); *An Angler's Hours*, H. T. Sheringham (1905); *An Open Creel*, H. T. Sheringham (1910); *Days Stolen for Sport*, Philip Geen (c. 1900-1910); *What I have Seen While Fishing*, Philip Geen (1905); *Lines In Pleasant Places*, William Senior (1920); *A Summer on the Test*, J. W. Hills (1924); and *Rod and Line*, Arthur Ransome (1929).

But we also had many other books including those on birds, flowers and country matters; reference and quotation books; Western novels; human palaeoanthropology books; several books on King Charles II, his favourite king; and all the C.S. Forester and Nevil Shute books in paperback. When he was ill I would fetch a dozen books, sometimes several times a week, from the Biggleswade Library. He was an avid reader.

Richard's memory enabled him to recite many things including the whole of Tennyson's 'The Revenge' and Shakespeare's Henry V speech before Agincourt, 'This day is called the Feast of Crispian'. These would be recited on long car journeys, together with encouragement for Robert, when he was tiny, with rhymes that we could sing to keep him amused ('He's a cheeky cheesy chomper' sung to the tune of 'John Brown's Body', for example!).

It was in the Seventies and Eighties that he became keenly interested in the study of man, and devoured any book published on the subject. Richard said that this interest in human palaeoanthropology started as a result of a question that he was asked as to why he and some three million others, nearly all males, liked to go fishing. After reading Professor Michael Day's book *Guide to Fossil Man*, he wrote a letter, on 29th January, 1981, asking if Michael Day could spare time to comment on some of his questions and ideas, writing, 'It is extremely difficult, when one has passed age 60, to progress beyond a rather limited point in study, with no access to published papers or to authorities, whose advice would be available if one could shed 40 years and re-enter University.' It turned out that Michael was a fisherman and knew of Richard, and he replied with a very long letter answering all Richard's queries. Due to the onset of Richard's illness they were not able to fish together, but kept in touch by telephone and letter. I had hoped that one day they would write a book between them with words that would be more easily understood by people like me.

Apart from angling books, another kind of book that Richard could have written, I thought, was a Western. That could have been a real money-spinner - he had read so many that I felt it couldn't have failed! He did venture into the world of children's stories, but was never published. In 1983 we acquired a female kitten and Richard found her a 'very engaging little beast', naming her 'Stripey Chufflecheeks Pussywillow Walker'. She was stripey, but also very pretty and he took photographs of her in a range of attitudes and performing various antics. He thought that 'as he could speak very fluent cattish', he could translate into English what Stripey would like to say to the readers of a little book, and he did write an engaging story.

Richard enjoyed writing doggerel and verse and I think, perhaps, that one of his verses should be included here. This is my favourite:

TIM TIGER

Tim Tiger was a stripey cat, his weight was sixteen pounds,
He lived in a palatial house, set in extensive grounds.
His nose was pink, his whiskers white, his fur all thick and glossy,
And everyone who saw him said: "Oh, what a handsome possy!"

Whenever it was wet or cold, he'd always stay indoors;
He'd sit and comb his whiskers or he'd manicure his paws.
But sometimes he would wistfully say: "I hope it's fine tomorrow,
For if it is, I'll go outside and try to catch a sporrow."

He woke one summer morning and started out at dawn.
He left a trail of footprints across the dewy lawn.
He said: "I'm after sporrows, but before it gets too hot,
I'll hide behind the compost heap and try to catch a rot!"

He waited very patiently, and then he heard a rustle.
He bristled out his whiskers, and he tensed in every muscle,
He switched his tail from side to side, he made a mighty leap,
And landed on a hodgeheg behind the compost heap.

His mistress heard him screaming and came to ask the cause.
He said: "I've got a lot of holes in each of my four paws.
I don't care if it's wet or fine, I'll stay indoors tomorrow,
And learn to spell some difficult words, like hodgeheg, rot and
sporrow."

Perhaps a brief mention should be made about politics. As a young man in the
early Fifties, when his mother was involved with the Conservative Association in
Hitchin and Letchworth - and working hard to try to get Nigel Fisher elected as
their Member of Parliament - Richard joined the Young Conservatives. As
Chairman, he also worked hard, and Nigel Fisher was duly elected.

Dick, in centre with trilby, supporting elected Conservative MP, Nigel Fisher.

Pat, Robert and Dick.

Robert enjoys fishing and is seen here fly casting.

James MacGibbon, Peter Maskell, Dick and Pat, at the launch of one of Richard's books, edited by Peter.

Richard always had a great knack of being able to communicate with people. I only heard him speak to a large audience once and all the way to the venue, a good hour's drive away, he kept saying things like 'why ever did I say I would do this', 'let's go back', 'I must have been a fool to say I'd be part of a forum'. However, when we got there - there must have been an audience of about six hundred people - and the questions started, mostly to Richard, he got the crowd eating out of his hand in no time. No sign of nerves at all! On that occasion we stayed at a hotel and I remember him telling me that he could never understand why clubs could not allow their visitor to speak first, and leave business matters to the end of the meeting. Most of the audience probably only had to go round the corner to get home.

Once after visiting my aunt in the City of London we took a taxi to the station. The taxi-driver thought he recognised Richard and after confirming that it was 'Dick Walker', he and Richard began a lengthy fishing conversation. I had heard about Richard being recognised by London taxi-drivers (and I understand that a lot of them are anglers) but now I could believe it. Richard was not allowed to pay the fare. So some of his tales are true!

And what of Richard, the family man? (Incidentally, he was always 'Richard' to me as from the first time I met him he was writing under that name in the *Fishing Gazette*.) Well, he was kind and generous, thoughtful and humorous. Soon after we were married I had to go to Surrey for family matters and on my return there were boxes of chocolates and flowers all over the house, with notes of 'welcome home' tucked in them.

Richard was a large man, broad and six foot two, but when I first met him I thought he was a bit 'skinny'. Much later on I discovered that he was very strong. It was after a very long day's fishing and a very long drive back to where we where staying, during which I had chatted to keep him awake. On arrival I was extremely tired but to my amazement he picked me up and carried me up a flight of stairs! Richard did put on weight after we were married, and later, due to medication, reached seventeen stone.

He was a much loved father and grandfather. His son Simon married Janet Williams, and Richard was proud to be made a grandfather when Iaan arrived in September 1971, followed by Paul in July 1974. Richard married Glenda Froy and their daughter, Charlotte, arrived in April 1974. Tim married Eileen Marshall and their daughter, Amanda, was born in October 1975, and their son Peter was born in October 1978.

Janet told me recently that she agreed with Eileen that they couldn't have had a better father-in-law: he was very much a kind, humorous man; he never interfered but he was always there if you needed him. Eileen remembers him as tall and distinguished, and said that at first she was a little in awe of the 'very famous fisherman' - she came from a small village in the north of England, and was young and rather shy in those days. Janet agreed and added that she found it difficult to know what to say, but that 'Dick' soon put her at ease - and she wondered if perhaps he was a bit shy of her, and wondered what to talk about! He was always kind and generous. Glenda felt that all the daughters-in-law liked him: he made them laugh, with his quirky sense of humour, they had sing-a-longs in the evening and Richard would play the guitar and sing folk songs with their husbands, who mocked him, jokingly, for his use of so few chords.

Eileen remembers going into his 'fishing office' in the back garden, which was actually a large caravan, and she was amazed at all the paraphernalia, feathers and fly-tying things. He taught her how to make a crane fly using part of a peacock feather. Eileen thought that they all regarded as very special their visits to 'Dick' and Pat - you just knew you were going to have a happy visit. His stories were great, the food was good and he always had a view on life which lifted the spirits. An irreplaceable human being.

Janet recalled the family gathering at The Hut, walking through the fields to get there (and she was eight months pregnant) - it was such a different and exciting evening. It was the time when my sister Mary and John Routley, Kate and Steve were enjoying a week there, and we had lots of good food, beer and wine, interlaced with much guitar music and jolly singing. My nephew fished there and used to join us trout fishing at Roxton, and has fished with me on the carrier.

When I queried with Richard why he, Simon and Tim did not fish, he thought that perhaps it had all been made too easy for them. They'd fished with their father and Pete Thomas, and caught large fish but going on their own would not have been so exciting. Now Simon says, "I just found it boring."

It is true that Richard was an entertainer, and would keep people enthralled with his stories, and jokes, which were tempered to the audience - but he was just the same at home, great fun. At mealtimes, sometimes, it was necessary to put a hand up to ask for permission to speak, as he could carry on at great length! Fortunately Richard and I were 'on the same wavelength', even driving similarly, which meant that we enjoyed, many interesting discussions on numerous subjects, although, as I've said, I was not so good on human palaeoanthropology. Football, in particular Arsenal, had to be watched and I could enjoy one match, but must admit to getting fed up on Saturday nights with highlights of the other matches! When Robert was very young, Richard would get down on the floor and play fierce, very fierce, tigers, and I know he enjoyed fishing the Ivel with Robert, and when he was very young teaching him how to net a trout at Roxton. I hope that he knows that Rob still fishes, and catches, trout from the carrier.

Richard had a motto *Ars longa, vita brevis* - do it now. This did not always work out, as, after we moved in to our home in Biggleswade, he wanted to put up a picture in the lounge over the mantelpiece, rather than wait for Ken and Den Taylor (who did lots of our odd jobs). He began by measuring (in a manner of fashion) and then started to fix. Gently, I said, "I don't think it is quite central." However, he persevered and only when he sat down did he discover I was right. So the Taylors had to repair the wall! That apart, Rob and I try to keep his motto.

Richard was also surprisingly superstitious. When out he would not pass a Salvation Army Officer without crossing their palm with silver, and seeing a nun was not a good omen for fishing, although a bullfinch was. When he saw a magpie - and there weren't many of them then - Richard said it was necessary always to be polite, to salute and say, "Good Morning, Mr (or Mrs) Magpie," for a good fishing day.

It concerned me to discover recently, that, after we were married, some of Richard's friends were disappointed that he did not go fishing with them as much. Certainly nothing could have stopped him if he had wanted to go. It must have just happened that way; although we did meet up with people, I suppose I was there too. When Richard was ill, we did not have a 'walk-about' telephone, and if he was not up to it, he would ask me to deal with the calls; certainly there was no idea of stopping anyone from speaking to him, or visiting him if he was well enough. Anyone who knew Richard well would know that and would also know how great he was at delegating jobs!

Richard also had a great love of music. He enjoyed strumming on his guitar and having a good old singsong, and when his sons joined in on their instruments, a tuneful, if noisy, evening ensued - 'The Streets of London' and 'The Wreck of The Old 97' being favourites. If there was a pianist at a hotel restaurant Richard would request 'Come Back To Sorrento' or 'Smoke Gets In Your Eyes'. He also enjoyed opera and started taking singing lessons. He used to sing various pieces to me and one was 'Nessun Dorma', which was well before it was taken up by the footballers. (Arias sung in the car were less pleasant - too loud for a confined space!) Richard was invited to take part in Desert Island Discs while it was presented by Roy Plomley, and chose a wide variety of music, which ranged from 'The Holy City' to 'Danny Boy'.

Richard was not a person who went to church, but he told me that during the war he had had some very strange experiences and so he could not say that there was not a god. He knew his Bible though and if Jehovah's Witnesses called at the door, he soon sent them, very nicely, on their way by out-quoting Bible passages to them. He was also on good terms with our vicar, the Rev. Canon Peter Hill. The vicarage was just round the corner, and during his illness when Richard went for a little exercise, Peter would join him and they would chat as they went. He used to tell Peter that he would go to church any time if they included 'Onward Christian Soldiers' in the service. This hymn was included in the Thanksgiving Service for Richard that was held at St Andrew's Church in Biggleswade, in October, 1985. Fred Buller gave the splendid address, and the church was packed with people from all over the country, mainly anglers. The service finished with 'Danny Boy'.

Once Richard knew that he had cancer, he said that he very much hoped to see Rob, who was six, at least into his teen years, and he always remained positive about the cancer, saying, "I'll beat it if it kills me!" A letter at the time from Jack Thorndike hoping that the treatment 'would halt and finally kill it' continued, 'You deserve so much better and because of all your good qualities, not least that of a fighter, I have great faith in my belief that you will be the winner. As always, your friend and admirer.' It was Richard's humour and positive outlook that shone through at this difficult time, but sadly Rob was only ten when Richard died.

Richard's early and cruel death is now nearly twenty-one years ago, but because of anglers' continuing interest it is almost as if my husband is still here, and this, at times, I find is very difficult.

As I have written, I met Richard as 'one of my contributors', first through working together and then gradually becoming very good friends. So I never thought of Richard as other than a friend, and then much later as a husband. My stepsons were young when we first met and I certainly did not want the family broken up.

In contributing to the making of this book I have been reminded of the many stimulating times we shared together, of much happiness, but also much sadness and anxiety. Of course we had our ups and downs, but not many disagreements. I do remember one occasion, when Rob was about four, when he came and stood between us and said that that was enough 'fighting', and we both burst out laughing - we couldn't even remember what we were arguing about!

One of my friends says that she thought that we made a good team and that I backed Richard as necessary, but that I was definitely (and she emphasised this!) not in any way subservient to this man admired by so many, and of course of whom I am justly very proud.

Since Richard's death I have from time to time thought about his eventual biography, and, fortunately, Barrie Rickards was persuaded by his angling cohorts to fulfil this need. We have had many meetings, and I have found that while working with Barrie the depth of our discussions about Richard have been most varied, interesting and enjoyable. My sincere thanks go to Barrie for all his endeavours, and also to Rosie and Jon Ward-Allen for their valuable contributions to bringing this book to fruition.

Patricia Marston Walker, Biggleswade, 2007.

Chapter 22

In the final analysis

DICK WALKER, as he preferred to be known in public, was the towering figure in angling during the second half of the twentieth century, a man whose premature death in 1985 dismayed anglers nationwide. I hope in this book I have managed to give some idea of the breadth of Dick's knowledge of, and involvement in, the sport, but possibly the most important thing he did was to speak *for* angling: he was the voice of angling in the last century.

All well known anglers have their critics. It simply goes with the territory and most get used to it and recognise that individuals can be ignorant or spiteful or both. But Dick had very serious critics too. Bernard Venables was an important figure himself in his time, helping to inspire many a young angler with his 'Mr Crabtree' cartoons. As we have seen, however, it is likely that B.V. was motivated a little by jealousy and the way angling was changing. Another vocal critic was the match and pleasure angler Frank Murgett, happily still with us, and given from time to time to fairly trenchant views on the philosophical principles of angling. Frank has told me several times that he now considers Walker to have been 'lucky', to have been in the right place at the right time rather than anyone out of the ordinary. There's probably an element of truth in this, but there was more to it than that: it was Dick Walker who *led* the charge so to speak, accompanied by a few who both recognised his vision and at the same time influenced him - people like Peter Thomas, Fred Taylor and Fred Buller for example. It is one thing to be in the right place at the right time: quite another to take the reins and ride with them!

Several of his friends have pointed out that he was one of those people who never really grew up fully, that a good part of him remained a youngster. This is something that is true of many great men, of creative people generally, and there are women who would say this was true of *most* men! The associated naievity can lead to a very trusting nature but it also has its downside. In

Walker's case his failure to actually exploit for his own end his unrivalled position in angling meant that when he died he was not a wealthy man by any means (a fact confirmed in the *National Dictionary of Biography*, recently published as a new edition).

Fred Buller told me that Dick was always a very fair and honourable man in his dealings with other people, despite having had his own personal problems at one time. He worked only in an open and honest way and with great kindness to people. True, he pulled the legs unmercifully of any new friend, but if they responded well he embraced their friendship and after that he'd not hear a word against them. Fred also confirms that it was not just in public that Dick was kind to, or about, people - he was never unpleasant in private either about people he didn't agree with. There was no snideness in his nature.

Walker saw angling as part of life's whole, as part of the social fabric of any modern society, with ancient roots going back to man's hunting days. In this he was like Izaak Walton. Walton surely lived at a time when fish were caught to eat - and that was the objective of going fishing - and yet in *The Compleat Angler* he sets angling in a social context too, just as Walker did, and in this he was well ahead of his time. Walker, as I hope I have shown earlier, achieved more than Walton. For a start, he wrote only from his own experience, and yet that experience was so vast, and his involvement in angling so wide, that his total contribution was concomitantly the greater, probably by quite a margin. One can imagine that had he not died so early there would have been in him one great book, one great masterpiece to rival and eclipse Walton's. As it happens we are fortunate enough to have such a treasure house of his writings that we are able to gauge the impact of it. And that impact has been incomparable. It is possible that there will never again be an angler of such stature, but I hope, indeed I am optimistic, that this will not be the case. Until such a figure emerges, Dick Walker will remain unquestionably the greatest angler in history.

Personal recollections of Richard Walker

collected by Pat Marston Walker

In anticipation of a biography of Richard, I thought it would be invaluable to have comments about him from his friends, those who knew him or had fished with him, while they were fresh in their minds. So, after his death, I wrote a number of letters to friends and colleagues asking for their memories, but, as Richard would wish, I hoped for honest appraisals. I said that I thought it would be good to include such a chapter in any future book. I was delighted to receive some marvellous material, for which I am deeply grateful.

TAG BARNES - 1991

There were two things I remember most about Dick, the first was his vast knowledge which covered an amazing range of subjects and secondly his unbounded generosity.

Anyone fortunate enough to spend time at his 'hut' on the upper Great Ouse would find plenty of 'goodies', and knowing of my life-long interest in natural history, when he turned up the first question would not be, "Have you been catching any good fish?" but, "Have you seen any 'good' birds lately?" On one occasion he excitedly told me that he had found otter tracks on the banks of a river where they had not been seen for years - not a lot of anglers would recognise otter tracks if they saw them!

We would talk about water snails and purple loosestrife; bats and rats; moles and mink, or how to tell the difference in the primary projection between willow warbler and chiffchaff. The discussion would have been just as interesting had you talked about music or combustion engines. Dick was a master of many things and we are indeed fortunate in that his first love was fishing. Wherever anglers gather together his knowledge on the subject will be discussed for many centuries to come.

CHARLIE BOWEN, Illinois, USA - 1991

My acquaintance with Richard probably began about 1957, when I read articles in the *Fishing Gazette* by him and Fred J. Taylor, whom I wrote to, and through Fred I heard from Dick. They urged me to visit England and both sent literature, books, and fishing tackle, including Dick sending me a Mk IV Avon rod to try.

My wife, sons and I came in 1966 and Fred and Dick gave us the exclusive use of their 'hut' at Deanshanger. My huge amount of fishing tackle was examined by Messrs Taylor, Walker and Fred Buller and it was suggested which items could be used effectively, and then I was given proper tackle, plus a great deal of patient tuition. They also took me to Romsey, and Dick remarked that it was unlikely that any Americans had fished the Test, Avon, and Two Lakes consecutively.

I have thought of Dick every time I tackle up for fishing, each time I slip on the old wellingtons he gave me, and slap on an old felt hat - which he reckoned more adequate than my 'Andy Capp'. I think of him when I read his books, articles and old correspondence - his generosity can't be described adequately, not so much for the countless things he gave and sent me, but for the time he took to explain the use of each item. When I catch a fish on Dick's tackle, how can I not hear him say, "Well done, old cock!"?

In his accompanying letter Charlie told me that his eldest son, George, an avid fly fisher, had cased the flies, floats and other items that Richard had sent him, to preserve for his progeny. Charlie says, 'I know Dick would have a fit if he knew this!'

GEOFFREY BUCKNALL - 1991

Geoffrey said that he did not know my husband personally, but that he liked subjects 'thrashed out', and had met him on Brain Trusts and had lots of telephone calls. Geoffrey says that he is glad that he did not know Richard too well, because it allowed him the smallest tinge of hero worship - which he confessed to, in spite of all the arguments in the angling press.

It is strange to recall that in a sense I acted as a foil to Dick's ideas, which was a good thing because it brought into discussion many controversial aspects of fly fishing, which otherwise might have passed without comment. Readers may recall some of those debates in various angling journals and one was about Dick's assertion that the static fly was a worthwhile technique, to which I reposted that 'legering wet flies was a waste of time'.

The most hilarious episode was when I patiently explained in the *Angling Times* the shotting patterns used in France by roach pole anglers, which the French call 'Logarithmic'. Dick headed his reply 'Logarithmic Cobblers' - which made me hoot with laughter.

I enjoy the memory of many small kindnesses from him. In my early years as an angling writer Dick stoutly defended me against a rather unpleasant review of an early book; when I started as a professional fly dresser, he arranged that I should supply his patterns to the, then, four Hardy shops; and on a legal action occasion, he intervened to arrange an apology to be published.

Whilst through his many talents and successes he dominated the angling world through a good part of his lifetime, I was always surprised that he didn't exploit this, as many another men might have done. I think he liked to be flattered, but he recognised flattery for what it was.

One last memory which honours his memory to me. I had to give a talk to a fly fishing organisation where I knew him to be a member, and I felt some trepidation that he might take over the event and, even unwittingly, 'make me look small'. My fears were completely unfounded. He sat with others in the body of the hall, joined in like everyone else and complimented me on my efforts.

One word to sum up? His kindness - and to say a person is kind, I don't think you can say anything nicer.

FRED BULLER - 2007

Richard Walker and the Magic Bay of Big Pike

The photograph overleaf shows Richard Walker and Peter Thomas fishing on Loch Lomond at Portnellan in 1967. Salmon and sea trout angler Jackie Thompson and his wife occupied the other boat. Jackie rented a wartime gun emplacement (hidden amongst trees) on the peninsula flanking the northern end of Portnellan Bay, converted it into a fishing lodge and spent the whole of his fishing summers on the loch.

This proximity allowed him to keep track of a huge pike (the very one that I eventually hooked and lost before it was found dead, choked by the trace wire that was round its jaws), a fish that was in the habit, as undisturbed big

Dick and Pete Thomas fishing at Portnellan in 1967. Jackie Thompson and his wife are in the other boat.

pike in Loch Lomond often are, of sunbathing close to the surface among beds of potomogeton weed. Strangely, few anglers bothered with Lomond's pike after Tommy Morgan gave up pike fishing soon after he caught his record 46lb 11oz fish at Portnellan in 1945. I started to fish Loch Lomond in the early 1960s and later took a team of fishermen there that included Dick Walker, Ken Taylor and Peter Thomas. For some three years or so, I had, with great good fortune, been kept informed about 'the big fish' in Portnellan Bay through London rod maker Robert Myslik who kept in direct touch with his Scottish friends (and great Loch Lomond anglers) Jackie Thompson and Harry Britton. Myslik was a political refugee from Czechoslovakia during the Second World War and was stationed near Loch Lomond.

Walker's influence was immediate, and emphatic; his premeditated plan to fish deadbaits on a rig of his own design changed our attitude to pike fishing forever - I don't think any of us has livebaited since.

So it was that the years I spent preparing an assault on the pike record, sorting out the logistics of catching livebaits (roach) from the river Leven and from Balmaha, transporting them across the loch in huge specially made livebait cans used in conjunction with an oxygen cylinder and then keeping them in good order in sunken fish boxes at Portnellan, were to all intents and purposes, wasted!

LT. COL. C. C. A. CARFRAE, MC - 1990
(From a chapter in a proposed book that Col. Carfrae was writing.)

Some time in 1970 I wrote to the famous fish-and-pen prolific angler, Richard Walker, and he replied at once, courteously and lucidly. We corresponded several times annually and I am the richer for his letters, finding no question bearing, however obscurely, on angling too trivial to have engaged his attention. If at times Walker's comments or expositions raised my eyebrows, subsequent reflection or experience has shown them invariably to be well-founded.

It is tempting to designate Walker the Dr Johnson of the angling world. But, within his chosen field, Richard Walker knew his facts better than the great Doctor always knew his. Omniscience, or something like it, was credited by his admirers to Johnson, but Walker would never have allowed such a claim to be put forward on his behalf, if - to fishermen who for years digested his books, his articles and indefatigable letters to editors of angling periodicals - he must have seemed to fall little short of it, regarding matters piscatorial.

Our fishing philosophies differed, our fly fishing interests diverged. Always logical, Walker believed in catching fish by whatever sporting means would prove most effective at the time. My concept is narrower, more hazy, based on sentiment rather than logic. But Richard was a veritable encyclopaedia of practical sense and knowledge which he had the gift of disseminating in words so unambiguous and cogent that the dullest-witted of fishermen should have been capable of grasping his meaning.

The late Pat Russell once arranged for us both to be fishing a beat of the lower Itchen on the same day. I will only say that his personality struck me as being both more ebullient and more brightly coloured than that of most men. Characteristically, Walker spent all morning laying siege to the one trout consistently feeding, testing its powers of resistance with a whole spectrum of flies. That trout had the impertinence or sagacity to defy him!

Richard dealt with many kindred matters important to me *at the moment*, he dealt with them in minute detail, as though having all the time in the world at his disposal. Nor did his generosity limit itself to correspondence. As well as sundry other tackle, he once gave me, unsolicited and out of the blue, as it were, a Hardy trout rod. Lacking a mentor in my fishing youth, my debt to Richard Walker is profound.

BRIAN CLARKE - 1991

I well remember where and how I first met Dick Walker. What enthusiastic angler of my generation would not? For anyone who came to the age of awareness in the 1950s or 1960s, a meeting with the sport's most brilliant and influential mind would be a memorable event to stand alongside other memorable events.

It was Jack Thorndike, then Editor of *Trout and Salmon*, that suggested that I should go to the Press Day of a small stillwater trout fishery, Latimer Lakes, in Buckinghamshire, in April 1973. He said, "You'll enjoy the day, and a lot of well-known names will be there, Dick Walker, probably, as well."

The weather was dreadful, and most of the anglers took their time in leaving the comfort of the fishing hut. When it was about half-empty, the door suddenly burst open and he arrived. He filled the door-frame; Barbour jacket, towelling scarf, glasses, balding; the great, wide-brimmed hat in a well-padded hand. Walker. Unmistakably Walker.

It would be going too far (perhaps) to say that the entrance was deliberately theatrical. But the effect was theatrical. Conversation momentarily hushed. Heads turned. He was dominating the room before he was in it, before he had uttered a word.

He seemed to savour the moment.

Then old friends waved and moved towards him, acquaintances nodded. There was a shaking of hands, and exchange of quips. Courtiers circled and sidled closer. In due course, I was introduced to the man I had held in awe since my schooldays, twenty years earlier. Eventually we all moved outside and the serious fishing got underway. Sensibly Richard had waited for the rain to stop, but, later, I saw him sitting on a low stool, back from the bank, catching fish one after another, just as I'd imagined he would.

After an hour or so - a blank hour for me - I moved up the bank and met Richard walking towards me. I excused my awful performance. He said there was nothing the matter with the way I was fishing, there were simply more fish where he had been, fewer fish along the bank where I had been. He bit the fly from his own leader. "Here, have a go with this."

And then he went to where I had been, I went to where he had been. At once he began to trundle in fish where I had scratched and scraped. I laboured mightily for two, where he had lifted a dozen.

We didn't speak again that day, as I recall. But later that week a letter arrived. It was from Dick. It simply said how much he had enjoyed the first article I had written and how he had admired the way I fished. He had no need to write that letter though, given the blizzard-like volume of his correspondence, it was, in reality, a tiny thing. But the thought was there and it further heightened my regard for him. Here was not only a great angler, but a warm and sensitive human being, as well.

My last meeting with Dick - many years later - was when Dick and Pat invited Fred Buller and I over for dinner. Dick was ill: we all knew how ill. And as it happens I had been ill myself for several weeks, not seriously as it turned out, but disturbingly. Dick put his arm around my shoulder as I walked into his study. "I was sorry to hear you've been ill, old son. Come and tell me about it." There was no reference to himself and no affectation in the fact. I was truly amazed at his capacity for concern about me, given his own, known, dire straits.

These two - to me - touching insights were bookends to a range of encounters and incidents over the years which showed something about Dick, or something about his impact on others, or something of both. From what I saw at both first and second hand, he was clearly a many-sided man.

In a fishing hut on the Test where he had been a guest a few days before, I once saw a note pinned on a beam. It was in the clear, fluid, unmistakable Walker hand. It said simply: 'I have no need to lie - R. Walker'. Beneath it someone else had written in large letters: 'Arrogant Bastard'.

And, of course, he was arrogant. It was a trait that sat alongside many traits and contradictions, which included modesty (but not false modesty); exhibitionism; puncturing sarcasm (reserved for those he considered fools or blimps); sensitivity; desire to give credit where credit is due; desire to provoke; desire to give help; willingness to accept correction; ever-present willingness to offer correction; utter objectivity.

One of the most interesting and, I think, understandably serpentine examples of Dick's objectivity came in our last, brief exchange of correspondence, shortly after I'd heard he was ill. I had felt it important to write to him, while there was still time, to tell him how great an angler I believed him to be. He didn't need me to do that, heaven knows. It was simply something that I very much wanted to do. I told him, 'You are unquestionably the most influential angler of this century; probably the most important angler of all time.' At once came the reply, rebutting my statements one by one. 'You overestimate me . . . I have had some influence but as regards really important things I stand far below others . . . I can think of two men in my own generation who have had more influence . . .' And so it went, for all the world as though we'd been academically disagreeing about some third party, naming names and giving reasons.

However, I am not naive and nor was he. I felt that, while all the points he made were true (and were unquestionably sincerely felt in the precise form expressed) there was an element of deliberate obliqueness to his reply: that he was responding to slightly different definitions of 'influence' and 'important' than I had clearly meant. I think that Dick not only knew of his own historical importance but dared to think that what I had written might perhaps be true; yet he could not - could he? - openly agree.

Looking back, it is indicative of Dick's stature to recall the influence that he had on other writers of his day. Always, in constructing a special article or making a particularly important case, one had to take account of Dick's possible reaction. Is this argument tight? Can I defend it? Can I defend it against *him*? This is not to say that one chose to write what Dick wanted to read or would agree with: of course not. But still, any serious writer had to take account of Dick's own great experience and strongly-held views, above all others. For the best writers and thinkers it was not a necessary discipline, but it was a healthy discipline, nonetheless.

Throughout his later life, Dick kept a kind of schoolmasterly order in the angling press: rapping knuckles, patting heads, putting the wellie in. It was an order, which, after his death, disappeared. Many writers began to make claims that few others could challenge on the basis of knowledge; or else could be bothered to challenge even if they knew the truth. Walker had the knowledge, the inclination and the energy to challenge always, at every turn. And not only other writers but 'fact', folklore and received wisdoms that did not stand the test of his own experience, observation and formidable power of reason.

Here is Dick's greatest contribution: that he caused vast numbers of coarse anglers to think to an extent that very few individual anglers had thought before. Almost single-handedly, because of the huge extent to which he communicated his ideas and attitudes, he drew coarse fishing out from the dark ages; brought science and logic to a sport that hitherto had largely been based on myth and potion. He gave every act a sense of clear purpose. Walker pulled around the tiller, setting a new course not only for his own generation but for all angling generations to come.

I believed when he lived, believe now, that Richard Walker was the most influential angler of this century, the most important all-round angler of all time. I do keep testing it, asking myself 'if not Walker, then who?'

But I cannot find even one runner-up.

JIM COVERLEY - 1990

Being an avid reader of the *Angling Times* since its advent in June 1953, and being a pleasure angler from my youth, I was soon to become enamoured by the writings of one of its contributors, a certain Richard Walker. He had already achieved eminence in the angling world by being the captor of the record carp 'Clarissa', a monster of 44lb - a record which he held for more than three decades.

I soon became a devout disciple of his teachings, and began to apply his methods on my local, somewhat polluted, 'Bridgewater Canal'. This I did with some acclaim by catching several specimen fish, notably a 10lb carp, a 3lb 10oz perch, a few more of this species in the 2lb-plus class. The result of which gave me rewarding publicity by the local journal and a very good write up by *Angling Times*.

In the meantime Richard had been going from strength to strength with his column in the *Angling Times*, his coverage had been expanded and was now affectionately called 'Dick's Patch'. Every angler, worth his salt, will be aware of the numerous innovations that Dick had brought to every aspect of our beloved sport. He was truly a legend in his own lifetime.

The pinnacle of my life was achieved when I had the audacity to ask him for an autographed photograph of himself. He readily responded to my request, the culmination of which led to numerous exchanges of personally hand-written letters, which I shall treasure for the rest of my life.

R. I. P. Dick, I will never forget you.

HELEN FORD - 1991
*A memory, from a brief non-angling friendship,
before they moved a distance away.*

My three sons, were teenage boys in the early Seventies, and we do remember Richard as being a very friendly and kindly man.

But the impression we were most strongly left with was that of Richard's skill at making flies. As we remember, his hands were generously propor-tioned, and yet he was able to handle the tiny components of the fly and manipulate them into the desired fish tempter.

This we will always remember with amazement and gratitude for a very happy memory.

JOHN GODDARD - 1991

Over the years I got to know Dick pretty well and apart from his amazing memory, he was an extremely gifted writer, and one of the very, very few anglers of his day who was capable of writing several articles nearly every week of his life. These articles were on a huge range of subjects connected with fishing, yet he rarely repeated himself, and to do this without any trace of plagiarism, was a great achievement.

He was a talented photographer and he also had a sound knowledge of engineering practices, which assisted him greatly in the many fishing tackle products he either designed or helped to design. In my humble opinion he was the greatest freshwater angler of this century, and it made me very cross when I heard, and also read recently, that John Wilson is now considered to be the greatest, just because he has appeared in a couple of dozen fishing programmes on television in the last two years.

I first met Richard in the mid-Fifties and, if my memory serves me correctly, I was introduced to him by Bernard Venables at a fishing tackle show. At the time I was a carp fishing fanatic, and I remember on that first occasion we spent over an hour discussing tactics. At that time Richard, Peter Thomas and the Taylor brothers were the big names in the carp fishing world, and I felt very honoured to meet him. Now although in those early days I never fished for carp with him, I did, on several occasions, fish with him, Peter and Fred J. on his stretch of the river Ouse, mainly for chub. In the early Sixties I gave up carp fishing as I was becoming increasingly interested in fly fishing for trout, and, eventually, when Richard also became very interested in this branch of our sport, I used often to meet and fish with him at such venues as Two Lakes, Pitsford, Grafham and Chew; on several occasions we shared a boat.

Whatever Richard took up he would always take it very seriously, and as he was such an innovative person he was always full of new ideas, or methods of fishing, and trout fishing was certainly no exception. At the time I was, and still am for that matter, a very keen fly dresser, and we used to spend many hours, on the bank or in a boat, discussing new designs for stillwater trout flies. Today many of his fly patterns are household names, and are popular all over the world.

By the early Sixties as a director of one of the up and coming manufacturers in the tackle trade, it was part of my job to design and test new products for the company; these were marketed under the name 'EFGEECO', which quickly became famous as an innovator for quality new accessories and equipment. Now Richard was also a very generous person, and over the years he assisted my company in the design of several new products, and yet he would never accept a penny for his services. He first assisted us in the mid-Sixties with a design for a new angler's shelter, which was an attempt to replace the large umbrellas most coarse fishermen carried. Towards the end of the Sixties he encouraged us to market a special groundbait for the coarse fisherman, based on an old country recipe, which was formulated by himself and Fred J. This we eventually marketed under the somewhat strange name of

'Pomenteg', under their insistence, and this sold very successfully for several years.

During the Seventies we spent some time together working out the design for a piece of equipment to contain the backing of the fly fisherman's line when using a shooting head, and this was eventually very successful, being marketed as the 'EFGEECO' line tray as recommended by Richard Walker.

Richard also assisted in many other diverse ways with many other new products, that we marketed over the years, during which time a lot of correspondence passed between us, as well as many hundreds of phone calls. We would sometimes meet for dinner at a mutually convenient restaurant and I can still recall the last meal we had at Woburn together with our respective wives. If I remember correctly our mutual very good friend the late Leslie Moncrieff and his wife Dora were also present to discuss some project in which we were all interested.

Richard over the years made an enormous contribution to our sport, and I can only hope that when the history of our sport is rewritten, he will be recognised for the giant of an angler that he was. A biography of Dick is long overdue.

FRANK GUTTFIELD - 2007

Richard Walker - Memories

It was October 1979. The venue was close to the Thames in London, the 'swim' was the 'snug' bar at the Waldorf Hotel on the Aldwych and the 'species' were James MacGibbon of David and Charles (the publishers), Dick Walker angling supremo and myself (who's place of work was next door). Our memorable and jovial lunchtime meeting had been convened to discuss two book projects with James. One had the working title of 'Angler's Almanac', the other and far more significant was the authorised biography of Richard Walker. I must emphasise 'authorised' biography because over the years others claim to have been asked to do likewise.

So back to 1979 when I was indeed surprised, honoured and humbled to be asked by Dick to do this important job. At our meeting we roughed out and agreed a draft contract for the book and all was set. Regrettably, for the next two or three years Dick and I were leading extremely busy lives with demanding 'day-jobs', new wives, new families and not very much fishing. However, we did manage to make a start and met for a tench fishing trip to Southill Park and made a tape-recording of more than an hour reflecting on the early days of the big fish scene. Sadly, that is where my biography ended. Soon after in

1982 when I was in New Orleans, I had a phone call from my old mate Mike Gale who looked after fishing books at Benn Bros (and published my *Big Fish Scene* earlier). Timothy Benn who was a good friend of Dick's had asked Mike to break the sad news to me that Dick had been taken ill with cancer.

There and then, I confess I made the wrong and perhaps selfish decision for which I now make a 'public' apology – I decided not to proceed further with Dick's biography. Why? At the time I was doing very little angling writing and not a great deal of fishing. I had often been critical of other angling authors who did far more writing than fishing and had this stupid belief that potential readers would think that Guttfield was 'cashing-in' on Dick's illness whilst he was still alive. Nothing could be further from the truth as unlike some angling writers of that time I did not depend on my freelance writing for a good living. My old fishing friends are still nagging me to resurrect this project; perhaps in another place I will. In the meantime I have plucked out some random memories of Dick that punctuated the thirty-odd years I was privileged to know him.

My first 'meeting' of Dick was circa 1948 in Arlesey when I was nine. We lived at 103 High Street and next door-but-one were Dora and Fred Proctor who ran the local chippie down the road. Dora's father was Reg Redd who was a pig breeder and at that time was top-gun in the rabbit (Belgian Whites?) breeding field. At that time Dick was emerging as a regular angling writer, his work appearing under the names of 'Water Rail', 'R. Stuart' Walker and 'Bedfordian' in publications like *Anglers' News* and the *Fishing Gazette*. At the same time Dick was still every much involved with the 'professional' rabbit breeding scene himself and Reg Redd was I suppose a mentor to young Dick and I remember old Reg as this gaunt man with two 'holes' in his cheeks from bullet wounds in the 1914-18 war. Dick was this six foot, blonde curly-haired man, who used to cycle on a dropped handle-bar racing bike from Hitchin about four miles away. Often he arrived with a guitar strapped to his back and he was pretty good at that too. At that time I, of course, had no idea who this man was who made such a marked impression on me as I had only just started to fish.

The next sighting of my idol and mentor was at Arlesey Lake in the early 1950s at the time of the big perch 'revolution' and Arlesey Bomb development - sitting behind two 'rested' rods (with empty line spool bite indicators) in the snow and dressed in an old army great coat and the legendary 'Walker' floppy trilby hat. I didn't actually speak to him and just watched him fish in awe. At Arlesey Lake (only a mile from home) I met great characters like Derek Davenport, Gerry Berth-Jones, Frank Murgett, Pete Thomas, Pat Russell and my great friend Bob Rutland. Dick also introduced me to whom he described as the best still-water angler living - the little heard of Ian French who taught me so much about water-craft. He had trained earlier as a paratrooper and was now chief test-pilot at Handley Page flying Victor bombers. That's another story!

My first proper meetings with Dick were a year or two later at his home at 11 Bearton Avenue, Hitchin, where I cycled once or twice a week for several years. On my very first visit I can still picture Ruth, Dick's vivacious raven-haired wife (she was about five-foot-nothing tall) cutting the front lawn with a pair of hedge-clippers. Dick was then the design director at his family firm Lloyds of Letchworth who made 'Rolls Royce' grass-cutting machines that were used on palace lawns, Lords and Wimbledon. It is difficult to single out memories of my evenings at Bearton Avenue - many were serious, many were funny. Let me give you an insight. Dick's whole approach to angling was practical, yet 'scientific'. One evening he decided he would do some 'striking practice' whilst listening to some opera. He produced two of his unique design carp rod rests secured in wooden blocks, then mounted his Mk IV carp rod in the usual way. I was then asked to shout 'strike' at random to sharpen his pistol-shot reaction time; Richard junior looked on in amazement. We would change over and take it in turns in the hot-seat. Hardly surprising that Richard junior (about eleven at the time) took little interest in angling - he was happier drinking beer from a can. Dick was a pretty liberal-minded father although he had Quaker family origins. I can't remember Dick, himself, drinking alcohol at that time.

It was during this period (circa 1954-55) that Dick taught me to cast a fly. I had watched him in awe when I was about thirteen trout fishing on the Oughton at Oughton Head but had not dared to approach my would-be mentor. What a great tutor to have and what an enchanting memory with Hugo Dalton (from the BBC TV *Tonight* programme) perched under the tall poplars practising his mandolin. Sadly, I believe the Oughton has long since been heavily abstracted and the once-famous Oughton Pond was filled in.

During this period I became actively involved in the Hitchin Angling Club (who had the rights at Arlesey Lake) and the famous *Daily Mirror* specimen fish competition. Dick master-minded and captained the winning Hitchin team. Other youngsters and Walker disciples in the team included Alan Brown, 'Titch' Collins, Trevor Lockhart, Bob Rutland, Peter Thomas and Pat Russell. At the award winners' presentation (at the Savoy Hotel) I remember Dick was dressed in brown corduroy trousers and a green roll-neck sweater. I was only just out of short trousers. VIPs present included Bernard Venables, Pat Winfrey, Howard Marshall, Peter Tombleson and Donald Zec the main 'showbiz' columnist from the *Mirror*.

Dick and a very young Frank Guttfield.

At about this time I remember cycling to Southill with Dick, Trevor and Bob to tench fish at about 3am. Dick asked us to slow up next to a pretty thatched cottage in the nearby village of Stanford to 'scrump' a bunch of red roses; he must have been in Ruth's bad books at the time and this was his way of making amends. But like everything in Walker's life, this mission was planned with precision - he had even packed the secateurs.

In 1956 aged sixteen, I caught a very big 'wild' brown trout from the upper Ivel in Bedfordshire near Astwick. It weighed 6lb 14oz and apparently was the biggest brownie caught on a dry fly in England for twelve years. Unfortunately the fish died and Dick kindly gave me a lift to col-lect the trout and together we made a plaster cast in his shed. He had every intention of painting it for me but unfortunately it was later lost or broken when he moved from Bearton Avenue to Flitwick. I believe it was at that time that Dick had the pleasure of meeting my Dad in Arlesey for the first (and probably last) time. My father did not really support my obsession for angling and he did not give my hero a very warm welcome to put it mildly! He virtu-ally told Dick to f***-off and told him to encourage me with my school work (I was coming up to O levels) instead of this 'mindless' fishing. Dick then put Dad in his place, extolling my talents and told him, "Your son could well become the next Richard Walker," or words to that effect, but that still failed to impress my non-angling father.

However, what my father lacked in encouragement Dick more than compen-sated for. It was really his idea for me to write an account of how I caught that big trout and with his help and advice Jack Thorndike (the Editor) published the six-hundred-word piece in *Angling Times* close to my sixteenth birthday.

A year or so later Dick collected me again from Arlesey in his Humber Hawk - that meeting was something to brag about to my mates, but I didn't know of Dick's hidden driving talents. At that time 90 per cent of the A1 was a single carriageway and somewhere near the Great Ouse at Tempsford he warned me he was about to 'undertake' a big lorry - he sped up on the inside of the lorry via a long lay-by and emerged gleaming in front of it. I froze in the passenger seat and have a feeling he had done that particular manoeuvre several times before. No wonder he chain-smoked over sixty Consulate menthol cigarettes a day! It wasn't too long after that my first white hairs appeared (Dick had been silver grey since I first met him).

Early in 1964 I had what I felt was an original idea for a book - a diary based on a fishing year. I had kept a fishing diary for several years but importantly the book idea was conceived after the particular year. Once again Dick was positive and volunteered to read the typed manuscript. I took it round one evening and he read it all the same night and later wrote in the Foreword '. . . I couldn't put it down and finished it at 3am in the morning'. What more of an accolade could a budding young writer wish for? I'm sure Dick's word would have been sufficient for the first publisher who saw it to say 'yes' and EMAP/Allen & Unwin published *In Search of Big Fish* for the princely sum of 12 shillings and sixpence! I'm told a pristine copy (with dust cover) can now fetch in excess of £200!

Talking of accolades, I remember being on the river Kennet at Theale with Dick when he was doing a film for the BBC TV peak viewing time news programme *Tonight*. After the programme the roving reporter/presenter six-foot four-inch bearded Fife Robertson described Dick as the most confident, knowledgeable, professional human being he had ever interviewed on the *Tonight* programme.

Yes, Dick was the consummate professional in every way and I'm privileged to be one of the dozens who benefited from Dick's great generosity. He gave far more to the sport of angling than he ever took from it.

He was by far the most influential angling figure since Walton and towered above other 'experts' past and present. That is why he was the only angler ever to appear on *Desert Island Discs* and that is why I reckon he should have been 'Sir Richard Walker'.

DOROTHY HANCOCK, Norfolk - 2006
The Sister in charge of me when pregnant, who,
with her husband, became friends.

What do I remember about Richard? Firstly his great kindnesses and generosity, there was always a bottle or fish or both to take home after a visit. I recall the first visit to your lovely home when I spotted a small mouse in your bookcase - I nearly died as I am terrified of mice, and even on a first visit I could not hide my fear and behaved rather badly. However, Richard soon had the situation under control, and did not make me feel like the idiot I portrayed.

JAMES L. HARDY, Northumberland - 1991

My late cousin Bill Hardy and I first met Dick at a lunch in London, which had been arranged by Fred Buller. There had been some disagreement between Dick and 'Hardy Brothers', which Fred thought should be healed; the lunch was to be the catalyst. I remember choosing carp from the menu, thinking it was an appropriate choice in Dick's presence.

When the Moncrieff Rod Development Company was set up, Dick became one of its members together with Leslie Moncrieff, Fred Buller and Fred Taylor. It was through the Hardy connection with the MRDC that we were to benefit from Dick's ideas and thoughts on fishing and fishing tackle. I particularly remember two occasions with Dick, which were to shape angling history. The first was a visit to Grafham in the early days of reservoir angling in the Sixties. Dick, Fred Buller and Pete Thomas took me out on Grafham water for the day, so that I could see for myself the kind of equipment that was required for this relatively new angling technique. From this outing we started to develop rods and reels specifically for reservoir angling.

The other occasion was when Dick drove me down to visit the Royal Aircraft Establishment at Farnborough to meet Leslie Phillips - one of the inventors of carbon-fibre. We talked fishing all the way, stopping for lunch briefly over a bottle of Blue Nun. I had done my tank training at Farnborough during the war when in the Royal Armoured Corps, so found the changing countryside most interesting. Our visit to the RAE led to the first carbon-fibre rods to be made from free issue material supplied by Leslie Phillips. These were exciting days for us all, and led to the patent on the use of carbon-fibre in fishing rods, being taken out in the names of Dick, Hardy and the Ministry of Defence.

John Jacobs and I met in the early Sixties when my wife and I started to play golf. John had a golf range just outside Newcastle, and we would have lessons from him on his visits north. In exchange I taught him fly casting - a good arrangement. It is very possible that I was instrumental in bringing John and Dick together.

I have met some wonderful people during the past forty years in the tackle business, all over the world, and I am proud to include Dick amongst them.

WILLIAM F. HARDY, Northumberland - 1983

The name 'Dick Walker' will undoubtedly mean different things to different people. There will be those who follow every word he writes with bated breath; there will also be those who condemn his articles, almost without reading them. This is the stuff of fame. I know that Dick never writes anything that he does not believe in. This brings me to my first contact with Dick, which was a great number of years ago, before the *Fishing Gazette* closed its last page. The famous *Fishing Gazette*, the demise of which marked the end of an era: many things, and more particularly, many attitudes, were changing at the time. The attitudes to fishing, which were enshrined in the *Fishing Gazette*, were those which probably knew their height with Halford and Skues. Of course Skues was a revolutionary in his day, but his philosophy of country sport was in tune with Halford before him and Dick after him. Dick was certainly vitally interested in maintaining all that is best in angling, but he was not averse to innovation, so long as it was consistent with preservation of his beloved sport.

My first contact with Dick was not an auspicious one. He had written something - I cannot even remember the subject now, which only shows how apt we are to take up positions for the flimsiest reasons - which was printed in the *Fishing Gazette*. I wrote to the Editor, who is now Mrs Richard Walker, to insist on a recantation. She obtained this for me, and a state of armed neutrality maintained. A mutual friend, in the person of Fred Buller, decided that this was not good enough, so he arranged a meeting at which Dick and I met for the first time. From then on we have been firm friends, and all past disagreements disappeared.

Dick has been instrumental in giving Hardy Brothers numerous good product ideas, among which the Richard Walker Reservoir rod, which was a conspicuous success. It was designed by him on paper, and was, therefore, a good example of the scientific approach to designing in the new materials. Later on came the Farnborough, named by Dick for another mutual friend, Leslie Philips of RAE, Farnborough; the man responsible for the development of the method of manufacturing carbon fibres in continuous lengths, which made the modern rod possible. These are only two examples of a continuing relationship with Dick, which benefited the company and, I hope, gave satisfaction to him also.

On a different tack, I should like to relate a visit I paid to Letchworth some years ago. Along with some colleagues I spent a marvellous evening with Dick and his mother, the redoubtable Mrs E. M. Walker. She is the soul of hospitality; and in her home she gave us a memory, which I hope, for one, will never fade from my mind. If my memory serves well, Dick and Fred Taylor cooked the evening meal, which consisted, for the main course, of fish, done to perfection. After the usual drinks, and when we were in a relaxed state of mind and body, Mrs Walker sat at the piano and played, while we stood around and sang carols, for it was close to Christmas. Afterwards we sat round the huge wood fire and talked. Why do we not allow ourselves more occasions like that in our lives? We seem to be always hurrying and scurrying from one appointment to another these days, without giving ourselves any time to savour the real joys in life, for which we do the scurrying in the first place.

One of the bonuses available to those engaged in the fishing tackle world, or in fishing itself, is the opportunity to meet so many interesting people. While their interest in fishing may be the prime reason for meeting, it is often qualities other than their ability to fish, which are more enduring in one's mind. On the other hand, it may be that people with that quality known to the Spanish as '*simpatico*', or to the French as '*sympathique*', tend to like fishing. Why do we not have a word in English to describe that particular sensitivity to others, and to things and places? Perhaps it does not go with the 'stiff upper lip' the English like to maintain.

From the foregoing one might think that Dick has lived an idyllic life, but like most of us, he has had his own problems, which I will not enlarge on. He also has had to make a living, like most of us. Together with his mother, who is a first rate cook, specialising in cooking game of all kinds, but also a considerable business woman, he had run the family firm most successfully for very many years. Just like Hardys, he makes only the best, and persuades hardbitten public parks' superintendents to pay for his expensive, but excellent, mowing machines.

As it happens Dick and I have not shared many actual fishing experiences. He lived in the south and I in the north, so we have gone our own ways in fishing. We have had many pleasurable hours of discussion on the technical details of rods and other fishing gear. It has to be understood that Dick has had a university training in engineering and electronics. During the war he helped to develop radar, and became familiar with RAE at Farnborough and this was the reason he was able to introduce us to Leslie Philips.

Being the man he was, he put all his abilities and learning into his ideas for better fishing tackle. He would have hit it off well with my grandfather, who had one overriding aim, to make better rods. What is true of Dick, and I am sure was true of my grandfather, was that he always enjoyed what he was doing. For a satisfying life this must be a prime requirement.

How do you end an article of this sort? It would seem appropriate to put into one sentence the epitome of all that is Dick. Such a sentence would tend to appear fulsome in the extreme. It would be almost as embarrassing for me to write as it would for Dick to read. (Shades of the 'stiff upper lip'.) However, something must be said, if only for the artistic reason that there has to be an end, not merely a stop.

In a life of sixty odd years one meets many people. Some are outstanding, some are not. Dick has to be amongst the top half dozen. He exemplifies so much of what, in England, we consider to be a real gentleman. My dictionary puts it thus: a man of good breeding, kindly feelings, and high principles, a man of honour.

JACK HARGREAVES - 1991

I meant to let you know earlier that I am myself getting a book ready for next Christmas and have decided that one of the chapters of it should be my memories of Dick. I haven't got to it yet but should do within the next month or six weeks. My own chapter will be about three thousand words at least, and full of gossip which is not perhaps appropriate to your needs. However, I will send it to you as soon as I have got it down in rough and you can take what you want from it for your use.

Sadly I did not receive a further letter, and Jack died in 1994. I contacted Jack's step-son Simon Baddeley but he was not aware of a book being prepared. He contacted Jack's great friend Len Smith who also did not know of such a book, but commented in an email to Simon Baddeley he could well imagine that Jack would have included such a chapter, and added that: 'Jack often said to me that Dick was the ultimate coarse fisherman.'

MAURICE INGHAM - 1991

When Maurice wrote this piece for me he had suffered his stroke, causing paralysis, and was unable to fish. But he kept very busy, as he told me: 'I am grateful for the other faculties that seem to be unaffected, and I have been doing quite a bit of writing and painting'. Maurice had written in another letter to me, that he liked to keep in touch with 'what was happening, and I take vicarious pleasure from other anglers' successes'. Rather like Richard, later in life.

Random Recollections of Dick Walker - the man.

If I were asked to choose just one word to describe Dick Walker the word that would immediately spring to mind would be 'generosity'. I believe Dick was the most truly generous person I have ever met. I discovered very early in our acquaintanceship that one should never express envious admiration of any of Dick's fishing tackle or indeed of any of his possessions or one was likely very soon to find oneself the embarrassed owner of those items. Readers of *Drop Me A Line* will know that before I even met him Dick was attempting, through our correspondence, to encourage me to take up fly fishing and that, as an additional encouragement, he presented me with a beautiful little built-cane fly rod that he had made entirely in his own workshop. Looking at it now, I marvel at the skill and the laborious striving for perfection that must have gone into the assembling of the minute sections of cane that form the top joint of that rod. I also treasure many other examples of Dick's generosity, probably the most highly valued of which is a wonderful collection of magnificent artificial flies, tied by his own hands.

But it was not in material things alone that his generous nature found expression. At a time when many anglers were, regrettably, secretive about the techniques that they had found successful, Dick derived great pleasure in sharing his knowledge and experience and he gave unstintingly of his time in advising and helping anyone who sought his assistance. I know he derived great satisfaction when a good fish was caught by a young protégé as a result of advice he had given. In his latter years when his declining health prevented him from wielding a fly rod for more than a few casts, he would sit beside an aspiring fly fisher, offering helpful tips and advice and he was almost as delighted when a good trout was caught as if he had caught it himself.

It was this desire to share his knowledge with other anglers that inspired the formation of the Carp Catchers' Club in the 1950s and also, I am sure, it was the main reason why for so many years he wrote his immensely popular columns for the angling press.

Of Dick's great angling skill and outstanding successes much has been written elsewhere and I do not wish to add to the tributes already paid, except to add my profound admiration, but there are other aspects of this multi-faceted character that are perhaps not so well known.

He was a delightful angling companion, always optimistic, cheerful and full of fun and, unlike some, when sport was slow he was not constantly wishing to move elsewhere. He always chose his pitch with great care and deliberation and, if it did not produce the sport he expected, he would regard that as a challenge - a problem to be solved and he always maintained that a solution would not be found by moving away from the problem. He always wanted to know *why* and in this, I am sure, lay the secret of his success. When he knew that fish behaved in a particular way under certain conditions, he was able to use that knowledge to his advantage when similar circumstances occurred in the future. Like all of us, Dick was not without his faults, but such as they were, his faults were minor ones. He was a great talker and could - and did! - talk very knowledgeably on almost any subject but, just occasionally, one was tempted to move away to a different pitch! I think it was Bernard Venables who, fanatical angler though he was, once said that Dick was the only person who could bore him by talking about fishing! His other 'fault' was that he was a reluctant participant in the chores that are inherent in camping by the water-side, such as making coffee (in almost constant demand), collecting firewood, digging latrines, cooking meals, washing up, etc. - in fact anything that for a few moments would take him away from his rods. As I recollect, Dick's main contribution to cooking was at the final meal of a session when he would make a gigantic 'nosh-up', by tipping into a frying pan the contents of the entire stock of unused tins - baked beans, sardines, spaghetti, stew - the lot! It looked a nauseating mess but, surprisingly, it was usually very good, but that was no doubt, a reflection of the state of our appetites rather than the quality of the food.

Dick had a lively wit and a Puckish sense of humour, but one of his most endearing characteristics was the almost childlike pleasure he derived from the small creatures of the waterside. I remember his gently fondling and 'baby-talking' to a small coot that he unhooked with exquisite care after it had taken a hook baited with a piece of bread crust intended for a carp. He habitually scattered small scraps of bread along the banks and in the shallow water in front of his pitch in order to attract rats, voles, mice and the small birds in which he delighted although he was not exactly delighted when a rat swam out and took a piece of crust intended for a Redmire carp. That was the first and only time I saw a rat fairly hooked in the mouth. His affection for small birds, however, did not extend to the larger species. Ducks he would tolerate within limits, but swans he detested for the nuisance and disturbance they caused and for their persistence.

He had an imaginative, romantic streak that, I am sure, was unsuspected by many of his angling acquaintances. I remember one wet night when we were fishing at Woldale. We had sought shelter in my tent from the cold driving rain and our conversation drifted comfortably from one subject to another until we found ourselves discussing in all seriousness which colours best represent the nature and characteristics of the various species of fresh water fishes. I cannot remember all the suggestions that we were agreed upon, but I do remember that we agreed that carp should be represented by purple, tench by olive green, pike by crimson, roach - blue, perch - orange, grayling - lilac, bream - brown, and so on. Not all Dick's fishing was conducted in a deadly serious vein. Occasionally as a relief from the more 'mature' sport of carp fish-ing we would indulge in light-hearted eel fishing sessions and impromptu mock-serious tiddler-snatching competitions. The latter usually developed into hilarious events with non-stop good-natured banter, and ribald comments greeting every missed bite or the capture of any unusually small fish. Not withstanding the prevailing atmosphere of hilarity I am sure we all did our utmost to outdo the others, although none would have been willing to admit it. It was all great fun - childish perhaps but highly enjoyable nevertheless.

Almost unsuspected, I am sure, by most of his angling associates was Dick's flair for writing humorous verse. No doubt a literary purist would describe it as doggerel but it was not written with any laureate aspirations but for fun and as such it achieved its purpose. The following is a small example:

> *There used to be a primrose here,*
> *But since I last passed by,*
> *It's been pooped on by a cow!*

R. W. KINGSLEY KEFFORD - 1991

I fully agree that Dick would not support other than an honest appraisal; with this in mind I have tried to concur with your wish, but in writing of a man with such superlative credentials it has been hard not to over-extol.

The late Denys Watkins-Pitchford ('BB') introduced me to Richard Walker in 1950, the outstanding common interest in our triple association being carp and carp angling. How importantly within the sport of angling has the subject advanced since those early days; today's knowledge owes a great deal to the early pioneers in the years immediately following the Second World War, of whom by far the greatest was Dick Walker; he improved many aspects of both game and coarse fishing techniques by thought, word, and deed.

Before those early days, carp fishing had been so neglected that suitable tackle was simply non-existent. Dick, who was a clever engineer, went to work and designed and built a rod - his Mk IV, which proved to be the best for its purpose that has ever been produced; he constructed a lightweight big landing-net; he thought out the useful bite-indicator and constructed the prototype. With the advent of nylon, which had its origin during the war years, and with all these new improvements, a few heavy-weight carp were starting to be caught - with occasionally a 10-pounder, a 'specimen' in those days.

A couple of instances concerning Dick's ingenious ways are well worth recall. Close to his home in Hitchin was Bearton Pond, and summer dawns might reveal Dick, almost hidden in the bank-side herbage, angling with crust-baited hook within a foot or two of the water's edge. He had previously discovered that this was the hour when, free of bankside disturbance, the big carp came close in-shore in search of discarded bait and sandwiches. The highly successful method of 'margin-fishing' had its birth!

August 1st, 1952, saw Dick and Maurice Ingham at Dagenham. On their arrival the local angling devotees assured them that carp fishing was a complete waste of time, for the lake-bottom was covered to a depth of several inches with a moss-like weed into which the legered bait must surely disappear. Deep in thought, the pair took a stroll round the further confines of the lake. The time was about midday; an occasional heavy fish was seen rolling on the surface far out. "Time to tackle up," said Dick. In a letter he wrote to me a few days later he told me: 'I put a running lead on my 9lb b.s. line, stopped with a shot 4 inches from the hook, which I baited with a biggish crust, a Mitchell reel and Mk IV rod, and a cast was made to the middle of the big bay.'

Within the ensuing four hours, two big carp were landed, the larger one, a fine common-scaled fish of 22lb 12oz was Dick's largest to date. What a simple, yet well conceived, and wonderfully successful outcome to the problem!

Six weeks later, on 13th September, Dick was to land his record fish at Redmire.

Dick had a constant wry sense of humour. Once I remember asking him if he had any exciting angling experiences to relate from when he was at Cambridge University. "Only when I was fished out of Girton pond one dark night," was his reply! Now I need hardly explain, Girton, in those days was a College of learning restricted to the attendance of young ladies!

Dick was one of the most generous of men; whether high, middle, or of low estate, class distinction meant nothing to him. Herewith, an instance: when we first fished at Redmire, the latter-day bailiff Eric Higgs was then a young schoolboy. Dick, in conversation with him, discovered the lad's fondness for cricket, so promptly bought him a quality new bat. Any item in a friend's tackle, which Dick decided was lacking in usefulness, would soon be replaced by a fine article, of his own construction. Refusing all offers of payment, he made me a Mk IV rod, which I have continued to use regularly to this day.

Very many people, and not only anglers, took pleasure from personal acquaintance with Richard Walker. Thousands have gained, and will continue to gain, inspiration from his written word.

Dick will never be forgotten.

DOROTHY MOODY - 1991
St Christopher School

Every school-day for a year, or perhaps two, I saw Dick in our small sixth-form room. I was a boarder and there were about eight boys in the Sixth, all boarders except for Dick and another boy, and two day-girls.

Dick interested me from the first, his strong likes and dislikes, his way of deliberately challenging all accepted views, such as vegetarianism, and his absolute delight in provoking the other boys to argument. He did this mischievously, sometimes rousing them by changing his argument in mid-stream, and contradicting a view he himself had put forward only a short time before. They were a nice lot of lads really, very individual and basically good tempered as Dick too certainly was. He was always very much in control of himself and I regarded him as more mature than most of them. I never saw him alone. My teenage heart-throb of that era was Noel, the other day-boy.

What did Dick look like? Well, tall, well-built really, with the odd distinction that his curly hair was tinged with grey. Sometimes he had a decidedly sardonic look, usually when he was trying to put someone down by using sarcasm. He was very good at finding the right words quickly. Sometimes there were fights, but it was a small room, which meant us being crowded together.

I often used to go to 'Old Scholars Weekend' and remember the headmaster Stephen Harris asking me about Dick, but I wasn't able to give him any news. He told me that he would have liked to have known if Dick was all right through the war, and added that he was the only man of that era that left saying that he never wanted to keep in contact with St Christopher, ever again.

If Dick had one outstanding quality, and I know he had many others, it was his honesty with himself and his courage in showing it. Not many people can do this and not many can think so clearly - it could possibly have made him a little difficult to live with at times.

We had occasional contact over the years and my opinion of Dick remained the same: he had great strength of character. To me he was a very fine human being with so much kindness and understanding, which his surface manner often hid, and hid deliberately. Why? I do not know. Yes, one of the finest men I have known.

JAMES MACGIBBON - 1990

Richard Walker was a model author. When I wrested from him the draft of his seminal *Still-Water Angling* he wrote abominably but, being highly intelligent, he accepted extensive editing, realising the merit of not using three words when one was adequate.

Later he paid me the compliment of saying that I had 'taught him how to write'. And he did, very quickly, write clearly and succinctly. Not that he was a modest man: he knew he was the best angler of his times and had a pretty good idea of himself. This, however, did not prevent him from paying tribute to his contemporaries in the preface to his famous book. He was always generous in this way.

Everything he undertook to do he did well, be it manufacturing grass mowers up to the mechanical standards set by Rolls Royce, angling and rod-making, and cooking. Richard's steak and kidney pie would have been approved of by Elizabeth David or Savarin himself.

Most importantly of all he was a loyal friend, and an enthusiast who delighted in seeing the new generations practising their skills with the rod, not just exploiting his theories but (as I believe he wished) extending them. I am sure that the angling expertise of his wife, Pat, gave him particular satisfaction.

JOHN NIXON - 1990

I have a multitude of memories, although I was never a close friend as I saw Richard Walker only occasionally, usually at fishing exhibitions. I must say that, in my younger days, I suppose my attitude was coloured by hero worship.

The very first time I met him was in the spring of 1952, after some correspondence following his carp articles in the old *Fishing Gazette*. My letters to the *FG* criticised 'Water Rail' for trying to popularise carp fishing, as I felt carp fishing would better retain its exclusivity if less people took it up. Of course I had no idea at that time that RW was 'Water Rail'!

Richard invited me to tea at 11 Bearton Avenue. I spent a fascinating afternoon in his den; he showed me all his new carp fishing rods and net and I met Bob Rutland, who had just caught a 31lb carp. I was thrilled that such a famous person should take such an interest in me - I was a seventeen-year-old apprentice in the RAF at the time - but that was typical of Richard, he always made time for keen young fishermen. To be perfectly honest, and no reflection on Richard, I will always consider that he did carp fishing no favours at all by writing so much about it, and that the present scene with gangs of high-tech anglers with multitudes of bite-alarms and snatch rigs on the banks of every water is a result.

During 1951 to about 1955 Richard kept me amused and encouraged in my carp fishing efforts with regular letters, and my second meeting with him was at Arlesey Lake in November 1952, when I also met Dick Kefford - a meeting which was to result in many happy hours carping all over the country.

My meetings with Richard were largely at the angling shows and one occasion was in 1959 at Alexandra Palace, which I think was when he first met his future wife. It was on that occasion that Richard rather blotted his copybook with my wife Valerie (then my fiancée) by saying that she would no doubt put a stop to my fishing after we were married - she never forgave him for that!

There was a trip to Weirwood Reservoir and I remember I made an idiot of myself by 'blowing' his carefully hatched plan to embarrass the then Pat Marston (Editor of the *FG*) in front of the bailiff by mentioning that we'd brought some maggots to try out there. He had telephoned the night before to brief me to go along with the plan, but whether through his bad briefing or my own slowness, I thought that it was purely a joke against the bailiff and that Pat was in on the joke. I will long remember Richard's exasperated snort in the car when I blew the gaff as we approached the reservoir.

I do not think anyone who ever knew Richard, however slightly, will ever forget the acquaintance. He was unique, a one-off personality of incredible intelligence and irreverent humour, a mixture of the schoolboy and the sage. I class him as the greatest British angler of all time and I shall long remember his many kindnesses and the encouragement he gave to me.

ALAN PEARSON - 1991

In my book *Trout Angler's Angles* I wrote thus of Richard Walker:

I knew the great man from about the mid-Fifties until his untimely death, and my memories of him are kaleidoscopic. More than anyone else he taught me to use my powers of logic, to think for myself and never accept tradition as fact unless I had investigated it, and to develop coherent campaigns against the fish I truly wanted to catch, rather than just adopt the standard 'chuck and chance it' systems adopted by so many. He also taught me how to laugh at myself for failing to realise that fishing must be fun.

It seems strange to think that I can never again pick up the phone to hear that warm drawling voice say, "Hello, my cock" - his standard greeting - and no more will I have my ears assailed with shaggy-dog stories retailed in a plethora of accents.

Someone recently said to me that he thought there was a total lack of new, logical thinking in angling these days, and regretfully we had to agree that this is because Richard is no longer around to needle us, to lead us into traps of our own making, or to persuade us to dig holes so that we could fall into them. We all of us, whether we realise it or not, miss his kindness, his warmth, his touch of sheer magic, his undoubted genius . . .

To me, Walker was the ultimate angler, possessed of mind-boggling skills with tackle, with pen, and with people. In helping others nothing was too much trouble, and there are many excellent anglers today who owe their beginnings to the man. My own indebtedness is great.

I wrote these words in 1990 and regretted only that the context in which they were written did not, in my opinion, permit much more to be said. Indeed, were I to catalogue the occasions of angling excitement that we enjoyed together, add in the severely technical discussions devolving upon the co-efficient of this or that, the modulus of elasticity of something else, and the varying necessities for introducing a constant (always known as 'K') into equations, and then leaven the whole with accounts of pranks and japes, of dreadful puns and none-too-tuneful singing to a rather twangy guitar - why, I feel that we could well be talking about a rather lengthy volume. And I was just one of his friends . . .

I well remember the day we were attending the angling opening session on Jubilee Lake, the second of the Church Hill Farm lakes. This was likely to be a most interesting day. As the retained fishery consultant, I had supervised the excavation of the lake and the construction of the immense dam; had estimated the length of time that it would take to fill, and had introduced the first stocking of rainbows - trout of some 2lb 8oz average - when I judged that it was about half full. In spite of a mild, dry period, the lake filled ahead of forecast and visual observation suggested that the trout had grown on well. How well we still had to discover.

What a morning we had. Both Richard and myself took trout up to a little in excess of six pounds, an amazing growth achievement. The star of the morning's session though, was undoubtedly John Cronin who achieved a marvellous catch with the best couple of trout each in excess of seven pounds. He, Richard and I sat talking on the banks, shortly before lunch, and our main topic was the growth achievement of the trout in such a short period of time.

"High protein diet, my cocks," said Richard. We looked askance and he pointed towards the lake margin, at our feet. There, all the way along the bank, as far as the eye could see, was a mass of drowned, drowning and escaping lobworms, driven from their normal habitat by the fast encroaching waters. We all agreed that we had never seen so many worms before. Easy pickings indeed for foraging trout.

Up at the clubhouse, Cronin - in a naturally excited state - was waxing lyrical about the size and numbers of trout that he had caught, and reeling off names of flies with gay abandon. Richard coughed dryly, and pointed to the floor at John's feet. There, in slimy disarray, were several fat lobworms trying to untangle themselves from each other.

"What sort of flies are those then, Cronin my cock?" asked Richard innocently. "Bet we'd have caught as well as you if we'd had some of them." There was a prolonged silence, eventually broken by mass hysteria as we gave way to the strain of watching the various expressions chase across John Cronin's face. We only quietened down after he threatened to put us all under arrest for behaviour likely to occasion a breach of the peace.

Richard was a great lover of animals, particularly cats, but he did seem to have a way with all creatures. I remember taking him to fish for big rainbows in a private lake in the Cotswolds, a beautiful place marred only by the presence of a pair of singularly ferocious Australian black swans. Indeed, these were so notorious, that no one actually dared go near the lake unless they were carrying a very long, stout cudgel because it was frequently necessary to beat them off. I told Richard about them as we were driving to the water, but he seemed singularly unimpressed, and I must admit thinking to myself that I was very likely to see the unflappable Walker in a considerable flap.

We started on a narrow arm of the lake, Richard one side, myself the other, and to start with the black beggars did not put in an appearance, so we were able to catch a good trout or two without hindrance. Then from the middle distance there was a flapping and a hissing, and up steamed the cob, black feathers very ruffled and red beak gleaming like freshly spilled blood. Richard was the closest, so the cob hurried over, hissing like a leaky steam engine, but infinitely more menacingly. When he was no more than a yard away Richard stooped over, putting his face on a level with the swan's red beak, and I have to admit that I cringed in anticipation of the mayhem that had to follow. Then he spoke to the swan, not loudly but with some passion: "You've been misled, someone told you that a swan can break a man's arm with one blow of its wing. Well, that is just not true. What is true is that *this* man can break your neck with one blow of his arm, and will very definitely do so if you don't piss off and leave me to fish in peace."

The old cob hesitated, stopped hissing, rearranged its puffed out plumage and quietly paddled away with scarcely a backward glance

"There you are," called Richard cheerfully. "It only takes a little kindness and some applied psychology." Shortly after that he caught a fine hen rainbow, well in excess of the then British record of 8lb 8oz, and returned it healthy and unharmed after carefully weighing it.

"Well, my cock, we had agreed to put all the hen fish back, and that was as pretty a hen as ever I've seen. Apart from that, this is a private lake, and you know I never say a word about any fish I take from private waters."

And yet that trout would have permitted him to achieve his lifetime ambition: to hold two British freshwater records simultaneously, because he had already caught the record carp.

One final short tale. One bitterly cold February day, we were fishing Richard's stretch of the upper Great Ouse and had a few good chub to our credit. Just as we were about to give up and enjoy a hot meal in the hut, he said that he wanted to try something. I watched him, at first with interest and then with mounting incredulity, as he rigged his terminal tackle in such a way that he could bait up with a whole slice of bread from a large loaf. He dipped this carefully in the water until it was well soaked, and then set it trundling downstream suspended beneath a sizeable trotting float.

"What do you think you're at, Walker?" I enquired, and as I spoke the float slid beneath the surface and quickly away, as a monstrous chub engulfed the whole soggy slice.

"Well, you never know, do you?" grinned Richard. And that's about the truth of it.

You never did know with Walker . . .

LESLIE PHILLIPS - 1990

The strange tale of how I met Richard Walker.

At an early stage in the development of carbon-fibre, the Ministry of Supply invited the BBC to broadcast an introductory programme and this was transmitted under the title 'From Strength to Strength' in the late Sixties. In it, I described the major properties of the new material and indicated some of its early uses in racing cars, boats and aerospace.

As an extra inducement, we announced that samples of the batch fibre (tows up to about 0.9 metres in length - a tow is a bundle of straight untwisted fibres containing a few thousand filaments) would be made available, without charge, for novel uses, in exchange for the results of any experiments, good or bad.

The public response was immediate and overwhelming!

Among the first of many visitors to beat a path to the departmental door, was the angler and writer Richard Walker, who brought with him J. L. Hardy of Hardy Bros, for whom Richard was consultant at the time. There was an enthusiastic meeting of minds. We agreed that carbon-fibre-reinforced plastics did seem to have the right properties for lightweight fishing rods and arranged to cooperate in production and testing of some prototype blanks, using fibre provided by RAE.

Within a few weeks, information began trickling back. The rods, while being both light and powerful, were really too violent in their response; flies were repeatedly snapping off their leaders during the cast.

Evidently it was time for a rethink. We needed a grade of fibre, which was a little less stiff, even stronger, with a higher elongation at break (the so-called type II fibre).

Happily such a product was already under development in the department, in the form of a thin but continuous tow. Possibly this could be woven? Early experiments with a small handloom showed real feasibility; and a contract was placed with James Carr and Sons Ltd, traditional weavers of narrow tapes, to mechanise production. There were many problems, first of all in the cleaning and sizing of the fibre. Then special creels had to be designed with low-friction guides to feed the tow safely through the loom without damage. The warp threads had to be held on individually spring-loaded reels, otherwise they wove unevenly. Special conductors were arranged over the surface of the fabric cloth to dissipate the high build-up of static electricity. Finally, around each motor to drive the loom an inflatable plastic bag was provided, blowing a current of air outwards, thus preventing loose fluff or fibre from entering and shorting-out the power supply!

The result of all this was a series of tapes or cloth, beautifully even, with their flattened carbon warps arranged in parallel array, held together with light glass-weft. Such fabrics became known in the trade as 'U/D (uni-directional) carbon cloth' and Richard took to them like a duck to water. He designed a series of superb rods with this material, one of which was called the 'Farnborough' rod in recognition of our period of fruitful collaboration. We did spend a most enjoyable day together fishing at Grafham Water, and it was very satisfying for me to see the rods in action.

Somewhere in the archives of the Materials Department at the RAE is our last letter from Richard Walker. In it, he says that the development of carbon-fibre and its application to fishing rods 'saved the British tackle industry'.

A fitting memory to a thoroughly nice man!

THE REV. R. J. REDRUP - 1991

My many years of correspondence with Dick started after he provoked, but entertained, me in an article in the *Trout and Salmon* magazine. I am happy to say that this culminated in friendship, and occasional fishing together. Dick's generosity is well known, but I found that his good deeds were usually conducted with great discretion. I remember him arranging for the Revd. Edward Alston (captor of the record rudd) to go for a day's trout fishing with me at Damerham. I told Dick that I would gladly pick him up as it was not many miles out of my way, and Dick insisted that he was not to know how the visit was financed. It was only when I arrived that I discovered that Dick had financed my own day's fishing as well. He was a perfect example of the biblical principle of doing good, by stealth.

COLIN ROGERS - 1985

Richard and I were friends from the late Fifties, when I had charge of the Lancashire Education Committee's playing fields, and we used to meet every year at the Groundsmens' Association Exhibition (of lawnmowers), sometimes at the Game Fair and sometimes on other occasions. He was most helpful to me both in connection with my work and also with the other interests we had in common, more especially fishing and photography. We corresponded regularly up to the time of Richards's illness: I still have every one of his splendid letters, which I value highly.

I also have all manner of other things he sent me from time to time, including some of his exquisitely tied flies. More than anything, I value the mass of information he passed on and all the advice he so generously gave.

During my lifetime I have been privileged to meet a number of people of genius, whom I regard it an honour to have known. Of these, none would I rank more highly than Richard, and certainly none has been more kindly and patient. He is one of whom I am constantly reminded, and one I could not possibly forget.

KEN SUTTON - 1983

When I first met Richard Walker in 1952, he gave me the privilege of reading the proofs of his forthcoming book *Still-Water Angling*. It left me with the opinion that his was certainly the most original mind in the angling world, in the first half of the present century.

Since then he has grown to tower over Britain's anglers as no one else has in angling history. As an angler, and a marvellously skilful craftsman, as a scientist, an innovator, an inventor, a writer and fountain of wisdom in angling matters, he has profoundly influenced angling at every level. Whether it is coarse fish or trout the angler seeks, the Arlesey Bomb he uses, the roller arm on the pick-up on his reel, the split-cane, glass fibre, or carbon rod he fishes with, the shooting-head line and probably the fly he uses, Richard Walker either invented or developed it.

FRED J. TAYLOR

In 1991 I asked Fred if I could use this piece that he had written, before he went to Australia, in connection with another book that he and Richard were planning.

To say that Dick Walker has simply been a friend for well over thirty years would be misleading. We met, as a result of his writings, in the early Fifties and it is true that, along with my brother Ken and my cousin Joe, I was one of his early disciples. Ours, however, was not an ordinary friendship. Somehow it developed into something deeper than that and, although our meetings are less frequent these days, that bond between us still exists as strongly as it ever did.

Dick once referred to Ken, Joe and me as a 'joyous crew'. We were indeed just that and we became even more joyous when he became a regular member of it. We have never quarrelled, as far as I can remember. We have had differences of opinion many times, and there have been occasions when he has irritated me almost to breaking point. Only the fact that I knew he was doing it deliberately restrained me.

He has always borne the reputation of being conceited, and it would be quite easy, on occasions, for a stranger to believe this to be justified. The truth, however, is that Dick Walker has often set out deliberately to antagonise. It has been his way of assessing character since the day we first met. It became more or less commonplace for him to subject visiting strangers to a great deal of mockery, in the sincere belief that anyone who could tolerate it, would prove to be acceptable. We found ourselves agreeing with that philosophy and it has stood us in good stead over the years.

I have heard Dick Walker described both as a 'big-head' and a 'dignified gentleman'. Both descriptions fit, depending upon circumstances and his mood at the time. "Big head he may be," said one acquaintance, "but after his achievements he's entitled to be one." (Paul Goss.) "He puts on an act of sheer arrogance," said another, "but in fact he is a kind, generous and dignified gentleman". (The late Jimmy James.)

I have seen him in all his moods. I have known him depressed, argumentative, arrogant, puzzled, hurt and joyful, and of all his many friends, with the exception, perhaps, of Peter Thomas who has known him longer, I believe I understand him as well as anyone. That in itself is simple and yet, at the same time so complicated as to be verging on the impossible.

My own life-style changed as a result of Dick Walker's influence and generosity. He would not thank me for saying so, and it is just possible that I may have carved out a niche for myself in the field of angling journalism without him, but I believe I owe most of my success to his kindness and encouragement. Without his prompting I might never have bothered. Whenever I have mentioned this to him, his reply has been that it is impossible to make a silk purse out of a sow's ear. Be that as it may, I have always known that my debt to Dick Walker can never be repaid.

He has always been a superb angler and his thinking has seldom been far off the mark. His achievements speak for themselves but it is a fact that, despite his competitive nature, he has always enjoyed the success of other anglers. Joe Taylor once said that Dick Walker enjoyed putting the landing-net under someone else's fish as much as if he had caught the fish himself. That is indeed the truth. My brother Ken once said of him, "You can't say he's always right, or that he's never wrong, but you'd better have the facts handy if you argue with him. And even then you'd better do so with great care!" That, too, is very true.

Bernard Venables once told me, "Dick Walker is the only person who can bore me talking about fishing."

Perhaps you'd have to know both Bernard and Dick to understand such a statement. I do not find it difficult myself, since I have known times when I too have been bored. Not from the content of the discussion, but from the sheer frustration of wanting to go to sleep while Dick Walker wanted to talk!

He can be as stubborn as a mule or as docile as a dove, depending upon the principles involved, but having made a decision, he has always been prepared to stand or fall by the outcome.

He has many faults but they are far outweighed by virtues, the greatest of which I believe is this great gift of bringing out the best in other people.

PETER THOMAS - 2006

My brother Stan used to fish with Dick in the 1930s, and I would join them. Later it was Dick and myself that became the 'two of us' to fish together, and it was long before he became famous. In due course Dick started writing, and when he became known for his carp fishing, his readers were unaware that as youngsters we had fly fished the Hertfordshire rivers for wild brown trout. It is sad to think of those rivers now, the Beane, Mimram and Oughton, and to know that the trout are gone, due to pollution or water abstraction. There has been improvement in many rivers, perhaps one day it might be possible to reverse the situation of 'our' rivers? There are a few trout in the Oughton now, but I can't think that any of the rivers will ever be a patch on what they were.

Gradually through Dick's articles, we met many anglers who became our friends, and who also became well known in the angling press. Friends who were initially local to us included Pat Russell and Bob Rutland, then there were the Taylor brothers, Fred Buller, Maurice Ingham and Peter Stone and gradually the circle increased.

Dick wanted people to know that he was not just a carp angler, but that he embraced all fishing, except sea fishing - he did not like the sea, but of all the species I think that roach were his particular favourite. Many of our visits to different waters produced the effect of Dick being a bit of a 'pied piper', as it was not long before a group of anglers gathered around him, watching him fish, or listening to him talking. We went together to give talks and demonstrations on fly dressing.

Dick's many achievements are being covered in this biography, suffice for me to add that my only contribution to his success was being an enthusiastic companion, who would warmly respond to any proposal to go fishing anywhere and at any time. We fished together for over fifty years. He was my dear friend.

ALWYNE WHEELER - 1991

I think that I first became aware of Dick Walker's name from his writing in the *Angling Times*, which I read from its very first issue. But it may have been as a result of his capture of the 44lb in 1952, which achieved an enormous amount of publicity in both the angling and national press. At about this time I was a frequent visitor to London Zoo, each visit including a trip to the aquarium to pay homage to 'Clarissa', and another to the 'Monkey house' to pay respects to Guy the gorilla. As time passed the *Angling Times* articles revealed Dick as a man who cared deeply for fish and the environment, which struck a chord within my own heart, and I developed a considerable respect for his work.

It was not until his articles turned to discussion of the identification of record fish (notably the co-equal Penney and Brown roach records) that I became involved with him on a professional level. His careful research into the two fish, and his forceful writing caused me to look into the details of his claim that Brown's fish was not a true roach. I became convinced that he was right. It had been a roach x rudd hybrid, but as neither the fish's body nor its pharyngeal teeth were available for examination I could not prove it.

However, in time Fred Buller gave me some massive 'roach' and rudd from Esthwaite Water, some of which were identical to the published descriptions of the co-equal roach record, and which proved as certainly as was possible that this had really been a roach x rudd hybrid. This study brought Dick and I together, if not directly, then through long (sometimes very long!) telephone conversations and a lot of correspondence.

The next concern of Dick's that brought us together was the heavy infesta- tion of chub in the Hampshire Avon, by the thorny-headed worm, *Pomphorhynchus laevis*. Dick had found that most of the chub there were in appalling condition, big-headed and terribly thin. Having his enquiring mind he opened up a few of the worst specimens, to find them full of these orange- coloured, maggot sized worms, attached to the gut walls. He preserved some examples and sent them to me. With the help of my parasitologist colleagues in the British Museum they were identified, and we then knew their life his- tory, because this is a common acanthocephalan parasite in Britain and Europe, even if unknown previously as severe infestations in the Avon.

What so impressed me about Dick was his eagerness to know the answers. Firstly, why were the chub so out of condition? Secondly, was it a result of this parasite? Then, what was the parasite and what was its life history? Finally, what could be done about it? His writings at this time reflected his interest and knowledge, and showed his quick grasp of the subject, and his ability to put over to the angling public what was quite a complicated story.

In the long term - long after Dick had died - it was discovered that this par- asite had been introduced to the Avon (as it has been elsewhere) by the intro- duction of infected barbel most likely from the river Kennet. Had Dick been alive when Professor Clive Kennedy published this paper, I can imagine his delight at dropping the last piece of this jigsaw into place!

Dick was also wonderfully generous. When he found that I was interested in obtaining spined loach for the Museum collection, he invited me down to his private fishery on the Great Ouse, near Stony Stratford, with advice on how to catch them. My suggestion that, being a weekend I would like to bring my wife and children along too, did not bother him at all. The resulting sum- mer's day spent paddling in the river catching loach and crayfish is now a most happy memory for us all. So, too, was the winter's evening I spent in his, and others', company over a meal in the Clock, Welwyn in Hertfordshire. Dick proved to be the model host, with a fund of good stories and enormously good company.

I now really regret that after all this collaboration and good relationship we finally fell out and never established contact again. In the early Seventies I had been busy monitoring the fishes returning to the tidal Thames, in the region of Central London, and spent five years doing so, and a year or more writing it all up. Of course, the story got a lot of publicity and the Greater London Council, who had laid out some £40 million (if I remember rightly) cleaning up the Thames, and a keen press office had made the most of it - and rightly so too.

Then came the day when Dick was reported by a national daily as saying it was all a press stunt, and the river was no cleaner than before, and the report inferred that fish did not exist in the river. Just why he said this I never found out, but I knew that Dick was not familiar with the Thames in this region at that time, and I also knew that I had several thousand fish in formalin, which had been caught there. My resulting letter to Dick asking him if he had been misquoted and if he hadn't, why he had said this, when plainly he was wrong - was pithy but not I hope rude. What amazed me was his phone call in reply in which he insisted that he had said it, and yes he didn't know anything about the subject, but that he was right!

I later found from mutual friends that Dick did tend to 'shoot from the hip' at times, and one friend in particular told me that Dick regretted the rift. But my professional life carried me into being busier, and took me to sea and abroad for long periods, while Dick became ill. I hope that he never recalled our disagreement or its cause; I had forgotten all about it until I was asked to write these recollections. Now I have done so I have to say that I am sorry the breach with Dick was never repaired - the good times had been so good, that a minor disagreement should not have overshadowed them.

COLIN WILLOCK - 1991

I first came in contact with Richard Walker through my then Managing Editor, Jack Hargreaves. I had succeeded him as editor of *Lilliput*. This was back in the Fifties. Jack had many contacts and for me was a powerful journalistic catalyst. Through his friendship with Howard Marshall, journalist, broadcaster and former war correspondent, Jack had heard that East Midland Allied Press, a powerful group of provincial newspapers, were keen to use the 'down time' on their presses to publish a tabloid specialist newspaper. Howard had suggested to R. P. Winfrey, the then Chairman of EMAP, that angling was the number one participant sport and that what the world was waiting for was a weekly angling newspaper. Thus was the idea of the *Angling Times* born. Jack Hargreaves suggested that I was the 'natural' for editorship, a claim that some would dispute, including, eventually, Chairman Winfrey. I did at least have the journalistic qualifications and was a fanatical if not highly skilled all-round angler.

Thus far, the idea was a good one. However, Howard Marshall and Jack Hargreaves had Rolls Royce ideas, when what was really needed was a Land Rover. To put it another way: Marshall and Hargreaves persuaded Wintrey that he needed Fleet Street talent to create his paper. Thus his key men were taken from Fleet Street at Fleet Street salaries. In his heart Winfrey knew that what he should be doing was making use of the perfectly good, though possibly not so widely based, journalists on his own provincial papers. In the end he was right, though his canny old fenman's instincts may have told him that he needed some bright sparks to set the new paper alight.

He also needed Bernard Venables as a 'name'. Bernard had made *Mr Crabtree Goes Fishing* famous as a strip cartoon in the *Daily Mirror*. Crabtree had originally started out as a gardening strip, which was not entirely successful. I believe that it was Jack Hargreave's suggestion to turn it into an angling cartoon. That's the way Jack told it, anyhow. Venables, Hargreaves and Marshall were all cronies at the Savile Club and that, no doubt, was where the *Angling Times* plot was first worked out. So Bernard, had to invent another name for his fishing strip, although all his characters had faces like potatoes and looked much the same, and did became an important ingredient of the *Angling Times* launch. Richard had, I seem to remember, just written the first edition of *Still-Water Angling*. Both Jack and I realised that the author had given a whole new approach to coarse fishing, an approach that would turn the sport upside down.

So, as Editor Designate, I took myself off to Hitchin where I was courteously, yet somewhat incredulously, received by Richard. His incredulity centred round the princely sum I was prepared to offer him for a weekly column. Richard, whose ideas of fair reward from the angling press had no doubt been conditioned by writing the occasional article for the *Fishing Gazette* and other fishing papers, quite genuinely could not see how any weekly angling paper could afford to pay £10 per week for a 1,200 word article. Once he had got over the shock he readily agreed to do the job. We decided on the name of the column there and then. It was to be 'Walker's Pitch'. Richard was to have a completely free hand to write what he liked.

From the start he struck the right note. He was often innovative, quite often controversial and even irritating. Most important of all, he was always entertaining. His readers may have resented his somewhat know-all approach, but if so they forgave him because inwardly they realised that if he didn't know it all, he knew a damn sight more than they were ever likely to do.

One of the nicest things about him was that he took endless pains to answer his readers' genuine problems and queries. I can still see his weekly copy and his replies to readers written in that clear hand, with scarcely an alteration or crossing out. I always assumed that his copy was so tidy because his mind was so damnably tidy.

I don't know if we ever fell out, anyway not more than is usual between Editor and contributor. I remember once asking him if he didn't need a fishing hat several sizes larger. He could at times appear to be arrogant, though I am perfectly certain that wasn't his true nature. I have heard frustrated anglers at the end of a day when conditions or the fish or both had beaten them, shout, "I'd like to see Richard Bloody Walker do any better." But even this was, in a way, a tribute because I suspect we all knew he almost certainly would have done better.

He certainly belonged somewhere near the top, if not at the very top, of the comparatively short list of really creative fishermen. What's more he could apply his analytical skills and undoubtedly scientific turn of mind to any branch of the sport and that, of course, included game fishing. I don't think he ever took to sea fishing, perhaps because he thought it too imprecise. If he had done, I've little doubt he would have made an impression on the vasty deep as well.

Richard rightly lasted far longer at the *Angling Times* than I or most of the Fleet Street contingent (except Bernard Venables). Once we had got the paper going, and at the end of the first six months, R. P. Winfrey handed over to his local boys who subsequently made a very good job of it and were conceivably more in tune with the real heart of the common man's fishing than we smart-alecs from the big city. I got at least a silver handshake and returned to editing *Lilliput* who had for some reason I have never understood welcomed me back. I had enjoyed the experience and I had certainly enjoyed the chance to give Richard Walker a weekly outlet.

DERMOT WILSON - 1985

You'll be receiving so many hundreds of letters about Dick that I hesitate to add to the volume. But I feel I simply must write. I've only today heard of the loss to you and to the whole fishing world, since I've been to the USA for the past two months. I couldn't possibly have come back to more dismaying news.

Dick's unique contribution to fishing and to fishing literature is bound to be the subject of many letters, as well as of many newspaper and magazine articles. He was certainly a giant among all too many pygmies. But I shall remember him best, and always, for the marvellous personal kindness he always extended to me, as indeed you did yourself. I recall that when I first met him I was rather frightened by encountering the great man, but I don't think anyone ever put me at my ease more warmly, or more quickly.

Later on, when Renee and I were at Nether Wallop Mill, Dick put himself out on countless occasions to help us - when he really had no need to do so. Once he even paid us a special visit to be photographed for our catalogue. Whenever I wrote to him for advice he took a great deal of trouble to reply in detail. When I was wrong he corrected me with courtesy, tolerance and wisdom. I learned more from him than from anyone else. I do think it's the mark of a truly great person that they can spare so much time for lesser mortals.

It's really no wonder that I liked him more than I can say. I never found him anything but good-humoured, thoughtful, stimulating - and fun. Renee and I always looked forward immensely to the visits that you and he paid to us in Nether Wallop.

Richard Walker by his mother, Elsie May Walker

S INCE MY Son, Dick Walker, became so well-known in the angling world, I have often been asked how and why he became so interested in this sport.

Basically, one might say it was inborn, since his father and one grandfather were dedicated fishermen, while all his ancestors were yeomen farmers and nature lovers.

Going back to a few years before Dick was born, my father's fields were bounded by the upper reaches of the river Lea near Hertford and there one could catch perch, chub and big roach.

Among my school friends were two keen anglers, Bill Johns (later to become Capt. W. E. Johns and famous as the author of the *Biggles* books) and Dick Walker, afterwards the father of my son, the present Dick Walker. Hertford was Paradise for fishermen, bounded and intersected by rivers. As well as the Lea, there was the Mimram, the Beane (full of dace), and the Rib, with big roach and chub and all of them free from pollution and water abstraction.

My father was an authority on the wildlife of the countryside generally, but not particularly interested in fishing, although he bought us a boat to enable us to get to the upper reaches quickly.

It was a family joke that his only real 'catch' happened after he saw a small moorhen seized by a pike; whereupon he grabbed a clothes prop, attached a length of wire, a butcher's hook and some bait with which he lured that pike to destruction. The 'tackle' was then dismantled and it's the last time I can remember seeing him 'fishing'.

The time came when a railway branch line was to be built across his land and he moved to North Herts, where some of his fields were alongside the river Oughton. By now, my friends and I had left school and gone our separate ways, although Bill, Dick and I kept in touch. Then came the 1914 War. Bill joined the Royal Flying corps and was later shot down over enemy lines and was a prisoner of war for two years. Dick joined the Royal Army Ordnance Corps and (after some training) his regiment was sent out to Gallipoli where, after fierce fighting, he was wounded and sent back to England. [Simon Walker tells us that Dick, and probably Bill Johns too, joined up *pre*-war, in 1909.]

When I next saw him, in hospital, we became engaged and later, when he was given a post in the Paymaster General's Department, we married. The following year our son (the present Dick Walker) was born. Sadly, my husband had never regained full health and one day, at his office, he collapsed and died.

I had relinquished my job, in the Civil Service, on marriage, but it was incumbent on me to earn a living for two and I accepted an offer to work, temporarily in the accounts department of a local firm. Somehow, I found myself very quickly promoted to other departments and permanently established.

My son went to a kindergarten school at three and by the time he was five he could read. He spent a lot of time with my parents, loving farm life and the animals and learning about wildlife generally. In the holidays he stayed with my parents-in-law at Hertford, where his grandfather Walker, himself a devoted angler, initiated him in river lore; his first attempts to catch fish were netting minnows and gudgeon, but among his books, mostly about angling, was a Hardy Brothers' catalogue, which showed beautiful rods etc. So he was given his father's greenheart rod and he began fishing in earnest. He also began writing stories and I recall an article on fishing (unfortunately not retained) which ended 'Hardys' Pennell minnows are the best'. His next ambition was fly fishing, but his pocket money wouldn't stretch to buying flies so, with some assistance from an angler, he made his own. He has been making them ever since, designing some new and successful ones described in his book *Fly Dressing Innovations*.

When at ten, he went to boarding school, he was given a split-cane fly rod (Hardy C.C. de France). It is a tribute to the maker's quality, that he used that rod for twenty-one years and then passed it on to his friend Peter Thomas, who fished with it for at least another ten years before giving it away.

About this time my father retired and he and my mother joined me in a new house at Hitchin. Within three hundred yards of our home was a deep two-acre pond containing various fish including carp. It belonged to a local doctor, who would give any schoolboy a permit to fish there, provided he could produce a certificate that he could swim. Since Dick was a first-class swimmer, he had no difficulty in obtaining permission and it was there he caught a carp weighing 16lb 5oz, at that time quite a feat. In 1931 he joined Hitchin Angling Club, as a Junior Member and in school holidays, fished in many ponds and rivers, within cycling distance, such as the Ouse, Ivel and Flit, Southill Lake and Tring reservoirs in addition to those Hertford rivers, where his father had caught dace, chub roach and trout. Taking him to Hertford one Sunday, he asked me to stop while he took a look at a stretch of water just off the road. In a few minutes he came back for his rod which was in the car boot, disappeared again and returned twenty minutes later with a 3lb trout.

As eighteen he went to Cambridge University to read Mechanical Science. There he wrote his first angling articles for the *Fishing Gazette* and other journals. In the vacations, he worked (on the factory floor) of various engineering firms, where he gained valuable practical experience and augmented his spending money (there were no student grants at that time).

When in 1939, our country was again plunged into war, Dick was transferred to a secret establishment in a remote country mansion to work on radar. There he had a brainwave - to rear rabbits to reinforce rations! His success in this venture [which he took up after the war], ending with his book *How to Breed Flemish Giants,* is another story. After a time, he was moved to the Royal Aircraft Establishment, where he managed occasionally to fish on the Basingstoke Canal or Mychett Lake.

The War over, Dick elected to join me in the firm of which, in 1937, I had become Managing Director. After six years of munition making, I was happy to have his help and scientific technical knowledge in re-establishing my normal business.

At Christmas 1946, he acquired *The Fisherman's Bedside Book* by 'BB' (Denys Watkins-Pitchford). On some minor point about carp, he disagreed with the author, whom he invited to 'go-a-angling' with him.

This began a close and lasting friendship which started his special interest in carp. For this, he acquired a new rod which, though designed for salmon spinning, served admirably for carp-catching.

One day, at Arlesey Lakes, he left this beautiful rod with other gear in the boot of his car at some little distance. Returning, he found all the items missing. The culprits were caught but, to Dick's dismay, the top of the super-rod was broken. However, he proceeded, with some split cane, to make a replacement and this was so successful that he launched into designing and making his own rods. He also wrote another book *Rod Building for Amateurs.*

For some time had had been corresponding with a young man in Lincolnshire, Maurice Ingham, who came to visit him and became another valued friend. They were persuaded (by 'BB') to publish their letters in book form. I was asked, casually, to suggest a title. I responded with 'Drop me a Line', which was adopted and those four words are my sole contribution to my son's vast literary output.

Dick was now a full member of the local angling club which, in 1951, won first prize in the *Daily Mirror* Annual Angling Competition. Prizes were presented at a Savoy Hotel luncheon and it was there he met several anglers, many of whom were later connected with the launching of *Angling Times* in 1953.

To this venture, Dick was invited to contribute a weekly column, which he has done ever since. In 1952 his book *Still-Water Angling* was published, a fourth edition of which has just been issued.

In recent years he has taken more interest in trout fishing in lakes and reservoirs and has designed special rods and flies for this class of angling. In the fishing fraternity there is a firm fellowship. Most anglers have contented minds and merry hearts. They love nature, peace and quiet, but enjoy a sporting challenge. Regardless of age, they all have a youthful enthusiasm which is endearing and which, over the years have given me many happy times.

E. M. Walker

291

Richard Walker by his son, Simon Walker

ORGIVE ME if I ramble somewhat; but the times of which I speak are a good many years ago now. I was born in 1950; Dick was planning to leave my mother in 1971 (she died in February of that year, before he could do so); and Dick himself died in 1985, over twenty years ago.

When I use the name 'Dick' I am referring to my father; most people called him Dick in the days of my youth, including we three boys. My elder brother, Richard, was generally referred to as Richard or Rick, and that's who I mean when I use either of those names.

We lived at 11, Bearton Avenue, Hitchin. It was a large, detached three-bedroomed house, built by Dick's mother, I believe in the early thirties. Pebble-dashed, as was fashionable at the time, it has I fear now been painted pink. The windows were iron framed, as were the French windows that looked out on to the back garden. It was on a double plot, because for some time my grandmother's parents lived there, and as they'd been farmers she felt they needed a bit of space. The only objection I had to the size of the plot was that it took ages to mow the lawn.

There were fruit trees - apples, plums, pears (several varieties of each); and bushes - blackcurrants and gooseberries, and raspberry canes. A path ran up the middle of the back garden; when I was small, the left side was given over to a vegetable plot. On the right was a lawn, and then a row of sheds. The plot backed onto Hitchin Town Football Club's practice pitch, which was surrounded in those days by elm, both scrub and trees. We had a gate that opened on to it, and it was generally referred to as 'the Wild'. We played there a lot as children.

Earliest recollections of Dick: games of rough and tumble in the sitting-room, in which Dick played the tiger, crawling about on his hands and knees; you were safe on the Chesterfield or the chairs, but as soon as you tried to cross the room he pounced. You knew this, and still did so in a delicious anticipation of being tickled. And Christmas, with a real tree. In those days you didn't have electric lights, you had candles, which fitted into clip candle holders on the tree. They were only lit occasionally and for short periods. They must have been awfully dangerous.

We quite often visited my grandparents at Stretham - my mother's parents - and sometimes we'd go on to Ely. The cathedral was immensely popular with us children, with its intricate tracery.

In those early days Dick was a good and caring father; I remember for example an occasion when my brother found a two shilling piece in 'the Wild'. I was aggrieved, but Dick recommended that I look carefully, and I might find one too . . . It was only later that I realised that the one I found he must have dropped there for me.

In the 1960s we saw increasingly less of him. He would leave for his job at Lloyds and Company (Letchworth) Limited after 9am, when we'd already gone to school; he came home for lunch; after his return in the evening, shortly after 5pm, we'd all have tea, but many evenings he'd go out. Later, when my mother resumed nursing, he lunched at his mother's house in Letchworth.

Regarding fishing, as children we all went on occasion, and we were all given rods, but none of us was very keen; I'm not sure why - I found it a little boring, with unpredictable results that were often a long time coming. I wanted instant results in my pastimes, and I didn't get them from fishing. I was not then very interested in plants, and the racket three children made scared any animals away long before we saw any of them (nowadays I am interested in all sorts of flora and fauna, which shows how one's tastes can change . . .). Nonetheless a good deal rubbed off on me, and I can't remember not knowing about the creatures to be found in and around water. This was before he did much fly fishing, and it was all coarse fishing with floats, or legering; of the two I preferred floats, because there was at least something to look at.

I can remember catching loach and crayfish by hand in the Ouse at Little Hill Farm, near Stony Stratford. The farm was run by Johnnie Marchant, a reticent man, but a nice bloke. Dick leased a mile of the river and a mile of the Grand Union Canal that ran nearby (or rather didn't run - it was stagnant in patches, and yielded a few small carp, I think, not much else). The Ouse was far more productive, and in one short stretch Dick and Fred Taylor both caught pike weighing around twenty pounds in the same year . . . And we children used to swim naked in the same stretch, a thought that almost frightened us, though we knew quite well that a pike, even of that size, would never attack anyone if it could swim away. The river held a variety of other coarse fish, including perch, roach, dace and tench, some a reasonable size. We sometimes spent short holidays there.

Dick, Fred Taylor, and the other Taylors - Ken, Den and Joe - designed and built a fishing hut near the river (the Taylors did most of the building). It was a timber (weatherboard) structure, built on stilts, and had three rooms. Lighting and cooking was by Calor gas, and later a water pipe was laid on from the farm. It had a hut next to it with an Elsan chemical toilet, and one of the less pleasant jobs was digging a hole and emptying it. As the years went by, it became increasingly difficult to find a spot that had not been used . . .

In the early days Dick built rods in a shed in the back garden. It was heated, I remember, with one of those upright Belling electric fires, but it was still pretty cold in there in the winter. It was quite a long building, with a bench along each side; bamboo for the rods hung overhead. There was a gluepot, and various tools, some of which I still have. I remember once we kids found a rusty tin in there, the label of which was illegible or missing. We just had to find out what it was. So we pierced the lid (I think we used a screwdriver). It contained pigs' blood, presumably for groundbaiting, and it had gone off. I mean, seriously off. It was under considerable pressure, and sprayed all over the place. The smell was appalling.

I can remember the introduction of several devices and techniques, for example the automatic bite-alarm, built into the rod-rest; beta lights for floats; fluorescent paint for floats; carbon-fibre for rods; and the Intrepid Elite reel. We found them interesting, but not as exciting as an angler might have done.

Photography was an important part of Dick's fishing career, and he sold a lot of pictures to the *Angling Times* and other publications. Of course, he also wrote a column for that paper for many years, and I recall on one occasion discussing writing styles with him; he said that he tried to write as though he was speaking to the reader, which seemed to work well for him, and works OK for me today. I can't remember what camera he used in the early days, but in the 1960s he bought a Pentax 35mm, which he swore by. I think he may have learned a good deal of his photographic skill from his step-father, Edwin Halford, who was a Fellow of the Royal Photographic Society. (The two of them got on well, and Dick took Edwin a perch from time-to-time, which he - Edwin - enjoyed fried). My twin brother and I had Kodak box cameras, and Dick said he'd replace them with decent cameras if we managed to produce some decent photographs with them. We never did. Rick had a somewhat posher camera, 35mm, I can't remember the make.

Dick was a man of passions. He threw himself into every new project with gusto and enthusiasm. For example, when he became interested in fly fishing, he spent hours in the back garden, practising his casting. This effort paid off when he won competitions at the Game Fair, casting into hoops at increasing range. (He was asked to appear on the TV series *The Saint* in the opening scene, casting - a role he declined, recommending Peter Thomas, who did it instead.) And there was a spell when he concentrated on catching large barbel in the Hampshire Avon, believing that there were record fish in the river. For a while both Dick and my mother became keen archers, and both had reasonably powerful weapons. As children we had bows too, though far less powerful ones. It was another phase, and died out after an arrow went through the kitchen window - I don't remember who fired it, but it wasn't me - narrowly missing a member of the household. It didn't shatter the glass window pane; it made a small hole, only marginally larger than the diameter of the arrow's shaft. Nobody bothered to repair the window, and it was like that for some years.

Other passions were rabbits, for which he won prizes; gardening and chicken-keeping, both of which were abandoned when rationing ended, or not long afterwards; and apiary. The hives were at the far end of the garden. My brother Richard and his friend Charles Eggington poked sticks into them, and were soundly stung for their pains. They came running down the path to the house with a swarm of bees after them.

Dick became deeply interested in palaeoanthropology in the late 1970s and 1980s, and corresponded with Doctor Michael Day of St Thomas's Hospital in London, who coincidentally was keen on fishing. My brother Tim and I visited Doctor Day on Dick's behalf (he was already ill then) at St Thomas's, and he showed us his collection of hominid fossils, along with casts made from other important examples from around the world. The one that struck me most was a cast of footprints - two adults, one smaller than the other, and a child's prints placed into one of the adult's footsteps. I thought, here are some prints, many hundreds of thousands of years old, and this child was doing the sort of thing children might do today. It brought the humanity of these early hominids home to me.

As a family, we used to take our summer holidays in Dorset (though on one occasion we camped in the New Forest, at Burley Lawn. We were in old ex-military bell tents, and on the first day I got lost. Later in the week I got kicked by a New Forest pony. I think Pete Thomas and Pat Russell, and their families, were with us). I know we once rented a cottage with the Russells, but I was pretty small, and I don't remember where it was. But I do remember that it was on a lake, and had no electricity or running water. There was a pump in the yard, and gas mantles on the wall. My elder brother Richard caught some tiny pike, almost transparent they were, but clearly pike, nonetheless.

When in Dorset, we stayed in guest houses, either in Southbourne or Christchurch, and on one occasion, I think in around 1960, Dick combined business with pleasure, and did an outside broadcast which was shown that evening on the television. All the guests gathered round the set, whether they were interested in fishing or not. Dick later said that the film crew said, after he'd set up his gear, "Right, now catch a fish." I think he did, but it amused him that they assumed that angling could be done to order.

One year we had our first encounter with a mink. It was an escapee from a fur farm. We'd rented a beach hut, and there were drainage pipes that ran through the concrete steps upon which the ranks of huts stood. The mink was spotted going down one of these pipes, and Dick grabbed a beach towel and set off to catch it. He positioned himself where he thought it might emerge, and he was right, too - it did, straight into the towel.

Mink have a defence mechanism that involves the release of extremely smelly liquids; a bit like a skunk. That's what happened. Dick dropped the towel, mink and all, with some haste. The mink legged it, and the towel was never the same again. In fact, it had to be thrown away, even after being washed several times.

In the 1950s we got our first car, and I seem to remember it was a Humber, perhaps a Hawk - we certainly had one of those later. I remember standing in the back between the seats - no seat-belts in those days - looking over Dick's shoulder as he pointed to the speedometer, and said, "There you are, sixty miles an hour. That's a mile a minute!" I think we were going downhill at the time. Later cars were Wolsley 6/99, Vanden Plas Princess (as much time in the garage as on the road, that one), Triumph 2000 & 2.5 p.i., and a string of BMW's.

Eels - Dick caught them from time to time, and brought them home for my mother to cook for the cats we always had (we bred Siamese for a few years, another of Dick's passions). He also brought home the occasional pike, which met the same end. Other fish, if they were big enough, were photographed, then returned to the water.

As soon as we were big enough (and that wasn't very big) Dick taught us to shoot. Both he and my mother were good rifle shots, and we all learned on air-guns. He believed that the ability to shoot decently was a skill everyone should possess. The basic rules drummed into us all were that 1) you don't point the gun at something you're not prepared to shoot, and 2) every gun should be treated as though it's loaded. Nonetheless there was the occasional accident, but no serious

Dick and his Triumph.

damage was done. We'd lie in the sitting-room and fire through the opened French windows at targets at the far end of the garden. During the Second World War Dick had been a sniper in the Home Guard, so he knew what he was doing.

My mother, Dick's first wife - Ruth Maud Burdett-Holcroft - was the eldest of seven children, six girls and a boy. She was born on Boxing Day, 1914, and always complained that people combined her birthday and Christmas presents. She was right. They did.

The Burdett Holcrofts lived in Old Pump Lane, Stretham, Cambridgeshire, where they stayed until about 1960. The children had all left home by then, and my grandparents then moved in with my Aunt Helen's family in Hertford (one of my mother's sisters).

Of the six daughters, three married Canadian servicemen, and emigrated; later, the son, Haydn, followed them. The other three girls stayed in England. Only one is still alive, my aunt Cynthia, who lives in Newton Abbott in Devon. I saw her this summer - it's hard to believe that she's in her seventies now.

I don't know exactly how or when Dick met my mother. I think it may have been when he was up at Cambridge. She lived with her family, and he used to cycle over to see her, a thirty-mile round trip. He must have been keen. They married in 1940, when he was twenty-two and she was twenty-six.

Ruth was a short woman, only five feet tall. She had dark hair and brown eyes, and was quite a looker in her youth. During the Second World War she was a nurse, a profession she returned to in the early 1960s. Her father was a watch-maker, though he trained as a Jesuit priest, and was in his last year when he met my grandmother, also named Ruth. She was even shorter than my mother.

My grandparents came to stay in our house whenever we went on holiday, mostly to keep an eye on the place and feed the animals. On one occasion we returned to a very puzzled pair of grandparents - there were more guinea-pigs than they'd been led to believe . . . One of the females had given birth, and as the little devils can run about pretty much as soon as they're born, she assumed that they were just small examples of the species.

My grandfather - everyone called him Pop - used to let us puff at his pipe, which had a silver cap to it, which he had made himself. Not the sort of thing you'd encourage children to do nowadays, and even then he only did it when no one was looking.

Dick disliked flying after his wartime experiences, and despite offers to fish in the USA and Canada, he always declined. He said there were only two aircraft he ever felt safe in - the De Havilland Mosquito, and the Short Sunderland. I don't think he ever flew again, though he once showed us children over an Avro Lancaster at an air show.

What sort of man was he? Immensely confident in his abilities as an angler, and despite other interests, committed to fishing in fresh water, in all its forms. Sea fishing never caught his interest somehow. He liked other sports too - football, cricket, boxing, motor sports, and on Saturday afternoons he often watched *Grandstand* on the BBC. He was charismatic and intelligent, interested in the world about him. He was perhaps opinionated, though if he thought he was wrong, he was prepared to say so. He reckoned it was less effort than trying to bluff it out!

He was certainly not over-modest! When Cassius Clay was fighting and used to say very loudly that he was 'the greatest', Dick took up the same cry. He was easy to get on with, and made friends with remarkable ease. And he was generous - he was always giving things away, sometimes to my regret (I wish I had that banjo . . .). Whilst on the subject of music, Dick played guitar, but tuned as a banjo in 'C' tuning - DGBD - and ignored the two lower strings. He had learned, I seem to remember him saying, during the Second World War, on a banjo, and this was the easiest way out. He played the melody, interspersed with chords, which was surprisingly effective. He had a good voice, and sang quite well. His taste in music varied from ballads (the 'Londonderry Air' was a great favourite) to the classics and opera.

Sense of humour . . . He made the most appalling puns, and revelled in them. When his mother sold one of Lloyds' mowers to a customer in Indonesia, he said, "there In-do-nesia place to sell them to . . ." For a while he took up the bizarre cry of "cheesewire!", which he shouted with gusto on any occasion, whether it made any sense or not. My mother managed to buy a cheesewire, and gave it to him for his birthday. As I got older, I saw a ruder side of Dick's sense of humour. He found barrack-room ballads amusing, and had a store of extremely vulgar songs. His view on such matters was that one should avoid offence; if one knew that a person would be offended by such songs, jokes or just plain swearing, then restraint should be exercised. If, on the other hand, he was amongst friends who habitually swore (and some of them did) he could 'eff and blind' with the best of them.

He was a great raconteur, and had a huge store of wartime stories, which we boys were always interested in; in those days - the 1950s - the Second World War was a regular subject of conversation still, and my twin brother and I especially were fascinated by it. One ghostly tale he told involved an aircraft with which he and his colleagues on the ground were in radio contact. It was a foggy night, and the plane flew into a hill, killing everyone on board. When the times were compared, they found they had been talking to the crew for half an hour after the crash. He swore the tale was true. I have my doubts.

He also said that he and his friends had bugged the huts of some WAAFs, and he learned more about women that night than he discovered in the rest of his days put together. He never thought about them in quite the same way again - he was amazed, he said, to find that 'they're just as filthy as we are!'

In those days there were small war comics that came out once a month. There were several series - *Air Ace Picture Library* and *War Picture Library* were two of them - and four of each came out every month. I expect there was a naval series, but I don't remember it. My twin brother and I read them all, and Dick read them too. In fact he often pinched them from us and read them before we did. Richard was less interested in such publications, being a more thoughtful and intelligent lad.

Dick was fond of his fellow man, and he'd say that ninety-nine out of a hundred people were fine - you'd only find one bastard. He was not easy to anger, though when he was angry, he was really angry. Letting off fireworks outside his bedroom window when he was asleep did the trick once, as I recall. So did firing air guns at the caravan in the garden he tied flies in. He threw my Webley Senior .177 pistol in the garden pond. (I retrieved it, but it took a lot of cleaning. I still have it.)

He was fond of animals, especially cats, and there were always quite a few in the household. We never had a dog, and he wasn't over-fond of them, unless they were a bit special - Peter Thomas's gun dog Ross for example, or Penny, a spaniel (Penny's owner turned up out of the blue one evening. He'd been to the local police station, asking where he might find lodgings, and for some reason they gave him our address - don't know why - we had never taken in lodgers in the past, and had not intended to in the future. Nonetheless, we took him in for the night, and he ended up staying for some time). Penny was wonderfully trained. When she later had a litter of puppies, her owner brought them all on a visit.

In those days tortoises were quite popular, and there were no restrictions on their import. We had several. One bit me in the leg once. Turns out they are not vegetarian - they'll scavenge meat too. For a while my parents also had tropical fish, but I fear that as a small boy I fiddled with the thermostat (I didn't know what it did) and I killed them all. I never confessed to the crime. Dick was a keen reader, with eclectic tastes. He liked Westerns, and read Louis Lamour novels with delight. In the 1970s Michael Morecock wrote a series of fantasy novels that Dick read too. Science fiction and war novels were quite popular too. Any technical inaccuracy received adverse comment, for example someone using a Colt Peacemaker during the American Civil War (it hadn't been developed then). Non-fiction included palaeoanthropology, as I have already mentioned; fishing books of course; history, both ancient and modern. Pretty well anything then, excepting romantic novels . . .

Simon Walker

Walker Family Tree

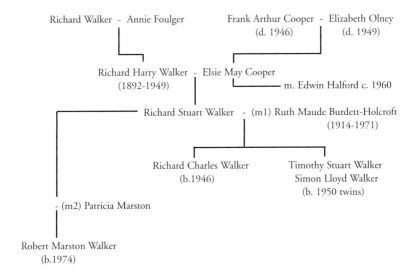

The Walker side of the family contained professional soldiers, including Dick Walker's father. The Cooper side were farmers in the Stanbridge and Tilsworth area, near Dunstable, Bedfordshire. Dick spoke warmly of his grandfathers, one of whom took R.W. fishing and set him upon the road from which we now all benefit. Grandfather Cooper taught him a great deal about wildlife although he was not himself an angler. Dick's father worked in London, at the War Office, so after the war, Dick was brought up by his mother and four grandparents. It was at least in part an idyllic countryside upbringing. His mother Elsie was renowned as a powerful personality, rising to be MD of an engineering firm and, incidentally, was a cousin of the actor Gary Cooper!

Richard Walker's Best Fish

Barbel 12lb 12oz Hampshire Avon
Bream 8lb 12oz
Carp 44lb (official record at time) Redmire Pool
Chub 6lb 14oz R. Great Ouse
Dace 1lb 5oz (larger than official record) R. Cam
Eel 5lb 12oz
Grayling 2lb 14oz Yorkshire Derwent
Gudgeon 4oz Redmire
Perch 4lb 13oz (unofficial record at time) Arlesey Lake
Pike 22lb
Roach 3lb 4oz R. Beane
Rudd 3lb 3oz Bedfordshire
Salmon 28lb Wye
Sea Trout 8lb Dorset Stour
Trout, Brown 12lb
Trout, Rainbow 18lb 4oz (unofficial record at time) Avington
Tench 5lb 14oz Bedfordshire

The exact weight and place of capture of some of these fish is not really known. In the documentation left by Dick he refers to having caught eels 'not much over 5lb', so we know there were several, but on the handwritten list shown opposite it clearly shows he caught one of 5lb 12oz. He also notes a pike of 22lb, though the biggest one I can find is 20lb 4oz from the Great Ouse. The note also shows a bream of 8lb 12oz, yet I can find only one of just 8lb, from Mapperley. The tench and rudd captures are almost certainly from Southill Park, but Dick's notes and *No Need To Lie* only give Bedfordshire. The implication from his writing is that his best grayling were from the Yorkshire Derwent, but it is not altogether clear that this is so. Nor is it certain whether the correct grayling weight is 2lb 8oz or 2lb 14oz; both are given in different documents. Dick was rather opposed to some aspects of record fish. It is well known that he did not officially claim his Avington rainbow trout as a record. What is less well known is that he didn't claim his 44lb carp as a record either. He told me this himself. Of course, in those days (1950s) it was not necessary actually to claim, for a fish to appear in the record list, because Record Fish Committee officials were simply trying their best to set up a list. However, there is an ironic twist to Dick's failure to claim the 44lb fish and it concerns Chris Yates' later claim for the 50lb-plus megacarp. Initially Chris' claim was rejected (C.Y.'s letter to Dick makes interesting reading) and Dick was outraged on Chris' behalf. He threatened to withdraw his 44lb fish from the list, but as he hadn't claimed it in the first place he couldn't! Fortunately, Chris' fish was eventually accepted, as well it should have been first time round!

The big dace on the list was just one of a series of spectacular catches on the Cam. On one occasion he had a 2lb roach and a 1lb dace on fly from the same swim on the same day. He pinpointed exactly for me the swim itself. The 1lb 5oz was one of three 1lb-plus dace that he caught in the same session, and from the same swim just referred to. The actual captures of many of the fish on this list are covered in *No Need To Lie*, which also gives a flavour of some of his other great catches - something that we cannot do here.

Barbel 12¾ lbs
Bream 8¾ lbs
Carp 44 lbs
Chub 6 lb 14 oz
Dace 1 lb 5 oz
Eel 5 lb 12 oz
Grayling 2 lb 14 oz
Perch 4 lb 13 oz
Pike 22 lbs
Roach 3 lb 4 oz
Rudd 3 lb 3 oz
Trout (Brown) 12 lb
      " (Rainbow) 18 lb 4 oz
Tench 5 lbs 14 oz .

An Article on the Inland Revenue

T HE FOLLOWING article by Dick was written many years ago but as far as I am aware it was never published. However, points from it were used from time to time in his columns and I remember his raising several of these points with me when, as a budding author, I had to deal with my own local Tax Inspector. It's possible that what follows was written for David Carl Forbes when D.C.F. was thinking of founding the Angling Writers' Guild. Much of what he says is as valid now as it was when written. Indeed, I have had an accountant check through it to confirm this. But my purpose in publishing it here is not to guide the modern writer, who should always obtain his or her own advice, but to show just how thorough Dick was in his writing. As I have argued in the main body of this book, Dick expected to be paid for his work when he dealt with professionals - but very often wrote free of charge anyway. I am more than ever convinced that he put *into* angling rather than took out of it, certainly in a financial sense, for he died far from rich.

Of course, editors liked to work with Dick because he produced his copy on time, in good order, well written and well illustrated. It is very clear from the many letters he had from editors and publishers that they regarded him as a friend. Because he produced what they wanted, when they wanted it, and gave them copy needing little attention, they used his copy. Hence he got the subject aired and the consequent publicity, but he could never be accused, in the widest sense of that phrase, of *using* the media.

There are several aspects of Dick's article that strike chords with me, not only from my own personal experience but from the rather strange case of Martin Gay. Martin wrote often, but not for money. Eventually the Inland Revenue came after him but Martin was able to show, with support from editors, that he had never received a penny from his writing, all monies going directly to charity. I tried, and failed, to persuade him to adopt the very proper strategy outlined by Dick.

INCOME TAX AND THE ANGLING WRITER

It is probable that many angling writers are paying more tax than they need, and that some need pay no tax at all.

What is taxable is the difference between the fees a writer receives, and the expenses he incurs in the course of his journalistic activities, in which photography may be included.

It is impossible to be an able angling writer without going fishing frequently and regularly. The experience of more than a century has shown that readers of angling journals and books will not accept the writings of people who are not regular practising anglers. In this, angling differs from other sports, in which armchair commentators and critics operate successfully, as a perusal of the sports pages of any newspaper will show.

Consequently, all the expenses an angling writer incurs in the course of his fishing activities are allowable in one's profit-and-loss account, which forms the basis for a tax assessment.

These expenses come under a variety of headings. For most people the largest expense is travelling, so let us consider this first.

Calculate the whole cost of running your car: petrol, service, replacement of worn parts, repairs, fuel, tax, insurance. Express this in terms of so much per mile.

Having arrived at a figure, make an appointment to see your Tax Inspector, and seek his agreement to a fair proportion of the use of your car; which proportion of its mileage is for fishing and which for other, non-allowable purposes. Be absolutely honest about this; tell the Inspector exactly what you estimate your fishing mileage to be, as a percentage of the total. You will find him absolutely fair and reasonable about all this, and if he sizes you up as an honest man, he will be prepared to accept a certificate of mileage from your local garage as evidence of the distance you have covered each year, instead of demanding a pile of receipts for petrol purchase, service, etc.

It is wise to keep a diary in which all your fishing trips, or other trips undertaken in connection with your journalistic activities, are entered. This can be used to justify the mileage you travel.

As regards depreciation of a car for tax purposes, there is a fixed Inland Revenue rate of 25% on the original cost at the time it is purchased, and 25% per annum thereafter on the written down value each year.

When the car is changed, the profit or loss arising by taking the difference between the proceeds of sale and the written-down value should not be charged in the Accounts, as the Inspector of Taxes calculates this separately, and sets it against the profit. In any business assessment there is a profit from which capital allowances (depreciation) is deducted. The Inspector of Taxes treats the capital allowances as a separate matter.

The next largest expense varies with the individual, but a common one is hotel expenses. These are allowable in full, but you should keep all the receipts in case you are asked to produce them.

Tackle is divided into two categories, though the division is debatable. Generally speaking, such things as rods, reels, waders, landing-nets, fishing clothes, and other items that last a fairly long time, can be treated either as capital investments subject to depreciation, or as items that need replacement from time to time, owing to wear or obsolescence, in which case no depreciation is allowable, but replacement cost is.

The Tax Inspector will probably allow you to choose whichever course gives you the lesser liability, but you must be honest about these charges.

Under the heading of obviously consumable or expendable items come such things as line, lead, floats, spinners, flies, plugs, and sundry other things that are often lost or damaged. The cost of these features directly in your accounts. The Tax Inspector will understand that once you have an initial stock, your annual expenditure represents your losses, more or less.

Next we have an item consisting of day or season ticket fees; subscriptions; water rent if any; boat hire, gratuities to keepers, boatmen, etc; rod licence costs, and anything else that, broadly speaking, comes under the heading of what it costs you to gain access to angling waters.

Whether subscriptions to anti-pollution organisations like the ACA, or other subscriptions that have no direct application to access to waters, are allowable expenses or not, depends on your Tax Inspector. Some allow them, some do not; it appears that Inspectors are permitted some degree of discretion.

If you include such charges and your Inspector tells you that he cannot allow them, accept his decision. He may be allowing you some other expense that he has discretion to refuse. Above all, don't cite some other journalistic colleague as having been allowed to charge an expense that you are not. The outcome will probably be that by so doing you will lose the allowance for him but fail to gain it yourself.

We now come to bait costs and these are entirely allowable. In some branches of fishing they can be considerable. It will be wise to obtain receipts for bait and consumable tackle purchases, but the Tax Inspector will not expect you to show receipts for every penny you spend, as a rule. If he believes you to be honest, he will usually accept an estimate by you, of the total cost under this heading.

If you pay a typist to type your articles, you will of course charge her fees: you can also charge postage, stationery and telephone calls. In the case of the last, it is usual to agree a percentage of your telephone bill with your Tax Inspector; for an active journalist, even a part time one, from 50% to 75% would be reasonable, but you may be asked to keep a record over a period of the calls you make, to form the basis for an agreement about the percentage.

If your wife assists you, you can pay her to do so and charge what you pay her, but you must actually pay her, and she must be actually working for you and you will be expected to state what she does for her money. It will not suffice to say, 'She answers the phone when I'm not in', or, 'She opens my letters and date-stamps them'. You must show that she does such work as would cost you what you pay her, if you had someone else to do it for you. A limit is fixed for what your wife's tax-free income may be; this changes from time to time.

Any periodicals and books you purchase count as allowable expenses; so does insurance for your equipment, not only tackle but books, stationery stocks, typewriter (whose depreciation and repairs are also allowable) cameras, fly-tying materials, etc. These will usually be covered by a comprehensive householder's policy, of which you can charge a proportion of the premium based on the value of the items concerned expressed as a percentage of the entire house contents, of which you should have an inventory.

If a room in your house is set aside for you to work and keep your equipment in, you can charge the cost of lighting and heating it. Do not, if you own the house, charge for this room a proportion of your house rates or mortgage, if any. If you do, you may run into trouble over capital gains tax if you ever sell the house.

Purchase of sensitive materials for your camera, plus processing costs, are of course fully allowable.

It is clearly advantageous to open accounts with regular suppliers, such as a local garage for your car expenses, a local chemist for photographic items, your friendly neighbourhood tackle dealer, and so on. You will then receive regular statements, which you pay by cheque, providing evidence of expenditure without amassing a huge pile of receipts for small amounts.

I now come to certain aspects of your relationship with the Tax Inspector who handles your tax affairs, which need careful handling.

The Inland Revenue will not stand for your claiming to be a professional writer, but making a loss on your journalistic activities and setting this loss against your income from other sources, year after year. Your journalism has to be, on balance, profitable. If it isn't, the tax authorities will tell you that your fishing, though writing about it is helping to defray its costs, is still a hobby and not a profitable business, and they'll be right.

If however you encounter an odd year now and then in which you make a loss, though in most years you make a good profit, then the tax authorities will allow that loss to be set against income from other sources. They judge each case on its merits and all my experience has shown that if you are fair and honest with them, they will be fair with you. They appreciate that freelance part-time journalism is a precarious occupation, in which you may do very well for a time, then have a bad year. This they accept.

The only point about which you may have to argue and if necessary appeal, is if your Tax Inspector says something like this:

"Now, Mr Doe, if you weren't earning money by writing about fishing, you would still go fishing purely for pleasure. Therefore such expenditure as you incur must apply partly to the fishing you do to provide material for your writing and partly to what you do simply for fun. We must arrive at a proportion, because I cannot allow such expenditure as you incur in your fishing for fun, as an expense to set against your income."

You must resist this suggestion very firmly. Don't lose your temper or use bad language, but say, "I cannot accept the argument that if I enjoy the work I do, the expenses I incur in doing it are not allowable. It is impossible to separate such fishing as I do for pleasure from that which I do to obtain material for my writing. Every time I go fishing, I am learning more about it and that makes me a better writer. I can never predict in advance of a fishing trip, nor say on my return from one, that it was useful to my journalism, or simply a pleasure outing. All my fishing is applicable to all my fishing journalism and I therefore claim all my expenses associated with that fishing."

The fact that you may have fished for years before you began writing about the sport, purely for pleasure, has nothing to do with the matter. You are not trying to recover any expenses incurred then, though they clearly contributed to your present journalistic ability. You're talking about your present situation; you have now become a professional, making a taxable profit, and the matter of how much of your work you enjoy is no business of the Inland Revenue whatever. If they raise the point, tell them so, politely of course.

Over the many years during which I have been writing about fishing, I have encountered this argument about how much of my fishing I enjoy several times, but I have always stood fast and carried my point.

If your journalistic activities are extensive, you may be well advised to employ a professional accountant to handle your accounts and deal with the Inland Revenue on your behalf. His fee is an allowable expense. He has a professional reputation, is already known by the tax authorities, and he can usually save you a good deal of time and trouble. The point at which it becomes desirable to engage an accountant is a matter for individual decision but as a guide, I would suggest that it could well come when your profit amounts to more than ten times the accountant's fee.

May I conclude by stressing that Tax Inspectors are almost invariably pleasant, reasonable, intelligent human beings, who, it is worth remembering, are taxpayers themselves. They don't want to charge you a penny in tax, above what you are liable to pay, but it is not their business to advise you on tax avoidance. That is the job of a professional accountant. Do not 'try it on' with your Tax Inspector. Declare every penny you receive, and resist the temptation to put in expenses which, however plausible they may appear, you know you did not really incur. Most taxmen can spot a liar or a 'fiddler' very quickly and accurately. Don't get yourself pegged as either for the sake of a few pounds. You'll live to regret it if you do.

Richard Walker's Books

I DO NOT claim that this list of Dick Walker's published books is entirely complete, but I have tried to include all new editions and major reprints, as well as some of the foreign editions of his work. It is widely thought that his first book was *Still-Water Angling*, but *The Book of the Flemish Giant Rabbit* was his first, published at the age of twenty-nine; and *Rod Building for Amateurs* was first published a year before the book that became his major work (and which ran to four editions). His first book on game fishing was in 1980, unless you include his other classic *Drop Me A Line* with Maurice Ingham (1953), which includes quite a lot on trout fishing. Several compilations and edited volumes appeared after his death in 1985. This bibliography does not include the many chapters Dick wrote for other people's books. I quailed at any attempt to produce a list of magazine articles, although it would be possible to produce a list of many hundreds, which, when added to his thirty-year *Angling Times* column, would amount to a minimum of 1500! - the list would never be complete. Dick told me that he threw away most of his manuscripts and typescripts, and this is confirmed by his files which retain only a few hundred at most. However, it is a clear indication of his integrity as a writer that there is a consistency in his ideas, a lack of contradictions, from year to year. He never wrote only to cause controversy; and certainly not for money. You will see that the last, fourth, edition of *Still-Water Angling* was in 1975. At about this time A&C Black had approached Richard, at my suggestion, with a view to a new edition, but it did not happen. For such a classic book I should say the time was right for a fifth edition.

As the reader will by now be aware Dick put great store by angling books and the extent to which anglers could learn from them as well as enjoy them. The story told by Chris Ball in Chapter 10 is worth repeating, for it shows how greatly Dick valued his books but also his generosity in giving them to those that really wanted them. Chris was sitting in Dick's den at the Flitwick home, staying with Pat and Dick, and whilst scanning through Dick's library came across a copy of 'BB's *Be Quiet and Go A-Angling*. At that moment Dick entered the room and said, "What you got there Boy?" Chris explained that it was the first time he'd seen the book and had been looking for one for ages. Dick's response was typical and immediate: he gave Chris the book on the spot. Later that weekend Chris was browsing through the book and discovered that it was a presentation copy from Dick to his mother and it was inscribed

'To mum from R.W. of the Magic Hat' which was a reference to 'BB's description of him in that volume (probably the first reference to Dick as a carp angler). Chris alerted Dick to this inscription but he refused point blank to take the book back.

I am especially grateful to Pat Walker, Tim Walker and Peter Maskell for help with aspects of this bibliography.

Walker, R. S. c.1947. *The Book of The Flemish Giant Rabbit*. Fur & Feathers. Idle, Bradford & London.

Walker, R. S. 1952. *Rod Building for Amateurs*. Belfield & Bushell Ltd. (Second edition 1954, same publisher; second impression 1963 following revised edition, 1961, published by *Angling Times*.)

Walker, R. S. 1953. *Still-Water Angling*. First edition. MacGibbon & Kee, London. (David & Charles Holdings Ltd.)
NB This is one of the classics of angling, possibly mentioned or quoted more than any other angling book. Yet this edition sold only 2000 copies.

Walker, R. S. 1954. *Kanjers. Nederlandse Vertaling van Hans deVries* (Introduction by Frans Domhof.) N.V. Leiter-Nypek, Maastricht.

Walker, R. S. 1955. *Still-Water Angling*. Second edition. MacGibbon & Kee, London.

Walker, R. S. 1959. *Walker's Pitch*. George Allen & Unwin Ltd, London. (Second impression 1966, East Midland & Allied Press; German edition 1960, Paul Parey; Little Egret Press 2003 with foreword by Fred Buller.)

Walker, R. S. 1959. *How Fish Feed*. An *Angling Times* publication.

Walker, R. S. 1959. *Fly Dressing Innovations*. Ernest Benn.

Walker, R. S. 1960. *Carp Fishing* (a reprint of carp chapters from *Still-Water Angling*). *Angling Times*, Peterborough, E.M. Art & Publishing Ltd. (Little Egret edition 2002.)

Walker, R. S. 1960. *Still-Water Angling*. Third Edition. MacGibbon & Kee, London. Reprinted 1962, 1965.

Walker, R. S. 1964. *No Need to Lie*. E.M. Art & Publishing Ltd in conjunction with George, Allen & Unwin & Co. (Illustrated by Reg Cooke.)

Walker, R. S. 1975. *Still-Water Angling*. Revised Fourth Edition with an additional chapter on zander by Doctor Barrie Rickards. David & Charles, Newton Abbot. (Five impressions; paperback edition 1978, Pan Books.)

Walker, R. S. 1979. *Dick Walker's Angling; theories and practice, past, present and to come*. (Foreword by Peter Maskell.) *Angling Times* in conjunction with David & Charles.

Walker, R. S. 1979. *The Shell Book of Angling*. David & Charles, Newton Abbot. (Edited with Leslie Moncrieff.)

Walker, R. S. 1980. *Dick Walker's Modern Fly Dressing*. Ernest Benn. (Line drawings by author; colour photographs by Taff Price.)

Walker, R. S. 1981. *Catching Fish; knowing their feeding habits*. David & Charles. (Edited by Peter Maskell.)

Walker, R. S. 1982. *Dick Walker's Trout Fishing*. David & Charles, Newton Abbot, in association with EMAP National Publications Ltd. (Edited by Peter Maskell.)

Walker, R. S. 1983. *Dick Walker's Coarse Fishing*. Patrick Stephens & EMAP National Publications Ltd. (Edited by Peter Maskell.)

Walker, R. S. 1988. *The Best of Dick Walker's Coarse Fishing*. David & Charles, Newton Abbot. (Edited by Peter Maskell in co-operation with Pat Walker.)

Walker, R. S. & Hardy, J. L. 1979. *Hardy's Guide to Reservoir Angling*. Hardy's, Alnwick, Northumberland.

Walker, R. S. 1997. *Dick Walker's Trout Fishing on Rivers and Stillwaters*. Swan Hill Press. (Edited by Peter Maskell.)

Walker, R. S. 1998. Letters in *The Carp Catchers' Club*. The Medlar Press, Ellesmere, Shropshire. (Eds. Maurice Ingham and Peter Rogers.)

Walker, R. S. 2001. *No Need to Lie*. Second Edition. Little Egret Press. (Limited edition. Introduction by Peter Thomas; illus. by Tom O'Reilly's sketches.)

Walker, R. S. 2002. *Big Carp*. Little Egret Press. (Limited edition. Three accounts of capture of 44lb carp by R.S.W., Pete Thomas and Tom O'Reilly.)

Walker, R. S. 2002. *Carp Fishing*. Little Egret Press. (Limited editions in leather and hardback, with a foreword by Kevin Clifford.)

Walker, R. S. & Ingham, M. 1953. *Drop Me A Line; being letters exchanged on Trout and Coarse fishing*. Douglas Sanders with MacGibbon & Kee, London.

Walker, R. S. & Ingham, 1964. *Drop me A Line; being letters exchanged on Trout and Coarse fishing*. Second Edition. MacGibbon & Kee, London.

Walker, R. S. & Ingham, M. 1953. *Drop me A Line: being letters exchanged on Trout and Coarse fishing*. Third Edition. H.F. & G. Wetherby Ltd, London. (Maurice Ingham and Pat Walker both disappointed with the production of this edition.)

Walker, R., Taylor, F. J., Buller, F. & Falkus, H. 1977. *Successful Angling. Coarse Fishing*. Stanley Paul & Co. Ltd, London.

Walker, R., Taylor, F. J., Buller, F. & Falkus, H. 1982. *Pesca Departiva. Méétodos y aperejos.* Ediciones Lidium, Buenos Aires.

Endpiece

I shall end this book with two sentiments I came across in Dick's file of correspondence which, I think, echo the thoughts of many people. One is part of a letter from Geoffrey Bucknall, the other an anonymous note.

29th November, 1983

Well, Dick. I don't hear much news of you these days. I miss your writing, but glad much of it is going into book form. We often talk and think of you in the shop. The carp anglers specially, and the feeling is that your book on *Still Water Angling* started all of this specimen hunting. Did you ever guess that anglers would sleep, with earphones connected to alarms, the monkey sticks and weird flavours? You started it, and the basics are the same.

Warmest wishes to you all.
Geoffrey Bucknall

21st July, 1983

Dear Mr Walker,
Thank you.

Signed: 'A Grateful Angler'

Sources

MANY ANGLERS today express surprise that there has been no Walker biography before now. Some starts have been made before, it is true, with all good intentions, but the task has never been completed. It could be that two things frightened people off. One was the sheer breadth of Dick's expertise. The other could have been that the sources of information are equally extensive: many people who knew Dick, or even fished with him, are alive today and when I put adverts in the angling magazines asking people to contact me with any artefacts, anecdotes or letters from Dick, I was almost overwhelmed with the response. Within weeks I had a file five inches thick of Dick's letters, mostly Xerox copies kindly donated by the people I have mentioned in the acknowledgements. I think I have now read almost one thousand letters either by or to Dick Walker. I have had phone calls from people who knew him, from the postman who delivered mail to the factory where Dick worked, to the man who serviced his family cars, and a neighbour who overlooked Dick's garden. Some individuals, such as Kevin Clifford and Chris Ball for example, have considerable collections of Walker-related materials, including letters and photographs. The newspaper *Angling Times*, for which Dick wrote his weekly column for thirty years, also has extensive archive material, mostly photographic. As a rule Dick did not keep copies of his *AT* articles, although files from later years of articles that were typed do exist. Consider though that thirty years, times fifty-two, equals more than 1,500 articles! Most of these, not being available in unpublished form, can only be seen by reference to a copyright library or to *AT* itself. In my case, I was fortunate to be able to use the copies of *AT* held by my publisher on behalf of the Angling Collection.

Dick also wrote many articles for other magazines, not always on angling matters. Very few of these exist in the unpublished form and tracing published versions is far from easy except from the magazines for which he wrote regularly over a period - the *Fishing Gazette* and *Fishing*, for example. However, many people have kept copies of these articles and have kindly forwarded them to me.

A great deal of anecdotal material is, quite naturally, held in people's heads. I have spoken to a great many anglers about Dick, and have received letters from numbers of others who I haven't had a chance to meet. In the former category the late Alan Brown and Fred Buller have provided invaluable information, Alan having known Dick probably better than most at a particularly formative period of Dick's career; and Fred at a later, more mature period.

I haven't even mentioned the family up to this point, and not surprisingly the family hold a great deal of relevant information, not just in the form of letters, tackle, and so on, but in their opinions and recollections. The latter are vital to an understanding of Dick's life as an angler-cum-engineer. The main source of information here is, of course, Dick's second wife Pat. She is the custodian of his library; a large filing cabinet of letters which is organised A-Z; his tackle, his artwork and photography; and many artefacts. She also asked Dick's friends and colleagues to give her an appraisal of Dick, through *their* eyes, after Dick's death; this provides an interesting archive at worst, and a very useful one at best (see Personal Recollections). She had also encouraged Dick to dictate to tape his life story and some of this forms part of the personal perspective she gives in Chapter 21. The recording was made during the last year of Dick's life and was later transcribed in full by Pat. (Some of it was incorporated in Peter Mohan's excellent *Coarse Fisherman* seven-part series.) Tim Walker also has a good archive of his father's things and has very kindly allowed me full access to letters and photographs. I have also been able to talk extensively to Dick's other sons, Richard, Simon and Robert, which has been a great help.

Richard Hunter's account in the *Dictionary of National Biography*, recently published, has been useful and there are other sources of published information too, such as *Dick Walker: a memoir*, a forty-six-page Carp Society booklet published to celebrate Dick at the Queensway Hall, Dunstable, Bedfordshire on Saturday, 4th June, 1988. This excellent volume contains recollections and appreciations by a range of famous anglers, including Pete Thomas, Jack Thorndike, Colin Willock, Tim Paisley, Chris Yates, Pat Russell, Fred Taylor, Chris Ball, Rod Hutchinson, Jim Gibbinson, Colin Dyson, Martin James, Ian Howcroft, Maurice Ingham, and Fred Buller. Finally, I should mention that a number of writers of national newspapers have provided snapshots of Dick's contributions to angling - for example, Brian Clarke (*The Times*), David Profumo, Conrad Voss Bark, and Maurice Wiggin.

All in all it is a monumental archive and I anticipate that the letters alone will provide a fruitful source of information, on a whole variety of topics, for years to come.

Index

A&C Black 310
Abu 71
Admiralty, The 25, 203
Albany Hotel 232
Aldrich, Bernard 231
Alexandra Palace 227, 274
Allcocks 210
Allen, Eric 58
Alnwick 59, 63, 64, 312
Ambidex 65
Anderson, Percy 171, 172
Andrzejczyk, Tad 237
Anglers' Cooperative
  Association (ACA) 78, 115,
  186, 306
Anglers' News 31, 33, 210, 217,
  222, 260
Anglers' World 159
angling books 42, 89, 239, 240,
  310
Angling Technical and Advisory
  Group 59
Angling Times 6, 9, 10, 14, 31,
  34, 35, 44, 61, 70, 109, 111,
  123, 161, 164, 167, 171,
  173, 174, 175, 180, 183,
  185, 210, 212, 223, 224,
  227, 231, 251, 256, 257,
  262, 282, 285, 286, 291,
  294, 310, 311, 314
Arbury, Len 79, 89
Arlesey 52, 53, 54, 73, 80, 109,
  111, 139, 172, 210, 213,
  222, 236, 260, 261, 262,
  274, 280, 291, 302
Arlesey Bomb 73, 111, 139,
  172, 236, 260, 280
Arte of Angling, The 52
Ashurst, Kevin 172
Avenue, The, Friends' School
  Magazine 20, 31, 215
Avington 233, 234, 302
Avington Lakes 233
Avon Tyrrell 82
Avon, river 41, 73, 82, 97, 137,
  229, 250, 283, 294, 302
Ayres, Pam 12

B. James and Son 212
Baddeley, Simon 267
baits, particle 67, 87, 99
baits, small 87, 137
Baitsbite Lock 218

Baldwin, Walter 197
Ball, Chris 6, 89, 97, 98, 310,
  314, 315
Bark, Conrad Voss 315
Barnaby, B. W. 70
Barnes, Tag 130, 249
Bartles, Bill 172
Basingstoke Canal 205, 291
'BB' 36, 83, 85, 142, 143, 212,
  220, 221, 270, 291, 310,
  311
BBC 39, 234, 261, 263, 277,
  298
Be Quiet and Go a-Angling 98,
  310
Beachampton 80, 109, 110,
  111, 112, 113, 116, 132,
  234
Beane, river 142, 144, 208,
  214, 219, 282, 289, 302
Bearton Avenue, Hitchin 27,
  30, 197, 213, 261, 273
Bearton Pond 24, 213, 221,
  270
Bedford School's Angling Club
  236
Beekay Publishers 89, 129
Beer, Stanley 197
Behrendt, Alex 42, 229
Belcher, Frank 109
Belfield and Bushell 212
Bellars, Vic 51, 80
Bennett, Tiny 173, 174, 223,
  224
Bernithan Pool 77, 80, 89, 224
Berth-Jones, Gerry 45, 83, 85,
  150, 176, 227, 236, 260
Berth-Jones, May 83, 85
Birch, Eric 46
bite-alarm 66, 69, 294
bivouacked 66
bivvies 66, 89, 134, 176, 181,
  228
Blagdon 157, 219
blanket weed 94
Boat Show 227
boilies 66, 67, 68, 101, 181,
  182
Book of the Flemish Giant, The
  210, 310, 311
Book on Angling, A 52
Booty, Colin 47
Bossington 232

Bowen, Charlie 250
Bowskill, Roger 95
Bray, Glen 207
bread flake 95
Brecknock, Ray 157
Bristol Waterworks 165
Bristol Zoo 78
Broadlands 231, 233, 237
Brown, Alan 6, 26, 27, 29,
  111, 177, 261, 314
Bruce and Walker 212
Bucknall, Geoffrey 161, 163,
  186, 250, 313
Buller, Fred 6, 11, 59, 60, 61,
  78, 82, 104, 124, 126, 127,
  148, 149, 158, 161, 175,
  183, 186, 226, 237, 246,
  247, 248, 250, 251, 255,
  264, 265, 282, 283, 311,
  314, 315
Burdett-Holcroft, Ruth 27, 203
Buss, Roger 6, 17
Buteux, Bob 6, 130, 176
Butler, Peter 133
Butt, Nick 39

Caius College, Cambridge 6,
  21, 23, 174, 198, 202, 211
Cam, river 23, 26, 156, 200,
  215, 218, 302, 303
Cambridgeshire Fens 126
Cambridgeshire Pike Anglers
  126
Cannon, Bunny 197
Cansdale, George 234
carbon-fibre 59, 61, 62, 121,
  160, 231, 264, 277, 278,
  294
Carfrae, Lt. Col. 253
Carlton Towers 138
carp, the record 44lb 76, 77,
  78, 302, 312
Carp Catchers' Club (CCC) 7,
  29, 66, 67, 71, 75, 83, 85,
  87, 88, 89, 91, 97, 99, 126,
  129, 133, 134, 137, 172,
  212, 221, 224, 268, 312
Carp Fishers' Club 221
Carp Society 134, 186, 315
carp, leather 95, 312
Carptalk Enterprises 89
Carpworld 79
Carter, Fred 105

cats 11, 191, 209, 221, 223, 276, 296, 299
centre-pins 168
Century of Carp Fishing, A 89
Charles II, King 15, 194, 239
Chator Leigh Manufacturing Company 201
Chew Valley 165
Chillingsworth, Bill 126
Chilvers, Basil 12
Christchurch 232, 295
chub 6, 7, 14, 27, 38, 53, 80, 87, 103, 109, 110, 111, 113, 115, 116, 117, 119, 120, 121, 132, 137, 152, 156, 169, 181, 202, 218, 233, 235, 238, 258, 277, 283, 289, 290, 302
Chub Study Group 6, 119, 120
Chubb's of Edgware 66
Church Hill Farm 234, 275
Church, Bob 6, 41, 130, 149, 157, 160, 161, 163
Clarissa 79, 99, 225, 257, 282
Clarke, Brian 6, 44, 77, 147, 149, 159, 161, 179, 180, 182, 183, 230, 254, 315
Clegg, Dick 130
Clifford, Kevin 6, 7, 10, 45, 77, 79, 87, 89, 95, 99, 312, 314
Coarse Fisherman 107, 161, 258, 267, 315
Coarse Fishing 221
Collins, Brian 27
Compleat Angler, The 71, 127, 179, 180, 181, 248
Conservative Association 241
Cooke, Reg. 57
Cooper, Grandfather 193, 301
Coulson, Dr Terry 13, 25, 139, 142, 144
Countess of Castlemaine 194
Country Fair 182, 234
Country Gentlemen's Magazine 238
Courtney Williams, Major 210
Cove, Arthur 149
Coverley, Jim 256
crayfish 119, 120, 137, 283, 293
cricket 19, 123, 197, 199, 271, 298
Crossman, John 35
Crow, Colonel Stanley 42, 229
Cursons, David 19

cycling 214, 217, 218, 262, 290

Daily Mail 210
Daily Mirror 78, 221, 222, 223, 224, 261, 285, 291
Damerham 155
Darwell reservoir 230
Day, Michael 240, 295
Desert Island Discs 39, 245, 263
Dick Walker's Modern Fly Dressings 57
Dick Walker's Trout Fishing 154, 312
Dick Walker: a memoir 175, 182, 186, 315
Dorset Stour 302
Drennan, Peter 114
Drop Me A Line 46, 70, 71, 74, 156, 157, 175, 176, 180, 226, 268, 291, 310, 312
Drury, Lt. Col. Esmond 229
dry-fly fishing 156, 219
Duke of Grafton 194
Dunn, Captain 157
Dymock, Karen 45
Dyson, Colin 315

E. T. Tackle 70
East Midland Allied Press 212, 223, 284
eels 53, 94, 95, 138, 213, 218, 296, 302
EFGEECO 258, 259
Emery Down 232, 233
Emmanuel College 21
Ernest Benn 12, 42, 311, 312
Esthwaite Water 283
Evening Standard 210

Falkus, Hugh 237
Farnborough 27, 59, 62, 203, 204, 205, 207, 210, 264, 265, 266, 278
Feare, Mr H. W. 211
Field, The 178, 210, 215, 224, 239, 281
Fisher, Nigel 241
Fisheries and Conservation Trust (FACT) 135
Fisherman's Bedside Book, The 220, 291
Fishing Gazette 31, 75, 79, 89, 154, 201, 210, 215, 217, 225, 226, 227, 228, 229, 231, 243, 250, 260, 265, 273, 285, 290, 314
Fishing magazine 139, 142, 143, 293
Flemish giant rabbits 29, 209
Flies
  'Chicken' 152, 294
  Amber Longhorns 152
  Amber Nymph 154
  big spiders 163
  Bob's Baby Doll 161
  Bumblebee 152
  Chomper 154, 239
  Crane Fly 152, 230, 244
  Daddy-long-legs 152, 161
  Dambuster 148, 153
  Dronefly 161
  Ghost Swift Moth 150, 152
  Green Longhorns 152
  Green-bodied Red Sedge 152
  Hawthorn Fly 152
  Leaded Shrimp 152, 161
  Mayfly 150
  Mayfly Nymph 153, 154
  Midge Pupae 153, 163
  Mrs Palmer 153
  muddlers 163
  Pale Watery 152, 153
  Perch Fly Streamer 150
  Polystickle 154, 159, 163
  Red Sedge 152, 153, 161
  Russell's Iron Blue 153
  Short Green Partridge 151, 152
  static fly 163, 251
  Sweeney Todd 153, 154, 159
Flit, river 235, 290
Flitwick 62, 98, 231, 235, 236, 262, 310
Fly Dressing Innovations 290, 311
Fly Fishers' Club Journal 147
Fly-Fishing and Fly-Tying 156
Flyfishers' Club 148, 149, 151
football 19, 197, 199, 209, 244, 292, 298
Ford, Helen 257
Fordingbridge 232
Forest of Dean 91
Fort, Tom 179
Foulger, Annie 192, 194, 301
Francis, Francis 52, 239
free-line tactics 137, 138
Friends' School, Saffron Walden 15, 17, 18, 20, 31, 195, 198, 215
Fuller, Commander Norman 149, 151

Fur and Feather 214, 217

Gade, river 219
gaffs 71
Game Fair 227, 228, 229, 279, 294
Garnafailagh 105
Gay, Martin 68, 182, 304
Gibbinson, Jim 6, 129, 315
Giles, Bill 123, 126, 127
Gillett, Brian 197
Goddard, John 257
Golden Scale Club 98
Goldstraw, Anthony 139, 140, 141
Gonville and Caius College 21, 23, 174, 198, 202
Grafham 147, 159, 160, 161, 164, 166, 219, 230, 231, 235, 236, 258, 264, 278
Grantchester Mill Pool 218
Grantchester 23, 200, 218
grayling 152, 237, 269, 302
Great Ouse 38, 80, 109, 111, 113, 119, 132, 164, 234, 249, 262, 277, 283, 302
Great Ouse River Board 119
Great Ouse Water Authority 164
Greig, Dr Mary 186
Grey, Zane 215
Grief, Harry 83
Griffiths, Eldon 163, 164
gudgeon 95, 205, 238, 239, 290, 302
Guinness Book of Records 209
Guttfield, Frank 6, 110, 259, 262

Halford, Edwin 28, 192, 207, 210, 223, 294
Hall, David 9
Halliday, Major Brian 134
Hammersley, Guy 236
Hampshire Avon 82, 283, 294, 302
Hancock, Dorothy 237, 263
Hanningfield 230
Hardy Casting Club de France 214, 290
Hardy's 59, 61, 66, 73, 214, 312
Hardy's Anglers' Guide 214
Hardy, Bill 62, 63, 64, 264
Hardy, James L. 6, 59, 60, 232, 264

Hargreaves, Jack 38, 39, 42, 43, 73, 234, 267, 284, 285
Hart, Frank 205
Harty, Russell 238
Haslemere 93
Hastings, McDonald 234
Hereford Museum 224
Heron bite-alarm 66, 69, 70, 103, 138
Herts/Chiltern Group 130
Hexton Manor, 221
Higgs, Eric 271
Hilton, Jack 9, 87
Hindle, Mr 197
History of Carp Fishing, A 77, 89
Hitchin Angling Club 213, 222, 261, 290
Hitchin Nomads 217
Hodson, Eric 38, 127, 130, 131, 133
Holland, Sam 233
Home Guard, The 206, 297
hook links, soft 87
hooks, barbless 87
House of Hardy 63, 64, 232
Howcroft, Ian 116, 234, 315
Hunt, Jimmy 197
Hunter, Richard 315
Hutchinson, Rod 315

Ickleford 220
Ingham, Maurice 29, 40, 41, 45, 46, 70, 74, 80, 83, 85, 86, 88, 89, 116, 156, 170, 176, 190, 212, 226, 267, 271, 282, 291, 310, 312, 315
Intrepid Elite 65, 169, 294
Intrepid reels 65
Inwood, Cyril 159
Ivel Gardens 47, 51, 56, 151
Ivel, river 216, 238, 245, 262, 290
Ivey, Dave 6, 91

J. B. Walker & Company 211
Jackson, Peter 129
Jacobs, John 232, 264
James, Martin 179, 183, 315
Johns, Bill (Capt. W. E. Johns) 289
Johnson, Dorothy 45

Kefford, Dick 83, 91, 95, 99, 274

Kefford, R. W. Kingsley 270
Kennet, river 229, 263, 283
Keston Ponds 67
Kite, Captain Oliver 42, 43

Lane, Billy 9, 167, 172
Lang, Sir John 55
Lapsley, Peter 149, 152, 156
Laura the rabbit 210, 216
Lea tributaries 219
leads 50, 87, 91, 93, 97, 109, 117, 121, 125, 137, 138, 139
leads, back 87
LEDs 66
Legering 121
Legerstrike 73
Lewis, Derek 6, 27
Lindsay, Lady Blanche 194
Little Brickhill Lake 236
Little Hill Farm 116, 118, 293
Lloyds & Co. 12, 27, 28, 45, 193, 207, 209, 261, 293, 298
loach 119, 283, 293
Local Authorities 55
Loch Lomond 38, 52, 82, 104, 124, 126, 251, 252
Locke, Colonel 'Tiger Rags' 42
Lockhart, Trevor 222, 261
London Camera Club, The 223
London Zoo 78, 282
Lowe's bar 67

MacGibbon, James 225, 226, 242, 259, 272
Maclean, Colonel J. F. 224
maize 87
Management of Angling Waters, The 230
Mapperly 80
Marchant, Mr 113, 117, 118, 119
Marks, Ivan 9, 171
Marsden, Graham 6, 161, 185
Marshall, Howard 261, 284, 285
Marston, R. B. 149
Marston, R. L. 208, 215, 227, 231
Maskell, Peter 14, 154, 182, 242, 311, 312
Matchmaker rod 238
Mead, Peter 135, 136
Mead Mill 232
Medlar Press, The 85, 89, 312
Midland Angler 210

Milton 23, 56, 126
Mimram, river 219, 282, 289
Ministry of Defence 59, 61, 62, 264
Miss Darby's School 15, 195
Mitchell 6, 27, 65, 168, 271
Mk III 97, 98
Mk IV 13, 62, 73, 74, 97, 98, 99, 121, 137, 212, 250, 261, 270, 271
Modern Specimen Hunting 129
Mohan, Peter 315
Moncrieff Rod Development Company 59, 60, 68, 264
Moncrieff, Leslie 59, 60, 61, 259, 264, 312
Moody, Dorothy 272
Morcambe, Eric 236
Morritt, Ken 47, 65, 169

Mr Crabtree 176, 177, 221, 247, 285
Mr Crabtree Goes Fishing 177, 221, 285
multipliers 168
Murgett, Frank 247, 260
Murphy Radio, Welwyn 25, 203
'Mycock, L. O.' 37
Mytchett Lake 205

National Anglers' Council (NAC) 35, 79, 133, 134, 135, 136
National Association of Specialist Anglers (NASA) 130
National Association of Specimen Groups (NASG) 13, 130, 133, 134, 135, 138
National Dictionary of Biography 248
National Federation of Anglers (NFA) 35, 134, 135
Nether Wallop 155, 287
Neve, Arnold 65
Nixon, John 91, 227, 273
No Need to Lie 57, 218, 255, 302, 303, 311, 312
Norfolk Broads 49
Norman, John 83, 87
Northampton rods 159
Northern Specimen Groups 130

Offord 27

Ogilvie, Ian 17, 21
Old Scholars' Association, the Friends' School 17
Opie, Dick and Jack 181
Oughton, river 193, 261, 282, 289
Ouse, river 27, 29, 38, 80, 105, 109, 111, 113, 119, 120, 132, 164, 234, 249, 258, 262, 277, 283, 290, 293, 302
Out of Town BBC series 38, 39, 73
Oyez, Mike 99

Page, Vic 201, 206
Paisley, Tim 79, 89, 182, 315
palaeoanthropology 106, 239, 240, 244, 295, 299
Parlour Pool 232
Passion for Angling 99, 178
paste 67, 95, 97, 105, 229
paste/crust balancers 97
Paxman, Jeremy 180
Pearson, Alan 233, 234, 274
Pembroke College 217
perch 7, 14, 51, 52, 53, 54, 80, 109, 111, 113, 115, 116, 117, 119, 121, 150, 201, 213, 218, 222, 225, 235, 257, 260, 269, 289, 293, 294, 302
Perrin, Tony 71
Peterborough Specimen Group 130
Phillips, Leslie 59, 62, 63, 264, 277
Philpott File 38
Philpott, Trevor 38, 234, 235
photography 7, 19, 69, 71, 73, 74, 223, 279, 294, 305, 315
Phragmites 195
Pickard, Dr J. N. 210
Pike Anglers' Club (PAC) 13, 56, 123, 125, 127, 128
Pike Society 126, 127, 131
Pitchford's Pitch 93, 94
Plomley, Roy 39, 245
poaching 206, 219
politics 17, 136, 241
polyzoa 94
Pomenteg 67, 259
Pomphorhynchus laevis 283
potato 67, 87, 95
potatoes, chipped 87
Price, Eddy 91

Prior, Wally 6, 29
Profumo, David 315
Prorok, Mike 38
Public Lending Rights (PLR) 54, 56, 57
PYM (Phillips' Yeast Mixture) 67

radar 25, 203, 204, 206, 266, 290
Radio Press 217
Raison, Bill 210
Ransome, Arthur 175, 239
Ravioli 79
Redmire 7, 14, 36, 67, 76, 77, 79, 80, 81, 82, 84, 87, 88, 89, 90, 91, 92, 93, 94, 95, 96, 97, 98, 99, 100, 175, 176, 224, 269, 271, 302
Redrup, The Rev. R. J. 279
Reynolds, Bob 83, 85
Reynolds, Hugh 126
Rib, river 219, 289
Richards, Bob 83, 87, 89, 91, 224
Richmond, Ken 220
Robertson, Fyffe 234
Rod Building for Amateurs 212, 291, 310, 311
rod-rest 69, 70, 161, 181, 294
Rogers, Colin 279
Rogers, Peter 85, 89, 312
Rohacell 63, 64
Ross, Hugh 6, 17, 21, 25
Roxton 190, 230, 235, 244, 245
Royal Aircraft Establishment 62, 264, 291
RSPCA 47, 50
rucksacks 72
Russell, Jean 231
Russell, Margery 6, 81, 231
Russell, Pat 82, 90, 148, 231, 232, 253, 260, 261, 282, 295, 315
Russell-Jones, B. 149
Rutland 52, 147
Rutland, Bob 52, 222, 260, 261, 273, 282

Saffron Walden 17, 195, 197, 198, 199, 200, 201, 214, 215
Sails, Tom 9, 167, 170, 172
Samuels 52
Sandholme Publishing 89
Sandys, Reg 126